SPIRAL GUIDE

SCOTLAND

D0259903

AA

Publishing

Contents

the magazine 5

+ Great Scots + Literary Scotland
+ Music and Movement
+ Crofting + From Sticks and Stones
+ Glasgow Style
+ The Edinburgh Festival
+ Oat Cuisine
+ The Angels' Share
+ Freedom's Sword

Finding Your Feet 31

+ First Two Hours
+ Getting Around
+ Accommodation
+ Food and Drink
+ Shopping
+ Entertainment

Edinburgh 43

In a Day
Don't Miss + Edinburgh Castle + Museum of Scotland
+ New Town
At Your Leisure + 8 more places to explore
Where to... + Eat and Drink + Stay
+ Shop + Be Entertained

Glasgow 67

In a Day
Don't Miss + The Burrell Collection + Merchant City
+ Tenement House + Kelvingrove Museum and Art Gallery
At Your Leisure + 15 more places to explore
Where to... + Eat and Drink + Stay
+ Shop + Be Entertained

South of Scotland 95
In Three Days
Don't Miss ✦ Burns Country ✦ New Lanark
At Your Leisure ✦ 10 more places to explore
Where to... ✦ Eat and Drink ✦ Stay
✦ Shop ✦ Be Entertained

Central Scotland 117
In Three Days
Don't Miss ✦ Loch Lomond ✦ Stirling and the Trossachs
At Your Leisure ✦ 10 more places to explore
Where to... ✦ Eat and Drink ✦ Stay
✦ Shop ✦ Be Entertained

Highlands & Islands 139
In Five Days
Don't Miss ✦ Road to the Isles
✦ Skye and the Western Isles ✦ Loch Ness ✦ Cairngorms
At Your Leisure ✦ 10 more places to explore
Where to... ✦ Eat and Drink ✦ Stay
✦ Shop ✦ Be Entertained

Walks and Tours 171
✦ 1 Whisky and Castle Trail
✦ 2 Walter Scott's Border Tour
✦ 3 Glasgow Walk
✦ 4 Great Glen Tour
✦ 5 Ullapool and Loch Broom Walk

Practicalities 187
✦ Before You Go ✦ When to Go
✦ When You Are There

Index 195

Atlas 199

Written by Hugh Taylor and Moira McCrossan
Where to sections by Elizabeth Carter

Copy edited by Maria Morgan
Page layout by The Company of Designers
Indexed by Marie Lorimer

A CIP catalogue record for this book is available from the
British Library.

ISBN 0 7495 2850 8

Published by AA Publishing, a trading name of Automobile
Association Developments Limited, whose registered office is
Norfolk House, Priestley Road, Basingstoke, Hampshire RG24 9NY.
Registered number 1878835.

Colour separation by Leo Reprographics
Printed and bound in China by Leo Paper Products

AA World Travel Guides publish over 300 guidebooks to a full range
of cities, countries and regions across the world. Find out more
about AA Publishing and the wide range of services the AA provides
by visiting our web site at www.theAA.com

10 9 8 7 6 5 4 3 2 1

the magazine

In a land whose greatest export has always been its people Scotland's latest offering is actually a sheep called Dolly, who became an instant media star when scientists at the Roslin Institute near Edinburgh created her as a clone in 1997. But Dolly is just the latest in a long line of world-famous Scots from all walks of life.

Scientific Excellence

For 200 years, Scots have been world leaders in areas such as medicine. Among the pioneers was James Young Simpson (1811–70), whose experiments with chloroform as an anaesthetic led to its widespread use for painless operations. Medical successes continued when Sir Alexander Fleming (1881–1955) shared the Nobel Prize for medicine in 1945 for the discovery of penicillin, the world's first antibiotic. More recently, Sir James Black also shared the prize in 1988 for the development of beta blocker drugs.

Fathers of Invention

There's no proof that a Scotsman invented the wheel, but Robert William Thomson patented the vulcanised rubber pneumatic tyre in 1845, yet never put it into production. It was another Scot, John Boyd Dunlop (1840–1921), who used the process on bicycles, which, coincidentally, were invented by blacksmith Kirkpatrick McMillan of Dumfries. And modern Tarmac road surfaces were developed from the process invented by road engineer John McAdam in the 19th century.

Above: Andrew Carnegie was a philanthropist who never forgot his roots

Shaping a Nation

This Edinburgh attraction focuses on Scottish people, past and present, famous and ordinary. Using the latest interactive technology, it features displays, hands-on experiments and quizzes, and ends with a memorable simulated tour around Scotland's other great asset – its beautiful and dramatic scenery.

✚ 198 off A2
✉ Fountain Park, Dundee Street (at the end of Fountainbridge), Edinburgh
☎ 0131 229 1706

Scots Abroad

Scots have made their mark beyond their native shores, and especially in the USA:

• **John Muir**
The founder of America's national parks was from the Parish of Dunbar.

• **William Smellie**
He founded the Encyclopaedia Britannica in 1768 from his printing shop in Anchor Close in Edinburgh's Royal Mile.

• **Andrew Carnegie**
The US iron and steel magnate was born in Dunfermline, and established a charitable library there.

• **Alan Pinkerton**
The former Glasgow trade-union agitator founded Pinkerton's, the world's first detective agency. He also designed the logo that coined the name 'private eye'.

Scots are also responsible for modern telecommunications through the work of Alexander Graham Bell (1847–1922) of Edinburgh, who built the first telephone in 1875. Besides inventing the television and making the first broadcast, John Logie Baird (1888–1946) also pioneered colour transmission and even held patents in fibre-optics, the advanced technology which carries telephone signals. And the ubiquitous silicon chip that now controls all electronics systems was first made by a team at Dundee University under Professor Walter Spear in 1976.

Sir Sean Connery, Alexander Graham Bell and Dolly show the diversity of Scottish talent

Scots

Media Stars

Among many well-known Scottish actors, Sir Sean Connery (born 1930) is arguably the most famous living Scot, having shot to fame as the original (and many say best) screen James Bond. A passionate Scotsman, despite living abroad, Connery was knighted in 2000 for his services to film.

Some Scottish Stars

Robert Carlyle	*The Full Monty* (1997)
Robbie Coltrane	*Cracker* (1993–6)
Billy Connolly	comedian and actor
John Hannah	*The Mummy* (1999)
Deborah Kerr	*From Here to Eternity* (1953)
Denis Lawson	*Local Hero* (1983)
David McCallum	*The Man From UNCLE* (1964–8)
Ewan MacGregor	*Star Wars Episode 1: The Phantom Menace* (1999)
David Niven	*Around the World in Eighty Days* (1956)

Literary Scotland

Almost 200 years ago poet and novelist Sir Walter Scott (1771–1832) developed the genre of historical novel in Britain. The publication of *Waverley* (1814) paved the way for many great writers and their memorable characters. Long John Silver and Captain Hook, Dr Jekyll and Mr Hyde, Peter Pan, and even the quintessential English detective Sherlock Holmes were all created by Scottish writers.

Devoured by an eager public in the 19th century, Scott's Waverley novels presented a romantic view of the Highlands and moorlands, but he didn't shy away from urban concerns, such as his depiction of Edinburgh's Tolbooth prison.

Later, the 'kailyard' school of Scottish writing portrayed a sentimentalised country of sweet grey-haired grannies, whitewashed cottages and kindly church ministers. J M Barrie's *A Window in Thrums* and S R Crockett's *The Lilac Sunbonnet* are typical of the genre.

By contrast, Lewis Grassic Gibbon's trilogy *A Scots Quair* provides an elegiac account of life in the farming communities of the northeast in the early 20th century, while George Douglas Brown's *House with the Green Shutters* examines the tensions below the surface of a small, rural community.

However, Barrie also produced the immortal *Peter Pan*,

while Crockett's *The Raiders* and *The Grey Man* are fast-paced adventures in the tradition of Robert Louis Stevenson's

Below left: Sir Walter Scott, lawyer and novelist

Kidnapped and *Treasure Island*. John Buchan followed with the much-filmed *The Thirty Nine Steps* (1915), the first popular spy novel of the 20th century.

Noted for establishing the detective story as a genre of popular fiction, Sir Arthur

Above: Sir James Matthew Barrie, creator of Peter Pan

The Writers' Museum

You can learn lots more about the works of three of Scotland's greatest writers – Robert Burns, Sir Walter Scott and Robert Louis Stevenson – in this great free museum housed in a 17th-century mansion, once home to the Countess of Stair, in Lady Stair's Close just off Edinburgh's Royal Mile.

Literary Pub Tours

In Edinburgh you can visit the favourite taverns of Scottish writers past and present. Tours start from the Beehive Inn in the Grassmarket and are run by Clart and McBrain, who argue passionately about the importance of pubs and drinking to the creativity of Scotland's writers, while they lead you through Edinburgh's closes, wynds and narrow streets. *En route*, you'll hear the stories and see the places behind the creation of Dr Jekyll and Mr Hyde, pass the nocturnal haunts of Robert Louis Stevenson and discover the bawdy poetry of Robert Burns. There are similar tours in Glasgow (tel: 0131 2266665; www.scot-lit.tour.co.uk).

Conan Doyle (1859–1930) modelled Sherlock Holmes on one of his professors at Edinburgh University who was a pioneer in the field of forensic science. However, Edinburgh's latest fictional sleuth couldn't be more of a contrast to the precise and fastidious Holmes. Detective Inspector John Rebus, created by novelist Ian Rankin (born 1960), is a maverick with a

Inspector Rebus Tours

Deep in the darkest recesses of the Oxford Bar you might spot a lone drinker with a pint of beer and a glass of whisky. He's middle-aged, with a beer belly and a face raddled from years of hard drinking, chain smoking and poor diet. He's the archetype of Ian Rankin's fictional detective, Inspector Rebus, and fans of the character are flocking to Edinburgh to visit his favourite pubs and the scenes of his most gruesome murder investigations. John Skinner of Rebus Tours (tel: 0131 5553065) will guide you on 'The Water of Death Tour', starting in Stockbridge, via the Dean Bridge and through the New Town to finish with a drink in the Oxford Bar.

Scotland's Book Town

Wigtown, part of the Machars Triangle near Stranraer, is a place where people vanish into second-hand bookstores, never to be seen again. The lovely beaches and mild climate of Galloway are as far south and west as you can go in Scotland, and if old, antiquarian and remaindered books are your passion then this tranquil backwater is the place to be.

J K Rowling and her magic hero

Left: Ian Rankin, one of Scotland's most popular contemporary novelists

drink problem, constantly assigned to obscure and peripheral cases. But somehow he always ends up solving the big headline case by unorthodox means, often unearthing uncomfortable facts which some would rather leave buried.

The latest literary star to emerge from Scotland is Harry Potter, the schoolboy wizard who has taken the world by storm. He came to life in an Edinburgh café where author J K Rowling wrote over a cup of coffee because she couldn't afford to heat her flat. With her books dominating the bestseller lists and dramatisations dominating the headlines, Rowling has secured Scotland's place as a literary leader.

Top Ten Scottish Reads

Robert Burns' poetry	
The Prime of Miss Jean Brodie	Muriel Spark
Robert the Bruce	Nigel Tranter
True Confessions	Liz Lochhead
Trainspotting	Irvine Welsh
The Silver Darlings	Neil Gunn
The Land of the Leal	James Barke
Para Handy Tales	Neil Munro
More Songs of Angus	Violet Jacob
The Bull Calves	Naomi Mitchison

Music and

Celtic music developed among the people of the Celtic fringe – remnants of the Celtic tribes of Europe now confined to its western extremities such as Wales, Ireland, Galicia in Spain, Brittany in France, Cornwall and the Isle of Man in England and, of course, Scotland.

Each country's traditional music is distinctive, yet a common thread runs through their dance tunes, airs, songs and ballads. Celtic immigrants to North America took their music with them and it was absorbed into a new society. Now their descendants are bringing it back across the Atlantic. Innovative musicians are fusing ancient tunes with jazz, rock and pop, and bag-pipes play alongside synthesizers. Singers collect old songs and teach them to children to ensure that the Celtic tradition continues to thrive.

The Traditional Music and Song Association (TMSA) in Edinburgh provides information about concerts, ceilidhs, folk clubs and pub sessions. Call 0131 6675587 or log on to the TMSA's listings section at www.tmsa.demon.co.uk/tmsa/home/TMListings.

Ten of the Best Celtic Musicians

Aly Bain and Phil Cunningham – Shetland's most famous fiddler teamed with the accordion virtuoso

Ivan Drever and Duncan Chisholm – Orkney singer-songwriter and multi-instrumentalist joins the fiddler with the band Wolfstone

Wendy Stewart – virtuoso of the clarsach (a small, wire-strung harp)

Battlefield Band – long-established Glasgow band

Black Eyed Biddy – popular duo from Dumfriesshire

Stravaig – Scotland's first all-female a cappella group, also from Dumfriesshire

Archie Fisher – elder statesman of the 1960s Scottish folk revival

Burrach – young, lively Edinburgh band led by Sandy Brechin, the wild man of the Scottish accordion

The Oatcakes – ceilidh band playing traditional but contemporary music, and classical tunes with a rock beat

Dick Gaughan – one of the greats

Celtic Connections

The brilliant three-week Celtic Connections Festival lights up the dark days of a Glaswegian January. It's a wonderful introduction to Celtic music, with singers and musicians from across the globe, vibrant musicians playing Celtic music to a rock beat or Beethoven in reel time. There are huge concerts and small, intimate, late-night venues, ceilidhs and pub sessions where anyone can join in, children's events involving local schools, and fascinating lectures and discussions.

The success of Celtic Connections has sent people in search of traditional music in other pubs and festivals. Street musicians will tell you where to find informal sessions, or you can head for the long-established haunts in the main cities. Glasgow's Scotia Bar in Stockwell Street has been a hang-out for musicians and poets since the 1960s. Close by, the Victoria Bar, the Clutha Vaults and the Renfrew Ferry offer variations on the Celtic theme. In Edinburgh check out Sandy Bell's Bar in Forrest Road, and you'll also find regular sessions in The Royal Oak in Infirmary Street and the Tass on the Royal Mile.

The Celtic Connections Festival Inset: Karen Mathieson of Capercaillie and Aly Bain, the Shetland fiddler

M@vement

Ceilidhs

If you see a ceilidh (pronounced 'kay-lee') advertised then chances are it will be a dance; but a true ceilidh is much more. Traditionally it was a gathering of people to sing, play music, dance and tell stories. You can find examples at many Scottish folk festivals – try those at Keith, Auchtermuchty and Newcastleton.

CROFTING
A Highland Way of Life

Crofting – tending small, rented farms with common pasture rights – was a 19th-century invention with its origins in the infamous Highland Clearances, when rapacious landlords discovered that sheep were more profitable than people and forcibly removed tens of thousands of inhabitants. These evicted communities were then resettled on small parcels of land (crofts) by the coast.

Before this, people lived in townships scattered all over the Highlands. The land was divided into narrow strips (runrigs), and the landowner allocated each family a selection of strips – some on good land, some on poor land.

A Harsh Life

Unlike the typical, romantic image of a crofter tending sheep while his wife span wool, the reality was of a harsh, inhospitable existence, incapable of sustaining life.

Kelp, a large variety of seaweed used in glass production, was profitable but notoriously difficult to harvest. This backbreaking work for meagre pay meant that landowners had problems hiring labour. But by resettling tenants and deliberately keeping the size of the first crofts too small to sustain life, landlords created a pool of cheap labour and crofters were forced to harvest kelp to augment their income.

When the kelp industry collapsed the crofters were left destitute. No longer needed as a workforce, continued evictions forced their mass emigration to Australia, Canada and the USA. However, some hardy souls remained and crofting became established; the first Crofting Act (1886) granted crofters security of tenure.

No Dogs Allowed

But the powerful landowners continued to make life difficult for tenants, instituting ridiculous rules like forbidding the keeping of dogs.

Contrary to popular myth, crofting was a hard way of life

This continued well into the 20th century, with successive unscrupulous, absentee landlords showing scant regard for the local population. Unhappy with affairs, the crofters on Assynt Estate in Sutherland launched a successful campaign to buy their land, and by 1992 they became the first crofting community to own their estate.

Out of the Frying Pan...

Even with modern agricultural techniques, crofts are essentially still not viable, and are supplemented by other activities. Telecommuting and Internet business have joined traditional jobs such as postman and bus driver, which crofters also do.

Crofting may seem trendy, and more people are opting out of stressful city lives to return to their roots. But demand is high and crofts are not easy to come by, as most remain in the same family and changes of tenancy must be approved by the Crofting Commission. Those who do leave the cities for a Highland croft must rise at 5am to feed the cattle before starting their 'day job', and still have to put in more hours on the land after work. So it's no wonder that some find they've simply swapped one rat race for another.

Top: Many crofts are now abandoned
Bottom: A crofter on Lewis weaving Harris Tweed

Some Crofting Statistics

- Locals bought Eigg for £1.7 million in 1997
- Assynt, Borve and Stornoway are also owned locally
- 77 per cent of the Western Isles is croft land
- There are around 5,000 crofts among 250 townships
- Sizes range from 0.5–50 hectares (average 5 hectares)
- Main products are lamb and beef, with some dairy farming
- Similar schemes operate in France and Norway

From *Sticks* and *Stones*

The modern sport of golf that millions watch each year has come a long way from the ancient Scottish game of gowf, developed over the centuries from the delight that early humans took in whacking a stone with a stick. In other countries different stick and ball games like hockey, hurling and shinty evolved from these humble beginnings, but Scotland gave golf to the world. And as the spiritual and historical home of the game, Scotland attracts golfers from around the globe to play on its famous courses.

The game was popular from the start – too popular it would seem. In 1475 (the earliest mention of golf) it was prohibited by the Scottish Parliament on Sundays because it interfered with archery practice.

In 1754 a handful of players founded a small club which they called The Society of St Andrew's Golfers. King William IV became their patron in the early-19th century, as was the fashion of the time, and they became The Royal and Ancient Golf Club. The R&A is the world authority on the sport, and it administers the rules and runs the British Open Championship. That small private golf club still operates, but nowadays it has 2,000 members.

Scotland's Gowf Club

In the Irvine Valley in Ayrshire golfers stubbornly cling to the old name for golf. Loudoun Gowf Club, beside Loudoun Castle, is on land that has never been ploughed, where gowf has been played for centuries. Turf from here was used to surface Hampden Park in Glasgow, Scotland's national stadium.

The Gutta Percha Ball

This invention more than any other made golf accessible to the masses. Early wooden clubs had evolved from a wooden stick or cleek. Balls, traditionally made from feathers, were expensive and often lasted just one round. They were also unpredictable and affected by the weather, making golf more a game of chance than of skill. Then in 1848 one James Patterson received a parcel from abroad packed in gutta percha – a tough coagulated latex similar to rubber. Patterson made an experimental ball from it and suddenly cheap, mass-produced, controllable balls became a possibility. They were also strong enough to be whacked by materials harder than wood, and so iron clubs were developed.

Above left: Mary Queen of Scots often played golf at St Andrews
Above right: Bunkered at St Andrews

Right: When Tiger Woods won the British Open championship at St Andrews in 2000, he became the youngest man to win the 'Grand Slam'

Top Ten Golf Courses

St Andrews (▶ 132) – www.standrews.org.uk
Turnberry Ailsa – www.turnberry.co.uk
Royal Troon – e-mail:
bookings@royaltroon.com
Royal Dornoch – www.royaldornoch.com
Muirfield – e-mail: hceg@btinternet.com
Carnoustie – www.carnoustie.org/golf
North Berwick – tel: 01620 892135/893233
Machrihanish – tel: 01586 810213
Nairn – www.nairngolfclub.co.uk
Turnberry Arran – www.turnberry.co.uk

Old Tom

Tom Morris Sr, four times winner of the British Open between 1861 and 1867, was largely responsible for the layout of modern courses. 'Old Tom', as he was called to distinguish him from his son, was greenkeeper and golf professional on the Old Course at St Andrews for 40 years. He pioneered the change from 22 to 18 holes and designed championship courses at Muirfield, Carnoustie and the first purpose-built 'modern' course at Prestwick.

How to Book a Round

Scotland has over 500 golf courses and most of them, including the championship ones, are open to the public. You can usually book by phoning the club; get the number from the local tourist office. It sounds simple, and in many cases it is, but for the top courses you may need to book a year in advance. Rules on admission vary from club to club, so check for any restrictions when booking.
The Scottish Tourist Board also produces a free map with details of over 300 courses (tel: 08705 511511).

you've either got or you haven't got...

The Glasgow Style, as defined by art historians, peaked at the time of the Glasgow exhibition in 1901, when art nouveau was sweeping through Europe. Fused with the Arts and Crafts Movement, it was the style associated with architect and designer Charles Rennie Mackintosh (1868–1928) and his contemporaries at the Glasgow School of Art, under the dynamic leadership of Francis Newbery (1855–1946).

True Glasgow Style is hard to define. It changes constantly, embodying many different traditions and trends. It's the confidence that built this magnificent city, it's the imaginative adaptations of old buildings for new uses and it's

Glasgow Style

the daring architecture of the late 20th century.

Mackintosh attended evening classes at the School of Art when he became an apprentice architect. He was an outstanding student, attracting attention not only for his architecture but also for his drawing and painting. Influenced by the romanticism of the pre-Raphaelites and the simplicity of Japanese design, he and his friends Herbert McNair and Margaret and Frances MacDonald became known as 'the Four', gaining a reputation in the art world for their striking designs using stylised natural forms.

The Glasgow School of Art is his masterpiece (▶ 87). Combining traditional Scottish baronial style with fluid metalwork and carved

Above and below left: the Armadillo; Below centre: Templeton's Carpet Factory; Inset: Glasgow's underground railway, the 'Clockwork Orange'

Glasgow Style...

• Puts a gallery of modern art in a grand classical building and decorates the pediment with primary colours and mirrors.
• Is wonderful buildings spanning two centuries – the Trades Hall, the Burrell Collection, the Egyptian building, Templeton's Carpet Factory, Kelvingrove Museum and Art Gallery, the Royal Concert Hall, the Armadillo.
• Is the 'Clockwork Orange', Glasgow's underground system.
• Is the Barras and the Golden Z, Glasgow's shopping heartland.
• Wears Versace with thrift shop finds or fine flowing silk with chunky Doc Martens boots.
• Above all Glasgow Style is about the people, the wit and panache that has reinvented the city as the Garden City, the City of Culture and the City of Architecture and Design, and underlying it is a humorous audacity which punctures pomposity with a wee touch of the ridiculous.

The Mackintosh Trail

Mackintosh design is everywhere in Glasgow. The Lighthouse, so-called because of the striking tower on the corner and built for the Glasgow Herald, is now the Mackintosh Centre (▶ 87). This series of exhibitions on his work makes a good starting point for following the Mackintosh trail around Glasgow:

• Take tea in the Willow Tea Room (▶ 87, 90), designed for caterer Kate Cranston.

• Visit a reconstruction of his home at the Hunterian Gallery at Glasgow University.

• Take the train to Helensburgh and Hill House, designed for the publisher Blackie, and now restored by the National Trust for Scotland. Visit the amazing House for an Art Lover at Bellahouston Park (▶ 84), designed in collaboration with his wife Margaret MacDonald.

stone, he designed a complete art nouveau building, including furnishings that are still in everyday use. Mackintosh and his wife moved to London in 1915, but the remainder of his life in England and France produced little to compare with the Glasgow legacy.

But Glasgow Style is more than Mackintosh: it's the tenement house in which most Glaswegians of the 19th and early-20th century grew up, and where the workers from the shipyard and heavy-engineering plants of industrial Glasgow lived. Although the houses were overcrowded and unsanitary, they were solid sandstone, bay-windowed terraces. Children played in the back yards, and women working in the communal wash-house would chat to each other from their windows (windae hingin'), and here the warmth and friendliness that is Glasgow was nurtured. Many of the houses that survived the architectural ravages of the 1960s and 1970s have now been impressively cleaned and renovated.

Charles Rennie Mackintosh and his distinctive designs

'Mockintosh'

All over Glasgow you'll find jewellery, ceramics, pictures and lettering in the Glasgow Style, affectionately known as Mockintosh. The distinctive lettering – tall, strong capitals softened by dots and lines – typifies the style. Soft fabrics or strands of hair escape from solid vertical lines, swirling tendrils of greenery entwine and climb around a grid and the stylised open heart of a rose lies delicately at the centre of an elongated ellipse. If you want a souvenir of Glasgow, there's an amazing range of these elegant designs, from china mugs to lamps and vases to delicate silver and gold jewellery.

The Edinburgh
FESTIVAL

It's Tuesday afternoon and the Royal Mile is closed to traffic. The motorists are exasperated but the assembled multitude thronging the steep cobbled street is oblivious to their anger. In the sunshine outside St Giles Cathedral a lone piper belts out a folk-rock version of some ancient Scottish reels. He's dressed in traditional tartan like an extra from the movie *Braveheart*. Beside him a native of the Gambia in national costume lays down a deep rhythmic African beat under the skirl of the pipes. They've only just met in a pub around the corner, but the crowd gathered round them would swear they've been playing together for years.

Further down the street a clown on stilts juggles some Indian clubs while the top-hatted flame-thrower at his side spews fire high into the air. On the next corner a theatre troupe performs excerpts from a show, while a woman dressed like the tin man from the *Wizard of Oz* does a robot mime across the street. It's like Mardi Gras meets medieval street fair, but it's Edinburgh in August so it must be the Festival.

This cultural extravaganza attracts thousands of visitors each year and for a month you can overdose on the arts whether you're into classical music, jazz, opera or theatre. There are open-air classical concerts in Princes Street Gardens and performances by renowned musicians or actors in every major venue in Edinburgh. Or there's the avant-garde, light-hearted or just plain ridiculous stuff of the Fringe – some shows are so dreadful that they attract a cult following, while others play to empty houses or an audience of one for their full run. Other shows, however, often become big names in London or even abroad.

The Edinburgh Festival's fringe performances showcase the weird and wonderful.

Festival Contacts

Edinburgh International Festival
The Hub, Castle Hill, Royal Mile, Edinburgh
EH1 2NE
☎ 0131 4732000; www.eif.scot.net

The Fringe
The Fringe Office
180 High Street, Edinburgh EH1 1QS
☎ 0131 2265257; www.edfringe.com

Military Tattoo
32 Market Street, Edinburgh EH1 1Q8
☎ 0131 2251188; www.edintattoo.co.uk

Edinburgh International Film Festival
88 Lothian Road, Edinburgh EH3 9BZ
☎ 0131 2284051; www.edfilmfest.org.uk

Edinburgh Jazz and Blues Festival
Assembly Direct
89 Giles Street, Edinburgh EH6 6BZ
☎ 0131 5534000/6677776 (box office);
www.jazzmusic.co.uk

Firework Finale
The spectacular Military Tattoo (pictured above) held on the Castle Esplanade throughout the Festival is always sold out, as is the final night concert in Princes Street Gardens, when the combination of music and fireworks bursting above the floodlit castle is truly magical. If you can't get a ticket, watch from Calton Hill (► 60) and listen to it on the radio.

Oat Cuisine

Oats are to the Scots what pasta is to Italians. A traditional, if unlikely, Scottish day might begin with a hearty dish of hot porridge oats, sprinkled with salt (not sugar). Main meals might include tatties and herring (potatoes with herring in oatmeal) or skirlie (fried oatmeal and onions). Rounding off the day's menu are oatcakes and cheese or cranachan, a luxurious mixture of oatmeal, honey, cream, raspberries and whiskey.

Below: Haggis is 'piped in' at a traditional Burns Supper Bottom: Dundee cake

But in these days of fast food, there's often little room or time for full-blown traditional meals in everyday life, and, as with the rest of Britain, the fish and chip supper is always a popular option.

Scottish cuisine has come a long way from the time when Highlanders could march for days on a sporranful of oatmeal mixed with cold water and a dram or three of whisky. Throughout Scotland there are small specialist restaurants cooking fresh local ingredients in an innovative way. Wild salmon, venison, lamb or beef may be served in an imaginative sauce, but the flavour depends on the freshness and quality of the ingredients.

Scots may be fond of oats, but they've become much more imaginative in the way they cook and serve them. Edinburgh's Stac Poly restaurants give a French spin to traditional Scottish food, serving filo pastry haggis parcels in a rich plum sauce. However, the French connection is nothing new, and dates back to Mary, Queen of Scots, who apparently imported lots of French ideas. And many Scottish words relating to food are of French origin, including haggis from the French *hâché* (chopped).

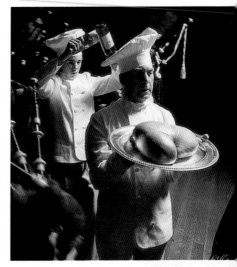

Classic Scottish Dishes

• **Cullen Skink**
Originally from the village of Cullen on the Moray Firth. Made from smoked fish, potatoes, onions and cream, this exceedingly rich soup is delicious, but don't count the calories. Try it at Wee Windaes in Edinburgh's Royal Mile, which specialises in traditional Scottish food.

• **Stovies**
Really hearty, filling peasant fare, this hotpot-type dish will set you up for the day, and

there are many variations. Some use no meat, while others include mince or sausages, but essentially the ingredients are potatoes, onions and sometimes carrots slowly steam-fried in meat dripping or butter. Sample them at Claire's, a small take-away in the Canongate on Edinburgh's Royal Mile.

• Haggis

The 'great chieftain o' the puddin race' is made from finely chopped offal mixed with oatmeal and heavily spiced. Historically, this mixture was then cooked in the stomach of a sheep. It's traditionally served with champit neeps and tatties (mashed turnips and potatoes). Haggis is now produced in a synthetic skin, and there's even a vegetarian version made from nuts and pulses. But nothing can compare to the original.

• High Tea

This particularly Scottish institution is now sadly dying out, but is still available in a few establishments, including Greenock's legendary Tontine Hotel. Served mainly between 5pm and 6:30pm, it consists of a main course of fish and chips or cold meat and salad, accompanied by gallons of tea and stacks of bread and butter, followed by an array of scones, cakes and shortbread on a tiered cake stand.

Simple but wonderful: the best Scottish restaurants will serve oatcakes and cheese, and freshly cooked salmon

The Angels' Share

Distillery workers will tell you that the whisky that evaporates from the barrels over many years of maturing is 'the angels' share'.
Whether or not you believe in angels, the prospect of a wee dram waiting for you is certainly a cheering thought.

From the Gaelic *uisge beatha*, meaning 'water of life', whisky is credited with all manner of medicinal and magical properties. It isn't really a cure, it's just that once you've had a few drams, you feel no pain.

Whisky wasn't always Scotland's national drink. In the 17th and 18th centuries claret was the favoured tipple, imported from Bordeaux to the port of Leith in huge barrels. Robert Burns testified to the copious quantities drunk in his song 'Gae bring tae me a pint o' wine'. It was the tax on wine that popularised whisky as an alternative, and many of today's famous distilleries were built on the sites of old illegal stills.

Whisky comes in two types: blended and single malt. Blended is a mixture of grain whisky and malt whisky,

Traditional methods: 'wash stills' at Talisker Distillery, and a cooper making barrels by hand

Bottle No 1 of a special edition of Glenturret, a snip at £25,000

Malts, on the other hand, have their own distinctive aromas and flavours, just like fine wines, and here it's the variations of malt, peat, water and cask that give each malt its taste signature. The Island malts in particular have a delicious, smoky smoothness imparted from the peat drying and the peaty water. The barley is malted and dried with peat smoke and, after distilling, the drink is aged in casks for many years. You can pay thousands of pounds for a rare 50-year-old malt.

while single-malt whisky is malt whisky only. The malt in the blends determines their quality. Aficionados on blended whisky can differentiate among the brands, but to ordinary drinkers they all taste pretty similar and are often mixed with lemonade or other soft drinks, so any special flavours tend to be lost.

You can have a great time comparing different brands in places like the Scotch Whisky Heritage Centre on Edinburgh's Royal Mile or in the bars of hotels. Just make sure to leave your car behind, then quietly raise your glass to the hovering angels before draining it dry.

Below: whisky-lovers are overwhelmed by choice in Scotland

Five Popular Malts
Islay, Bowmore
The Macallan, Craigellachie
Glenmorangie, Tain
Talisker, Carbost
Balvenie

Best for Malt Whisky Tasting
• Scotch Malt Whisky Society, The Vaults, 87 Giles Street, Leith
• Scotch Whisky Heritage Centre, Castle Hill, Edinburgh
• The Whisky Shop, Princes Square, Glasgow
• Cairngorm Whisky Centre, Inverdruie, near Aviemore
• Lochside Hotel, Bowmore, Islay
• Taychreggan Hotel, Loch Awe near Oban
• For a memorable taste of Scotland, also explore the Malt Whisky Trail (▶ 172–5).

FREEDOM'S SWORD

For centuries Scotland's identity has been moulded by its relationship with England. Scotland was self-governing from the 14th century until 1707, a right the people had fought for against their more powerful English neighbours, and their strong sense of identity has been fiercely defended ever since.

The long Scottish Wars of Independence that Scotland won at Bannockburn near Stirling (➤ 126–9) in 1314 started with an unhappy chance in 1286 when Alexander III, King of Scots, fell from his horse and over a cliff to his death. As all his children had predeceased him, arrangements were made

With no obvious monarch in waiting, the guardians who had been appointed to run the country in Margaret's infancy asked King Edward I of England to adjudicate on the many claimants to the throne. But Edward asserted his own claim to the country, making the contenders swear an oath of fealty to him.

The statue of Robert the Bruce at Bannockburn

for his three-year-old grand-daughter, Margaret, to succeed him. Unfortunately, she was in poor health and died on the boat journey from Norway to her new realm.

It eventually came down to a decision between Robert the Bruce (1274–1329) and John Balliol (c1250–1313), and Edward chose Balliol, who was little more than the king's

The Gothic Wallace Monument was near the site of William Wallace's most famous victory at Stirling Bridge

Below: Robert the Bruce and his horse De Bohun

puppet. When Balliol began to show some resistance to Edward's wishes, Edward simply removed him and invaded Scotland in 1296, carrying off the potent symbol of Scottish monarchy, the Stone of Destiny on which all Scottish monarchs had been crowned (▶ 48). With Scotland under English domination, one man emerged who was to become the country's greatest hero.

Braveheart

Sir William Wallace (c1270–1305) was a shadowy figure about whom little is really known before his uprising. He routed the English at Stirling Bridge in 1297 and continued to wage an out-standing guerilla war against them. His actions found favour with the Scots nobility, who knighted him and appointed him Guardian of Scotland. He was eventually captured after the second English invasion and taken to London, where he was tried for treason and hung, drawn and quartered – a gruesome death even by the brutal standards of the period.

Meanwhile, Robert the Bruce was advancing his claim to the Scottish throne. After murdering one of John Balliol's leading supporters, the Red Comyn, in Greyfriars Church, Dumfries. Bruce seized the castle and the town and advanced through the southwest. He was crowned king at Scone, and although his fortunes rose and fell for a few years, he finally won a decisive victory against the English at Bannockburn. This led to the English withdrawal and left Bruce free to tackle opposition to his rule within Scotland. He spent the next few years ruthlessly destroying all those against him. But it was not until the Treaty of Northampton was signed in 1328 that Scotland was acknowledged as 'independent of England for all time'.

An Uneasy Union

But this was not to be so, and almost 400 years later it was not war that ended Scotland's independence but economics and, some would argue, greed. The English wanted the union of the two countries for reasons of national security. Embroiled in a major war in Europe, the last thing they wanted was trouble from their northern neighbour. Scotland's economy meanwhile was in disastrous straits and union would allow them free trade and access to a huge market. The Act of Union of 1707 was almost universally unpopular but was pushed through in the face of heavy opposition by the 31 Parliamentary Commissioners, ably assisted by huge amounts of English money for the purpose of buying support. Robert Burns later declared in song, 'We were bought and sold for English gold', describing the commissioners as 'a Parcel of Rogues in a Nation'.

Although Scotland prospered from the Union, the shifting of political control to London was seen by many as being taken over. However, despite the political union, Scotland's legal system has remained separate from

England's. A notable example of this are Scotland's more enlightened and liberal licensing laws, which have long been the envy of drinkers south of the border.

Enough is Enough

In the late-20th century the voting patterns of Scotland shifted considerably from those of southern England, with Scots consistently voting for the more socialist policies of the Labour party but being ruled by the right-wing Conservative policies of the London-based government. During the 1980s, when the Conservative Prime Minister Margaret Thatcher was in

Supporters of the Yes Campaign in the referendum for a Scottish Assembly can't contain their delight as the results are announced

The Parliament Building

Harmony has not been a hallmark of the search for a permanent home for the new Scottish Parliament. The old High School on Calton Hill, originally identified as the Parliament building, was rejected as being too difficult to modernise. The competition to design a new building to modern high-tech specifications was won by the Catalan architect Enric Mirales amid controversy about both the design and the site at Holyrood. Even before the foundations were laid, the original estimate of around £80 million had increased to £109 million and MPs demanded closer scrutiny of the project. The building is due for completion by the end of 2002, but unfortunately Mirales will not see it, as he died of a brain tumour on 3 July, 2000, aged 45.

power, many Scots perceived themselves as guinea pigs for new government policies: the ill-fated 'poll tax' of 1989–90, first tried out in Scotland, proved unpopular throughout the whole of Britain. These policies damaged Scotland's morale and by the final election of the century no Conservative members for Scotland were voted into to the Westminster Parliament.

Meanwhile, the Scottish National Party (SNP), was making inroads into traditional Labour support as many Scottish people felt a need to reinforce their national identity. Labour pursued a policy of devolution, promising the Scots their own parliament but stopping short of full control. Policies such as immigration and defence would still be the province of Westminster. When Labour won the general election in 1997 the Scottish referendum that followed produced an overwhelming majority in favour of a devolved parliament. The Scottish Secretary (and, later, First Minister of Scotland until his death in October 2000) Donald Dewar declared 'There shall be a Scottish Parliament'.

The New Scottish Parliament

On 12 May, 1999, the veteran Scottish Nationalist Winnie Ewing declared 'The Scottish Parliament, which adjourned on 25 March, 1707, is hereby reconvened'. The abolition of the Parliament, as part of the 1707 Act of Union, had been likened at the time to 'the end of an auld sang'. Winnie Ewing added 'All of us here can begin to write together a new Scottish song, and I urge all of you to sing it in harmony – fortissimo'.

Scotland's inaugural First Minister, Donald Dewar, and the Queen at the opening of the Scottish parliament in May 1999

Finding Your Feet

First Two Hours

Arriving By Air

Scotland has three main airports: Edinburgh (code EDI), Glasgow International (GLA) and Glasgow Prestwick International (QPIK), and all have a choice of onward transport. Public transport is generally reliable. Edinburgh and Glasgow International have Tourist Information Offices.

Ground transport costs (excluding tip)

£ = under £5   ££ = £5–10   £££ = £10–20

Edinburgh Airport

- Scotland's **main airport** (tel: 0131 3331000; www.baa.co.uk) is 12km west of Edinburgh.
- **Taxis** are available from a rank in front of the terminal. With fares of around £15 to the city centre, cabs are good value for groups of up to four people travelling together, and are the most convenient option if you have a lot of luggage.
- **Guide Friday** (tel: 0131 556 2244) and **Lothian Region Transport** (tel: 0800 232323 or 0131 554 4494 / 555 6363) run coach transfers to Waverley railway station adjacent to Princes Street, via the smaller Haymarket Station. Services run every 15 minutes during peak hours, and 30 minutes at off-peak times (£). The journey takes 30 minutes, or around 45 minutes during the rush hour.
- If you're **driving**, take the A8 east and follow the city centre signs. It is a 20-minute drive to the city centre.

Glasgow International Airport

- Glasgow Airport (tel: 0141 8871111; www.baa.co.uk) is in **Paisley**, 13km west of Glasgow city centre.
- **Paisley Gilmour Street** railway station is 3km from the airport.
- **Taxis** (tel: 0141 848 4588) are available from the front of the terminal building for transfers to central Glasgow (£££) or to nearby Paisley (£).
- **Airport Express** (tel: 0141 553 1313) and **Scottish Citylink** (tel: 0870 5505050) shuttle buses run to Glasgow city centre every 15 minutes during peak times and every 30 minutes in the evening (£). Local buses also run to Paisley station every ten minutes (£).
- **Drivers** should take the M8 west and follow signs for the city centre. Glasgow airport is about 20 minutes' drive from the city centre.

Glasgow Prestwick International

- **Prestwick** airport (01292 479822; www.glasgow.pwk.com) is 72km from Glasgow city centre, about a 45-minute drive.
- **Trains** run every 30 minutes to Glasgow Central Station and take 30 minutes (££).
- To **drive** from Prestwick airport, take the A77 north following the signs for Glasgow, but expect delays at peak times.

Train Stations

Waverley Railway Station

- Situated at **Waverley Bridge**, Edinburgh. Exit via the Waverley Steps to reach Princes Street.

■ East coast mainline services from **London King's Cross** station arrive hourly and take 4–5 hours.

Glasgow Central Station

■ Situated at **Argyle Street** in the city centre.
■ Terminal for West Coast mainline trains from **London Euston** station, with average journey times of 5–6 hours.
■ **Trains** to towns in the immediate vicinity of Glasgow also leave from Central Station.
■ It is a ten-minute walk through the city centre to **Queen Street Station**, from which services leave for the rest of Scotland.

Bus Stations

St Andrew Square Bus Station

■ Situated in **Clyde Street**, Edinburgh, the heart of the New Town and five minutes' walk from Princes Street, along which principal city buses run.
■ **National Express Coaches** (tel: 0870 5808080) arrive here from England and Wales. **Scottish Citylink** (tel: 0870 5505050) covers all of Scotland.

Buchanan Street Bus Station

■ Situated in **Killermont Street**, Glasgow, about ten minutes' walk from Central Station or George Square (tel: 0141 3327133).
■ Well served by the **National Express** and **Scottish Citylink** network covering most destinations in Britain.

Tourist Information Offices

The main tourist offices in Edinburgh and Glasgow provide an excellent service, including help with reservations and comprehensive what's on information. Both offices have outlets at Edinburgh and Glasgow airports.

Edinburgh

■ 3 Princes Street, above Waverley Shopping Centre
■ 0131 4733800; e-mail: esic@eltb.org; www.edinburgh.org
■ Mon–Sat 9–6, Sun 10–6, Oct–Apr; daily 9–7, May–Jun and Sep; Mon–Sat 9–8, Sun 10–8, Jul–Aug

Glasgow

■ 11 George Square, opposite Queen Street Station
■ 0141 2044400 (general), 0141 221 0049 (reservations); e-mail: tourismglasgow@GGCVTB.org.uk; www.seeglasgow.com
■ Mon–Sat 9–6, Jan–Easter and Oct–Dec; Mon–Sat 9–6, Sun 10–6, Easter–1 Jun; Mon–Sat 9–7, Sun 10–6, Jun and Sep; Mon–Sat 9–8, Sun 10–6, Jul–Aug

Scottish Tourist Board Central Information Department

■ 23 Ravelston Terrace, Edinburgh; telephone 0131 332 2433; fax 0131 315 4545; www.holidayscotland.net/os. Telephone and written enquiries only.
■ Mon–Thu 9–5:30, Fri 9–5; all year

Admission Charges

The cost of admission for places mentioned in the text is indicated by the following method:

Inexpensive = under £3   Moderate = £3–5   Expensive = over £5

Getting Around

In main towns and cities the public transport network is fairly extensive.
Glasgow has Scotland's only underground system and is also well served by
urban trains and buses. Public transport is the best option in well-populated
areas, but for rural and remote areas a rented car will be more convenient,
as buses and trains may run infrequently.

Ticket deals for rail and bus travel

- **Freedom of Scotland Travelpass** – Available for 4, 8 and 12 days, it covers
  all rail journeys within Scotland, all internal scheduled CalMac ferries,
  Strathclyde PTE ferries and some Scottish Citylink bus connections.
- **Strathclyde Passenger Transport** (tel: 0141 332 7133) – Zonecards and Day
  Tripper tickets allow unlimited travel within western Scotland and also
  Glasgow underground, bus services and the Gourock Kilcreggan Ferry.
- Check the Scottish section of the **UK Public Transport Information** website
  (www.pti.org.uk/docs/scotland.htm) for up-to-date rail and bus timetables.

Trains

- For rail information, use **National Rail Enquiries** (tel: 08457 484950).
- **Scotrail** (tel: 0345 484950 for enquiries or 0345 550033 for bookings)
  operates most rail services within Scotland.
- **GNER** (tel: 0345 225225) operates the main east-coast London to
  Edinburgh intercity route.
- **Virgin** (tel: 08457 222333) also operates services on the main intercity
  routes and to the rest of the UK.

Journey times by train from Edinburgh:

Aberdeen 2 hours 30 minutes	Glasgow 48 minutes
Dundee 1 hour 20 minutes	Inverness 3 hours 30 minutes
	Perth 1 hour 15 minutes

Buses

- **Scottish Citylink** covers most of Scotland and also the rest of the UK (tel:
  0870 5505050; www.citylink.co.uk/index.html).
- Numerous small **local companies** link areas not covered by the main operators. Information and timetables are available from tourist offices.
- The **Royal Mail Postbus** service, which operates in the Highlands, Islands
  and remote rural areas, carries passengers in addition to the mail (tel:
  01463 256273).

Journey times by bus from Edinburgh:

Aberdeen 4 hours	Glasgow 2 hours
Dundee 2 hours	Inverness 4 hours
	Perth 1 hour 30 minutes

Ferry Services

- **Caledonian MacBrayne** (CalMac) has an extensive car-ferry service covering
  the main island destinations on the west coast, including Arran, the
  Western Isles, Skye and the smaller islands. Its website has full details and
  timetables (tel: 0870 5650000; www.calmac.co.uk).
- **P&O Scottish Ferries** sail regularly from Aberdeen to Orkney and Shetland all
  year round (tel: 01224 572615; www.poscottishferries.co.uk).

Internal Air Travel

- **Loganair** flies from Glasgow and Edinburgh to over 25 destinations in the Highlands and Islands, including the Western Isles, Orkney and Shetland. With average flight times of around 90 minutes, this is the quickest way to reach these destinations but it is expensive (tel: 0141 848 7594; www.british-airways.com/inside/wrldwide/partners/franchise/docs/loganair.shtml).
- **British Regional Airways** has scheduled flights linking the main cities in the UK and provides a regular service to the Islands (tel: 0345 222111; www.british-regional.com).
- Flights may be delayed or cancelled in **poor weather**.

Taxis

- In cities and larger towns the standard **black hackney cabs** ('London' cabs) are licensed, have meters and should display a tariff.
- **Taxi ranks** are usually found near stations and larger hotels and in the main shopping centres. Raise your arm to hail a cab in the street when its light is showing.
- **Minicabs and private hires** are also licensed and may have a meter. If not, agree a price before you get in. To hire a minicab, phone one of the numbers in the Yellow Pages or telephone directory. They are not allowed to pick up fares in the street, but many ignore this rule.

Driving

Driving in Scotland, particularly outside Glasgow and Edinburgh, is enjoyable and the best way to see the country. Roads are in good condition, but the further north you go the narrower the roads become, and in many areas they are single track with passing places. A bonus is that there's less traffic the deeper into the countryside you drive.

- If you bring your **own car** you'll need its registration documents (and a letter of authorisation) and valid insurance for the UK.
- Drive on the **left**.
- Drivers and all passengers must wear **seat belts**.
- **Speed limits** are 48kph in towns, 96kph on other roads and 113kph on motorways unless signs indicate otherwise.
- The **legal alcohol limit** for drivers is 80mg alcohol per 100ml blood. Drivers will be breathalysed when involved in an accident or when stopped by police and transgressors will be locked up, brought to court, heavily fined and banned from driving. The safest policy is not to drink when driving.
- **Fuel prices** vary but are much higher in the Highlands and Islands (but generally cheaper than the rest of the UK). Best prices are at supermarket filling stations. There are some 24-hour stations on motorways and in large urban areas, but filling stations are few and far between in rural areas.
- You'll find **emergency telephones** at regular intervals along motorways. The Automobile Association (AA) operates a 24-hour breakdown service for its members and for members of organisations with reciprocal agreements (tel: 0800 919595).

Car Hire

Most major companies have facilities at airports and major towns and cities. Book in advance to save money and to avoid lengthy waits at peak times. Car hire is usually available to over-21s only, and you'll need a full driving licence or international permit and a major credit card.

Avis 0990 900500	**Connect** 08707 282828
Budget 0800 181181	**Thrifty** 01494 442110

Accommodation

Standards of accommodation are generally high throughout the country, and wherever you stay the Scottish people are warm and hospitable (as long as you don't call them 'Scotch').

Hotels

- **Rates** are normally quoted per person and include VAT (value added tax). Luxury hotels can cost over £200 and the average price in Edinburgh or Glasgow is about £70–150 for two people, including breakfast. Elsewhere, expect to pay £50–90.
- Scotland is noted for its **country-house hotels**, most of which were built in the 19th century by rich industrialists to indulge their sporting passions. Often remote and set in vast estates, fishing (and occasionally shooting) is generally included in a very expensive deal, but these places do give you the chance to experience the pampered world of the super rich. Other grand houses stand beside world-famous golf courses and give you the chance to play a course that would otherwise be out of bounds.
- Few locations can match the romance of a Scottish **castle** and the unique opportunity to glimpse Scotland's turbulent history *in situ*. Although most genuine castles are privately owned, a few have been converted into hotels where you can enjoy all the atmosphere of a castle, but without the associated deprivations. Resplendent in granite and castellation, often complete with hexagonal towers, they bring an intimate yet refined atmosphere and, although prices are high, comfort and luxury are second to none.

Other accommodation

- For traditional Scottish hospitality and a chance to rub shoulders with local people, a **bed and breakfast** (B&B) is the best option. Most of Scotland's B&Bs and guest houses are family homes, and even inexpensive B&Bs usually have simple *en-suite* facilities. The hosts are usually a wonderful source of information, can help in planning itineraries and recommend the best places for visits, shopping, eating and entertainment. You'll often find a selection of local guides and maps that you can browse during your stay.
- **Guest houses** are more like small hotels than ordinary family homes (even though many have resident proprietors) and offer simple accommodation at reasonable prices.
- **Coaching inns** were once integral to Scottish life, when they were staging posts for weary horses and travellers who might have ridden for days over the glens. These attractive historic buildings can be found in practically every town centre. Traditional décor is standard, and there's usually a restaurant serving regional, home-cooked food in an informal atmosphere.

Booking Accommodation

- It's always wise to book ahead as major cities, especially Edinburgh and Glasgow, are busy all year. Elsewhere, many attractions and a lot of the accommodation closes from October until Easter.
- May to August is the **peak season** so any visit off-season in early spring or late autumn may avoid the crowds and bring discounted accommodation.
- If you're touring by car and have a flexible schedule, a network of Tourist Information Centres offers a **Book-a-Bed-Ahead** scheme and, for a small fee, they will reserve a room for you. Contact Edinburgh and Scotland Information Centre at Waverley Market, 3 Princes Street, Edinburgh, tel: 0131 4733800; fax: 0131 4733881.

Breakfast

- In mid- to top-range hotels, breakfast may not be included in the price of the room, and it may turn out to be an expensive and disappointing option. It is often better value, and more fun, to find a local café instead.
- Food in the smaller establishments is usually restricted to breakfast, but most hosts take great pride in their breakfasts, offering traditional Scottish fare such as bacon, eggs, sausages, tomatoes, mushrooms, black pudding and haggis, as well as a range of regional variations. A typical B&B breakfast will beat most served by hotels, and the portions often seem generous enough to keep you going until evening.

Alternative Inexpensive Options

Camping and Caravanning

- Despite the damp climate, camping and caravanning is a popular choice for locals and visitors alike. Camping is the most practical option for those wishing to explore the spectacular countryside in depth, particularly as Scotland is one of the last areas in Britain where it is possible to pitch a tent away from recognised campsites (but it is wise, and polite, to ask the landowner for permission first).
- Roads which are unsuitable for towing caravans are usually marked clearly. However, take extra care when towing a caravan along a single track road that you are not causing a blockage, as it is an offence to hold up a following vehicle.
- Although welcome at dedicated sites, caravans are not permitted to park overnight in lay-bys or other car parks. Barriers may be placed across entrances to prevent this from occurring.
- There are over 400 official, licensed camping and caravan sites in Scotland. Listings and directions can be provided by local tourist offices.
- *Scotland: The Official Where to Stay Caravan and Camping* is published by the Scottish Tourist Board.

Youth Hostels

- If you're on a tight budget but don't want to camp out in the cold, youth and backpacking hostels provide cheap alternative accommodation. The simple lodgings are usually in the form of dormitories, which also provide an opportunity to meet fellow travellers. Washing and cleaning facilities are also provided, although at some hostels you will be expected to clean up after yourself.
- The Scottish Youth Hostel Association (tel: 01786 891400) offers an extensive network of properties, some of which are in fascinating old buildings such as croft houses, converted churches, abandoned schools and even a Highland castle.

Information Sources

- AA *Bed & Breakfast* and *Hotel Guide* – annual publications with comprehensive sections devoted to Scotland. You can also check listings and book online at www.theAA.com.
- *Scotland Bed-and-Breakfast* and *Hotels and Guest Houses* – directories of over 1,700 B&Bs and over 1,500 hotels and guest houses, published by the Scottish Tourist Board.
- **Classic Scotland** Queen Anne House, 111 High Street, Fort William PH33 6DG (tel: 01397 704422; 01397 700022; www.classicscotland.com) provides listings of castles and country house hotels.
- The Scottish Tourist Board also publishes an annual guide to **self-catering** properties and provides practical information for **visitors with disabilities**.

Food and Drink

Eating out is one of the highlights of a visit to Scotland, with everything from traditional Scottish classics to the latest culinary innovations on offer. The secret is good-quality local produce, with the best menus featuring such delights as Aberdeen Angus beef, salmon, venison and lamb, an array of fresh vegetables and a bewildering selection of cheeses.

Scottish Cuisine

- The best-known Scottish delicacy is haggis (➤ 24) – sheep's offal mixed with beef suet and lightly toasted oatmeal, and then boiled in the synthetic skin. With a rich, spicy flavour it tastes better than its description might imply. Haggis is traditionally served with 'neeps' (turnips) and 'tatties' (potatoes). You'll find it in butchers' and supermarkets everywhere, but the best-known haggis makers are Charles MacSween & Son of Edinburgh.
- Local cooking is widely available either in its traditional form or with a continental spin such the haggis in filo pastry parcels covered in a rich plum sauce found in Edinburgh's Stac Polly restaurants.

Traditional Scottish dishes to look out for include:

- **Scotch broth** (hotch-potch) – a light, thin soup of mutton or beef, pearl barley and vegetables.
- **Cock-a-leekie soup** – chicken, leeks, rice and prunes.
- **Cullen skink** – a soup made from smoked (finnan) haddock, milk and mashed potatoes.
- **Forfar bridies** – a pie of flaked pastry filled with minced beef and suet.
- **Scotch pies** – similar to bridies but with a delicious watercrust pastry, found in fish and chip shops along with other deep-fried delicacies like black and white puddings. But avoid the deep-fried Mars bar at all costs.
- **Scottish cheeses** are among the finest in Europe and range from hard, cheddar-like varieties to soft, creamy types flavoured with herbs, oatmeal or garlic. They are eaten with oatcakes – oat-flour biscuits baked on a griddle. Edinburgh cheesemonger Ian Mellis stocks the very best.

International Cuisine

- A wealth of international culinary styles is available, from cheap and cheerful Chinese takeaways to Greek, Turkish and Thai food. Most small towns have an Indian resaurant or two, even in the Highlands.
- Hotels often have excellent international restaurants, for example the Sheraton Grand, Channings and the Howard in Edinburgh, the Taycreggan on Loch Awe and Culloden House near Inverness.

Informal Eating

Café-bars and bistros are a growing trend in Scotland. Youthful, informal, irreverent and buzzing with atmosphere, they serve a variety of foods, from American to French, alongside British standards like bangers (sausages) and mash. Excellent examples are Barga and 76 St Vincent Street in Glasgow, Hubbub in Dumfries and the inimitable Fouters Bistro in Ayr.

High Tea

Traditional Scottish high tea is served in many hotels, tea rooms and cafés. Unlike English high tea, it often includes fish and chips or cold meat in addition to sandwiches. Also expect local specialities such as Dundee fruit cake, shortbread and scones or Scotch pancakes served warm with butter and jam.

Best for High Tea
■ **Café Gandolfi**, Glasgow (➤ 90)
■ **The Gleneagles Hotel**, Auchterarder (➤ 136)
■ **Kailzie Gardens Tearoom**, Peebles (➤ 112)
■ **Kind Kyttock's Kitchen**, Falkland (➤ 134)
■ **Old Pines Restaurant with Rooms**, Spean Bridge (➤ 167)

Eating Out

■ **Breakfast** is served from about 7:30 to 10:30am; **lunch**, noon to 2:30; high **tea** or early dinner, 4:30 to 6:30pm; **dinner**, from about 6:30 to 10:30pm. Last orders are often taken 45 minutes before the restaurant closes.
■ Some prices include a 10 per cent **service charge**, otherwise tipping is discretionary and can be anything from 10 to 15 per cent.
■ Many places offer good value early-evening or pre-theatre **menus**. In top restaurants, lunch may be a comparatively inexpensive option.
■ **Dress codes** are increasingly relaxed and although a few restaurants insist on a jacket and tie, smart casual is usually acceptable.

Drinking

■ Pop into a bar or pub, where the choice for many is a 'dram' (a glass of **whisky** – the Irish and American varieties are spelled with an 'e'). Known as the water of life, there are two basic types of whisky: single malt is the most expensive and the product of a single distillery; blended whisky is less expensive, more popular and is a mixture of malts from several distilleries. When you're drinking malt whisky, make sure you add nothing but water to it – anything else is an insult.
■ **Beer** is not known by the English term 'bitter', but is described as 'export', 'heavy' or 'special'.
■ There's been a significant revival of small, traditional **breweries**, including Belhaven of Dunbar, Traquair of Innerleithen (➤ 110), Tomintoul (Ballindalloch) and Edinburgh's Caledonian, producer of the excellent Golden Promise organic ale.
■ **Licensing laws** are different to those in England. Pubs tend to be open later – until midnight during the week and 1am on Friday and Saturday nights, or even after 2 if they have a late license. Pubs do not open until midday on Sundays, however, and cannot serve alcohol until 12:30. They may not open at all on a Sunday where the Sabbath is strictly observed.
■ The **minimum age** for buying alcohol is 18.
■ It is usually prohibited to drink alcohol, or even to carry opened bottles, in the street and the drink will be confiscated by police if you are caught.
■ The **non-alcoholic** choice is Irn-Bru, the Scottish soda drink (➤ 53), although some might argue that this is an acquired taste. Tea and coffee are also generally available in pubs and bars.

Best Pubs
■ **Babbity Bowster**, Glasgow (➤ 90)
■ **The Byre Inn**, Brig o'Turk (➤ 135)
■ **Café Royal**, Edinburgh
■ **The Crown**, Portpatrick (➤ 113)
■ **The Drover's Inn**, Inverarnan (➤ 135)

Useful Publications:

■ The **Taste of Scotland** Scheme encourages its members to dedicate themselves to a high standard of traditional cuisine. The organisation produces an annual restaurant directory of the best places to eat and stay.
■ AA *Best Restaurants* guide is also available on CD-ROM.

Shopping

Shopping opportunities are abundant in Scotland, not only in modern city malls but tucked away in individual craft and specialist shops, and in smaller towns and villages. Traditional favourites such as tartan scarves, Celtic brooches, silverware and glassware make ideal gifts. Souvenirs range from the cheap and tacky (Loch Ness monsters or Highland cattle in the form of soft toys, fridge magnets and ornaments) to the upmarket, from cashmere to a crafted silver quaich (a traditional drinking cup).

Tartans, Tweeds and Knitwear

Good purchases are traditional kilts, jackets, skirts, suits and sweaters, especially if hand-made, and durable high-quality goods are widely available. Edinburgh's Royal Mile and Princes Street are two of the best places to browse, and bargain hunters can't beat the mill factory shops in the Borders.

Crafts and Jewellery

You'll find a vast array of arts, crafts and kitsch everywhere from high street shops to country craft stores, but the **House of Bruar**, just off the A9 north of Pitlochry, and the **National Trust for Scotland** (NTS) gift shops are the best places for Scottish crafts. Gift ideas include Scottish crystal glasses, vases and bowls created by Edinburgh Crystal or Caithness Glass (➤ 170). There are small, traditional potteries all over Scotland, including the Lighthouse Pottery at Portpatrick and the Borgh Pottery on Lewis.

Also popular and widely available is **pewter and silver jewellery** crafted to traditional Celtic designs copied from ancient illuminated books and manuscripts. Antiques shops and second-hand shops are good for unusual Victorian jewellery, but also look out for the work of new young designers in the trendy shops of Edinburgh and Glasgow.

Food and Drink

Scotch whisky makes an excellent gift and what you don't drink while you're here you can take home. It's available everywhere, but it's more fun to try before you buy at a distillery (➤ 172–5).

Food also makes great souvenirs, but check your home country's food import regulations first. Good buys include smoked salmon and Loch Fyne kippers, or try oatcakes, shortbread and Dundee cake in traditional tartan presentation tins. An option for those with strong teeth is Edinburgh rock, a hard, sugary treat available at sweet shops and souvenir shops throughout Edinburgh and beyond.

Entertainment

The Scottish entertainment scene features everything from incomprehensible avant-garde theatre to traditional Scottish shows of the 'haggis and heather' type. Tourist information packs in hotels and guest houses usually include listings. In Edinburgh or Glasgow buy a copy of *The List* magazine, published every two weeks. It's the best guide to what's on and covers cinema, theatre, clubs, concerts, the arts and readings by local and visiting authors. Elsewhere, the *Herald*, one of Scotland's quality newspapers, publishes national listings in its Saturday supplement.

Theatre, Music and Dance

■ Scotland has a strong tradition of theatre and modern and classical productions, musicals and pantomimes are staged throughout the year. Venues include the Dundee Rep, Pitlochry Festival Theatre, Tron and the Citizens in Glasgow, the Traverse in Edinburgh or the Theatre Royal, Dumfries, Scotland's oldest working theatre.

■ Opera, classical concerts and most other forms of music are available in abundance in the main cities. Try Glasgow's **Royal Concert Hall** for a varied programme or the **Queens Hall**, Edinburgh, which is also home to the Scottish Chamber Orchestra (see also ➤ 12–13).

■ For classical dance lovers the acclaimed **Scottish National Ballet** is the main company.

Pubs and Clubs

■ The pub scene has changed greatly over the years and most bars now serve food as well as drink. If music is featured it's usually free when in the main bar and you'll find music to suit all tastes, from traditional Scottish to jazz.

■ Clubs range from ceilidh (pronounced 'kay-lee') dance venues to the latest high-tech dance houses, with the best choices in the main cities (➤ 12–13). There's a useful website for Edinburgh and Glasgow clubs at www.webflyers.co.uk.

Outdoor Activities

■ **Golf** is one of Scotland's major attractions and many visitors come to play on its world-class courses (➤ 16–17). With over 500 courses to choose from, you can get full details from an excellent searchable website: www.scottishgolf.com/course_directory/ index.cfm. You can also get a list of local courses from area tourist offices.

■ Scotland is ideal for **hiking and climbing**, with challenging peaks in the Highlands, gentle hill walks in the Lowlands and a series of waymarked, long-distance paths, including the West Highland Way and the Southern Upland Way (➤ 122).

■ Most tourist information offices have books, leaflets and maps covering walks in their area. For general books on **walking** in Scotland, maps, clothing and safety equipment try Graham Tiso's shops in Edinburgh (Rose Street and Princes Street) and Glasgow (Buchanan Street).

■ For practical information and locations of walks and trails check www.visitscotland.com/outdoor/walk.

■ **Safety note:** Scottish hills and mountains can be lethal even in summer. Before undertaking any walks or climbs make sure you are skilled and fit enough to complete them, with adequate footwear and outdoor clothing for the terrain and the necessary safety equipment.

■ There's some excellent **fishing** to be had, whether by fly in the lochs and famous salmon rivers, beach casting from spots round the coastline or sea fishing from purpose-built boats. Great information can be gained online from www.where-to-fish.com/2.html, or contact the area tourist offices for details on close seasons, local fishing spots and where to get permits. Many hotels also offer fishing for guests.

Spectator Sports

■ **Football** (soccer) is a passion for the average Scot and you'll have plenty of opportunities to watch a game. The season runs from around August to May and most league matches are held on Saturday afternoons, with some Sunday and midweek evening games. Most large towns have at least one league team and local rivalry, such as between Rangers and Celtic in Glasgow, can be intense. National and local newspapers carry fixture lists.

- **Rugby union** is almost an obsession in the Scottish Borders towns, but for an unforgettable experience try to catch an international match at Edinburgh's Murrayfield stadium, particularly during the Six Nations Championship and especially if Scotland is playing England for the Calcutta Cup. The post-match atmosphere in the city's pubs and clubs is beyond description.
- **Shinty**, the national sport of the Gaels, originated some 2,000 years ago with the ancient Celtic people. Played by teams of 12 with a ball and stick, it's been described as a 'warlike version of hockey'. Details of fixtures can be found on the Camanachd Association website: www.shinty.com.

Festivals

Festivals and gatherings of all descriptions take place in most Scottish towns and villages. From highland games to cultural events, there is rarely a time of year when there is not a festival to visit.

- **Edinburgh's International Arts Festival** in August is perhaps the best known and attended (➤ 21–2), but festivals featuring traditional Scottish or Celtic music are held most weekends throughout the country. A good cross-section of the best includes:
- **Celtic Connections**, Glasgow, mid-Jan (tel: 0141 3538050; www.grch.com; ➤ 12–13)
- **Girvan Traditional Folk Festival**, May Bank Holiday weekend (tel: 01465 712123; http://welcome.to/girvan)
- **Newcastleton**, early July (tel: 013873 76254; http://members.netscape online.co.uk/newcastletontmf
- The **Traditional Music and Song Association** (TMSA) at 95 St Leonard's Street, Edinburgh, produces a comprehensive calendar of events (tel: 0131 6675587; e-mail: e.cowie@tmsa.demon.co.uk; www.tmsa.demon.co.uk).

Other Festivals and Village Galas

- **Up Helly Aa**, Lerwick, Shetland, last Tuesday in January – Viking Fire Festival with no allowances made for the weather (➤ 165).
- **Inverness Festival**, last week in February – covers the whole gamut of music, from classical to traditional.
- **International Science Festival**, Edinburgh, early April.
- **Glasgow Art Fair**, mid-April – art from selected galleries displayed in marquees in George Square.
- **Beltane**, Edinburgh, evening of 30 April – a celebration of the start of the ancient pagan summer on Calton Hill. Some smaller towns hold similar events around this time.
- **T in the Park**, Balado, Fife, second weekend in June – mega rock festival attracting big name bands as well as big crowds. A campsite is provided for those staying for the whole weekend.
- **St Magnus Festival**, Orkney, third week in June – superb arts festival.
- **World Pipe Band Championships**, Glasgow, mid-August – a sea of tartan invades Glasgow Green.
- **Cowal Highland Gathering**, Dunoon, last weekend in August – the world's largest Highland Games.
- **Braemar Gathering**, Aberdeenshire, September – quintessential Highland Games, including caber tossing, tug o' war and pipe bands, usually attracting one or two members of the royal family.
- **The Mod**, changing locations, second week in October – festival and competitions for all areas of Gaelic culture.
- **Hogmanay**, 31 Dec–1 Jan – enthusiastic New Year's celebrations occur throughout Scotland, but Edinburgh's Princes Street is *the* venue for this massive outdoor party.

Edinburgh

RARE OLD
WHISKIES

Royal Mile
Whiskies

In a Day 46 – 47
Don't Miss 48 – 57
At Your Leisure 58 – 60
Where to… 61 – 66

WHISKY

Getting Your Bearings

Edinburgh is one of the most beautiful and well preserved historic cities in Europe. Set among the volcanic plugs of Castle Rock, Arthur's Seat and Calton Hill, the medieval Old Town and the Georgian New Town provide contrasting historical insights. The narrow closes, steep winding alleys and tall tenements of the Old Town recall the overcrowded conditions of 'Auld Reekie' (Old Smokey) in the Middle Ages, and it's easy to imagine the black smog from a thousand chimneys which gave old Edinburgh its nickname. Go from here to the light, airy squares of the New Town, with spacious avenues, elegant terraces and spruce gardens, to see how things were different for the wealthy citizens who moved to these streets.

Despite the hills, Edinburgh is best explored on foot. Wherever you turn there's a breathtaking view and in summer there's greenery everywhere, from the great open space of Princes Street Gardens to the enclosed gardens of the New Town or the tiny hidden corners in the Old Town. The architecture of the 1970s made few inroads in Edinburgh, with the notable exception of Princes Street. Viewed from the gardens, try to picture these buildings before they were encased in unlovely concrete boxes. The castle dominates the city, peeping over the tenements, silhouetted in the sunset or towering over Princes Street. There's always a buzz about Edinburgh, with plenty of cafés and pubs in the Royal Mile, excellent restaurants and a lively nightlife centring on the Grassmarket and the Cowgate. In August the city explodes into life, with the Edinburgh International Festival attracting thousands of visitors to its bewildering choice of shows and exhibitions throughout the day and night. The Festival spills out all over the city with street theatre, buskers and craft stalls. Wander the streets, sit at the pavement cafés and absorb the vibrant atmosphere.

This figure of Ensign Kennedy carrying a wounded comrade is on display in Edinburgh Castle Museum

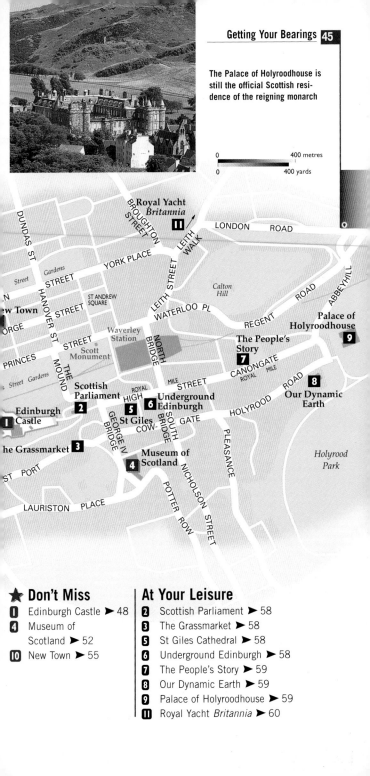

The Palace of Holyroodhouse is still the official Scottish residence of the reigning monarch

0   400 metres
0   400 yards

Royal Yacht *Britannia* **11**

LONDON ROAD

DUNDAS ST

BROUGHTON STREET

LEITH WALK

YORK PLACE

LEITH STREET

Street

Gardens

STREET

HANOVER STREET

New Town

ST ANDREW SQUARE

WATERLOO PL

Calton Hill

ORGE

GEORGE ST

Waverley Station

REGENT ROAD

ABBEYHILL

Palace of Holyroodhouse 9

PRINCES STREET

Scott Monument

NORTH BRIDGE

THE MOUND

The People's Story 7

CANONGATE ROYAL MILE

s Street Gardens

MILE STREET

Scottish Parliament 2

ROYAL

HIGH

Underground Edinburgh 6

Our Dynamic Earth 8

HOLYROOD ROAD

Edinburgh Castle 1

5 St Giles

GEORGE IV BRIDGE

SOUTH BRIDGE

COW- GATE

PLEASANCE

The Grassmarket 3

Holyrood Park

ST PORT

Museum of Scotland 4

NICHOLSON STREET

LAURISTON PLACE

POTTER ROW

★ Don't Miss

- **1** Edinburgh Castle ➤ 48
- **4** Museum of Scotland ➤ 52
- **10** New Town ➤ 55

At Your Leisure

- **2** Scottish Parliament ➤ 58
- **3** The Grassmarket ➤ 58
- **5** St Giles Cathedral ➤ 58
- **6** Underground Edinburgh ➤ 58
- **7** The People's Story ➤ 59
- **8** Our Dynamic Earth ➤ 59
- **9** Palace of Holyroodhouse ➤ 59
- **11** Royal Yacht *Britannia* ➤ 60

From the castle, wander in medieval streets with bizarre and fascinating shops, through pleasant gardens to restrained Georgian terraces.

Edinburgh in a Day

9:30am

Start the day by exploring **Edinburgh Castle** (pictured right, ➤ 48–51) for an hour and a half.

11:00am

Head down Castle Hill, cross over Johnston Terrace and walk down Upper Bow to Victoria Terrace. Take the steps down into colourful Victoria Street. The shops here include an intriguing brush shop and a wonderful flea market called Byzantium. Take tea in its old-fashioned tea room, from where you can watch the market stalls below. Alternatively, the **Grassmarket** (➤ 58) at the bottom of Victoria Street has still more quirky shops and pubs with pavement tables.

Noon

From the Grassmarket head up Candlemaker Row. At the top on the left look out for the statue of the Skye terrier Greyfriars Bobby (pictured), who guarded his master's grave for 14 years and is the only dog to have been awarded the freedom of the city. Cross the road to the new **Museum of Scotland** (➤ 52). Allow a couple of hours for a visit, including lunch in the Tower Restaurant with a great view over the castle, or have a snack in the café of the adjoining Royal Museum of Scotland.

2:15pm

From the museum, head along George IV Bridge and pop into the **Scottish Parliament Visitor Centre** (► 58). At the Royal Mile turn right into the High Street for a quick look at **St Giles Cathedral** (► 58) and then turn back towards the castle, exploring some of the closes on the way. The excellent Writers' Museum (pictured left) in Lady Stair's Close is free, and Gladstone's Land, a medieval merchant's town house, is also worth a look. Halfway up Castle Hill turn into Ramsay Lane to look at the houses in Ramsay Garden.

3:30pm

Walk down the Mound and turn into Princes Street Gardens (its floral displays provide a welcome dash of colour, below). Stop for afternoon tea at the café in the park if the weather's fine. If not, head for the tea room in the church crypt at the end of the gardens.

4:00pm

Cross Princes Street into **New Town** (► 55–7) and turn up Charlotte Street to Charlotte Square. The headquarters of the National Trust for Scotland are at No 28, and you can go in for some information before heading for the Georgian House at No 7. Last entry is at 4:30pm.

5:00pm

From Charlotte Square stroll through the New Town to appreciate the elegant Georgian terraces, tenements and mews. It's worth thoroughly exploring this handsome old area of the city. Head down to Queen Street, cross over and go down Forres Street to Moray Place. Walk clockwise around this massive classical circle and along Darnaway Street to exclusive Heriot Row. If you have time turn left down India Street as far as Royal Circus, taking the first right and back up to Queen Street by Howe Street and Queen Street Gardens West. Turn left along Queen Street and continue up Hanover Street to George Street. Turn left into George Street to St Andrew's Square and cross the square to West Register Street and the Café Royal for a pre-dinner drink.

8:00pm

Le Chamertin in the George Intercontinental Hotel on George Street (► 63) provides an intimate atmosphere to end the evening. Alternatively, Henderson's, round the corner in Hanover Street, offers imaginative vegetarian dishes. Finish the day with a tour of the pubs in Rose Street.

Edinburgh Castle

Over a million people visit the castle every year, and if you only have time to see one attraction in Scotland, make it this one. Perched high on a craggy outcrop, the 800-year-old castle has served as a royal palace, a military garrison and a battleground. This great sheer rockface dominates the view from every direction as you approach Edinburgh, and it must have looked awesome to tired and footsore infantry marching from England. Yet the castle is not as impregnable as it looks, and has often changed hands over the centuries.

Once through the gate, keep climbing the curving cobbled road up to Crown Square, then work your way down. The entrance to the **Crown Room,** housing the ancient Honours of Scotland – the oldest crown jewels in Europe,– is in the corner of the square and you may have to queue. After a short trip through Scottish history through a series of excellent tableaux, the Crown Room itself is undoubtedly the highlight. The crown, made for King James V, is richly decorated with pearls, precious gems and ermine, and incorporates the gold crown of Robert the Bruce. It has been frequently repaired over the years, but remains an important national treasure. The fine gold sceptre topped with a sparkling crystal orb is decorated with religious icons. It was originally given to James IV by Pope Alexander VI in the 15th century, while Pope Julius II presented the sword, its great two-handed hilt and scabbard intricately decorated.

Next to these glittering icons lies an equally potent but surprisingly mundane symbol of Scottish sovereignty – the **Stone of Destiny.** A coarse pink sandstone block with iron rings attached to each end, it was the coronation stone on which the kings of Scotland were inaugurated for over 400 years. Stolen by Edward I of England in 1296, it became the coronation stone of England and, later, the United Kingdom and was kept in Westminster Abbey. It was temporarily 'repossessed' by four Scottish students at Christmas 1950 but was returned to Scotland in 1996.

Left: In the Castle Museum, Private McBain is part of a re-creation of the 17th-century Battle of Maplaquet

The crown was made with gold mined near Scotland's highest village

Also on public view are the **Royal Apartments,** particularly the chamber where Mary, Queen of Scots gave birth to the future James VI. The rooms have been refurbished and sensitively restored to their original 16th-century splendour, including beautifully carved wood panelling, replica wall coverings and ornate fireplaces.

Above: Edinburgh Castle rises majestically above Princes Street Gardens

On the south side of Crown Square, the **Great Hall,** with its massive wooden vaulted ceiling, once housed the Scottish Parliament, and is still used for receptions and state functions by the First Minister of Scotland.

On the north side of the square, the **Scottish National War Memorial** is a moving tribute to the dead of all wars. Behind the War Memorial is Edinburgh's oldest building, the tiny 12th-century **St Margaret's Chapel,** which has survived demolition by marauding armies for 800 years.

From Crown Square, descend to the dank, chilling corridors of the **Vaults**, which are built into the solid rock. They have been used variously as stores, bakeries and prison cells. Look for the graffiti left by French prisoners incarcerated in this dismal hole in the 18th and 19th centuries. Also here is the great 15th-century siege gun Mons Meg, along with the enormous stone cannonballs it could fire over a distance of 2km. Known as the Muckle Murderer, it was used at the Battle of Flodden in 1513.

Right: The Great Hall with its massive stone fireplace and part of the armour collection

TAKING A BREAK

After trudging round the castle, you can eat, have a coffee or just sample the huge range of whiskies at the **Scotch Whisky Heritage Centre** next to the castle.

✚ 198 B3
✉ Top of the Royal Mile
☎ 0131 2259846
🕐 Daily 9:30–6 (5 in winter), Apr–Sep
🚉 Waverley
💷 Expensive

Below: The firing of the one o'clock gun is tradition which has continued, unbroken, since the 17th century

EDINBURGH CASTLE: INSIDE INFO

Top tip Get your picture taken astride the cannons on the Argyle Battery.
• Try to be at **Mills Mount Battery** at 1pm for the firing of the gun. This was originally for the benefit of ships in the Firth of Forth, but now Edinburgh folk just check their watches by it. On Calton Hill look for Nelson's Monument, a strange telescope-shaped feature with a suspended ball at the top. Watch for the ball dropping when the one o'clock gun fires.
• Even if you're short of time, don't be so keen to see inside the castle that you miss the panoramic views of the town and surrounding countryside. The best viewpoint is from the battlements in front of St Margaret's Chapel, where the formal plan of the New Town is laid out before you with the Firth of Forth and the Lomond Hills of Fife beyond.

Hidden gems Just below the battlements of the Argyle Battery is the tiny and always beautifully kept **Pets' Cemetery** , the resting place of soldiers' pets.
• Just as you enter the Esplanade, look out for a small iron wall-fountain known as the **Witches' Well**, where women found guilty of witchcraft were once burned at the stake.

One to miss West of Crown Square in an 18th-century barracks is the **Scottish United Services Museum**, with a comprehensive display of uniforms and weaponry. Unless you're particularly interested in military history, you could give this a miss, but do try to see the model ship, the *Great George*, made by French prisoners of war.

Museum of Scotland

Opened in 1998, the Museum of Scotland is housed in a wide, round sandstone tower with asymmetric windows, described as 'the finest Scottish building of the 20th century'. The museum complements the adjoining Victorian Royal Museum of Scotland and tells the story of the country from its geological formation to the end of the second millennium. Over 10,000 of the nation's greatest treasures are displayed alongside countless everyday objects, over several floors.

A good starting point on Level 0 are the abstract human figures sculpted in bronze by Sir Eduardo Paolozzi (born 1924), displaying the rings, necklaces and amulets of shadowy early generations. In the 'Dead and Sometimes Buried' section is a skeleton lying in its burial position on a bed of flat stones in a reconstructed Viking grave.

On Level 1 you'll find one of the museum's most important objects – the **Monymusk Reliquary,** a tiny 8th-century casket that once held a relic of St Columba. Revered and treasured as a holy shrine, it was carried to the army of Robert the Bruce before the Battle of Bannockburn in 1314. Here too are the **Lewis chess pieces,** intricately carved in ivory by invading Vikings and discovered in the 19th century. Also on this level is the gruesome but compelling **Maiden** (pictured opposite right), Scotland's guillotine, used for public executions in the Grassmarket from the 16th century. A multimedia display demonstrates its workings, complete with chilling sound effects.

The tiny Monymusk Reliquary is a masterpiece of the medieval craftworker's art

The entrance to Level 3 takes you under the royal arms into the United Kingdom. The succession was bitterly contested in the rebellions of 1715 and 1745, and the full story is told in **The Jacobite Challenge**. Jewellery, portraits and glassware inscribed with the image of Bonnie Prince Charlie

For the Children

The **Discovery Centre** on Level 3 is a hands-on zone where children can touch the exhibits, reconstruct ancient pottery, delve into a Roman centurion's knapsack or dress in period clothes.

(Charles Edward Stuart, 1720–88) testify to the cult that grew in the years following his defeat at the Battle of Culloden in 1746. But pride of place goes to his personal items, particularly the silver travelling canteen that he abandoned at Culloden along with his sword and targe (shield).

Levels 4 and 5 move from romantic legends to an age of machinery and factories, when Scotland became one of the most industrialised countries in Europe. The Victorian steam locomotive *Ellesmere* dominates the railway engineering display, and you can learn all about whisky distilling around the huge copper still.

The spectacular architecture of the Mueum of Scotland is as much a draw as its contents

Some Modern Scottish Icons
- **Irn-Bru:** A non-alcoholic soda drink, Scotland's popular answer to Coca-Cola.
- **Doc Martens:** Tough and very comfortable 'air-soled' shoes and boots. Named after their German inventor and made for the British market in England, they are very popular in Scotland. Once a symbol of aggression, available only in black and worn by trouble-makers, they are now fashion items available in a variety of colours, patterns and sizes.
- **Oor Wullie:** Perhaps Scotland's most famous cartoon character. This mischievous wee laddie and his pals have tormented the local policeman for decades in a weekly strip in the *Sunday Post* newspaper.
- **The Broons:** Often described as 'Scotland's first family', their adventures also appear in the *Sunday Post*.

The Twentieth Century on Level 6 brings the story bang up to date. Scottish people were asked to choose the artefacts that they thought best represented 20th-century Scotland, and they came up with a pretty diverse selection, including things like Doc Martens boots, Irn-Bru and Oor Wullie (see panel on page 53). Televisions, tubeless tyres and teddy bears share space with the Queen Mother's tartan sash and former motor-racing champion Jackie Stewart's racing helmet. The Prime Minister, Tony Blair (born 1953), chose a Fender Stratocaster guitar, recalling 'a time when everyone wanted nothing more than to be in a rock band'. Sir Sean Connery's milk bottle with a copy of the Declaration of Arbroath (Scotland's claim to nation-hood of 1320) rolled up and stuck in the neck unites his Scottish nation-alism and his early days as an Edinburgh milkman.

John Logie Baird's 'Televisor', the world's first television set, on display in the Royal Museum

TAKING A BREAK

The **café** in the adjacent Royal Museum building is great for a quick coffee or a light lunch. For a bigger bite, the **Tower Restaurant**, overlooking Edinburgh Castle, one of the city's top eating places (➤ 61).

➕ 199 D3 ✉ Chambers Street ☎ 0131 2474422; www.nms.ac.uk
🕐 Mon–Sat 10–5, Tue 10–8, Sun noon–5
🍴 Café in Royal Museum (£), Tower Restaurant (£££)
🚌 14, 7, 8, 87 from Princes Street (east end); 21, 33, 30, 3, 31, 36, 69 from west end
🚉 Waverley
🎟 Inexpensive; season ticket expensive

MUSEUM OF SCOTLAND: INSIDE INFO

Top tip It's well worth buying a **season ticket** which, for just a few pounds more than a single entry, gives unlimited access to several of Scotland's national museums for one year.

Hidden gem The **roof terrace** on Level 7 has breathtaking views over Edinburgh, the Firth of Forth and the Pentland Hills.

The New Town

Stray into the quiet Georgian streets of Edinburgh's New Town and not even the parked cars can break the spell of a time warp where the last 200 years have simply disappeared. It richly deserves its status as a World Heritage Site and even in its day would have been an outstanding collection of buildings. You can quite easily wander for hours around the cobbled grid of parallel avenues, backstreet mews, private gardens and curving terraces.

Moray Place, the most visually stunning part of Edinburgh's New Town

The area was a pioneering venture in town planning, prompted by the desire of Edinburgh's wealthy merchants to escape the medieval squalor of the Old Town where rich and poor lived cheek by jowl. The young architect James Craig won the competition to design the New Town in 1767, with a simple grid design of three parallel streets with a square at each end. Central to the design is the broad avenue of **George Street** while below, **Princes Street** looks out over the Old Town and the castle, and **Queen Street** enjoys uninterrupted views to the Forth and Fife. Between the broad main streets, narrower **Rose Street** and **Thistle Street** provided service access, and this part became known as the First New Town while development continued around it. The New Town now encompasses the series of crescents arching west as far as Haymarket Station, the terraces of Dean village and the quiet streets below Queen Street Gardens. Linking these are the magnificent sweeping curves of **Moray Place, Ainslie Place** and **Randolph Crescent,** with their neo-classical façades.

Other famous architects and engineers also contributed to the New Town. The elegant north side of **Charlotte Square** has been described as Scottish architect Robert Adam's (1728–92) masterpiece, while further north artist Alexander Nasmyth (1758–1840) designed the Pump Room on the Water of Leith, and Dean Bridge was the work of Scottish civil engineer Thomas Telford (1757–1834).

At No 28 Charlotte Square, arguably the finest Georgian square in the UK, you'll find the headquarters of the National Trust for Scotland. There are exhibitions, information and a restaurant, as

well as a Georgian drawing room with original furniture. For a better idea of life in these elegant town houses, head for the **Georgian House** at No 7, where the domestic life of Edinburgh's 18th-century gentry is faithfully re-created, from the china and furniture to the wine cellar and kitchen. The light, airy rooms and the open vistas of the square contrast significantly with the tiny windows, low ceilings and cramped

Above: 18th century elegance in the Georgian House
Below: A Town House in Moray Place

conditions of the Old Town. To make the comparison, visit **Gladstone's Land**, a typical 17th-century merchant's house in the Royal Mile. The official residence of the First Minister of the Scottish Parliament is next door to the Georgian House at No 6, Bute House.

Just below Charlotte Square on the other side of Queen Street, Moray Place was certainly the grandest of the New Town developments. Walk all the way round to absorb the scale of the huge classical-pillared frontages surrounding the central private garden. Robert Louis Stevenson lived at 17 **Heriot Row**, overlooking Queen Street Gardens – still one of the most desirable addresses in Edinburgh. Many original features remain, including fan lights, lampposts and boot scrapers at the doors. At the bottom of **India Street**, with its tall tenements stepping down the hill, the two matching crescents of **Royal Circus**, designed by William Playfair (1789–1857), are restrained and simple compared to the massive scale of Moray Place. **St Stephen's Church** in Howe Street is another Playfair building. Its distinctive classical frontage can be seen clearly down the length of the street.

Footbridge across the Water of Leith to the picturesque Dean Village

TAKING A BREAK

Have lunch or tea in the **Roxburghe Hotel** overlooking Charlotte Square. It's easy to miss because, in keeping with the architecture of the square, there's no obvious hotel sign.

THE NEW TOWN: INSIDE INFO

In more depth If you have time, explore the **northern extremities of the New Town**. It's a lovely walk from Telford's graceful Dean Bridge along the Water of Leith to the Pump Room at St Bernard's Well. At the end of Dean Terrace, look for Ann Street, possibly the most beautiful in the area, with miniature country houses with attractive gardens on each side.

At Your Leisure

🔢 The Scottish Parliament

After a gap of 300 years, Scotland's Parliament reconvened in 1999 following devolution (➤ 27–30). Until its new building is ready, the Parliament meets in the Assembly Rooms of the Church of Scotland at the top of the Mound, where you can go and see the new Scottish democracy at work. You don't need a ticket, and, unless there's a particularly controversial debate, you won't even have to queue.

➕ 198 C3 ✉ Visitors' Centre, George IV Bridge ☎ 0845 278 1999; www. scottish.parliament.uk 🕐 Mon and Fri 10–5, Tue–Thu 9–5, during Parliamentary session; Mon–Sat 10–5, during recess 🍴 Café (££–£££) 🚌 Guide Friday tour bus 🎟 Free

🔢 The Grassmarket

The Grassmarket, with the castle looming over it, has been a focal point and market-place for the town for over 500 years. Public executions were carried out here on the infamous Maiden (➤ 52) and it was here that the notorious 19th-century bodysnatchers (William) Burke and (William) Hare sought victims for their nefarious trade in cadavers.

Maggie Dickson's pub in the Grassmarket

The area is now a lively nightspot, its streets swarming with revellers wandering from packed pubs to the latest nightclubs. By day you can visit idiosyncratic shops such as Mr Wood's Fossils and Armstrong's, a fabulous second-hand clothes shop, or just relax at one of the pavement tables.

➕ 198 C3 ✉ Grassmarket

🔢 St Giles Cathedral

Dating from 1120, and featuring the 15th-century Crown Spire, St Giles has been at the centre of Edinburgh's turbulent past. This fine building is famed for its superb stained glass and grand organ. The small Thistle Chapel is dedicated to Scotland's highest award for chivalry.

➕ 199 D3 ✉ High Street ☎ 0131 2259442 🕐 Mon–Fri 9–7, Sat 9–5, Sun 1–5, Easter–Sep; Mon–Sat 9–5, Sun 1–5, Oct–Easter 🎟 Free

🔢 Underground Edinburgh

The modern streets of Edinburgh conceal a maze of ancient streets below, as any new buildings simply used the existing streets and tenements as their foundations. Several guided tours explore these streets, but the most interesting centres on **Mary King's Close.** This area suffered particularly badly from the plague, which frequently swept through the polluted streets of the Old Town, and the entire close was sealed for a period in around 1645. The guide provides a lively insight into life in the multistorey tenements, including details of some of the actual inhabitants and graphic descriptions of the sanitary arrangements. There are lots of walking tours of Edinburgh, based around a number of themes – look for details on boards around the Mercat Cross, near St Giles Cathedral.

🔢 199 D3 ✉ High Street ☎ 0131 5576464 🕐 Phone for booking 💷 Moderate

🔢 The People's Story

This tiny museum in the **Old Tolbooth**, a former prison and one of the oldest buildings in the Royal Mile, tells of the hard lives and work of Edinburgh's ordinary people. Displays include a prison cell, a cobbler's workshop and barrel-making, and there are re-creations of life in Edinburgh's tenements at different periods. Near by is the fascinating Carson Clark Gallery, which sells 17th-century maps of Edinburgh depicting the Tolbooth.

🔢 199 E4 ✉ Canongate ☎ 0131 5294057 🕐 Mon–Sat 10–5; (also Sun 2–5 during Edinburgh Festival) 🚌 Guide Friday tour bus 💷 Free

🔢 Our Dynamic Earth

Housed in a futuristic dome close to the Royal Mile, this exhibition explores the geography and geology of the world through lots of interactive screens and displays. Children of all ages will love it. Highlights are the floor pad to stamp out your own earthquake, the time machine with fantastic wide-screen effects and trembling floors, the enormous curved block of ice to touch and the realistic model of a tropical rain forest to explore.

🔢 199 F3 ✉ Holyrood Road ☎ 0131 5507800; www.dynamicearth.co.uk 🕐 Daily 10–6, Apr–Oct; Wed–Sun 10–5, Nov–Mar 🍴 Café (£) 🚌 Guide Friday tour bus 💷 Expensive

From a gentle walk to a steep climb, head for Holyrood Park and Arthur's Seat

'Wha'll buy my Caller Herrin'?' Model of a Scottish fishwife, once a common sight, in the People's Story

🔢 The Palace of Holyroodhouse

At the end of the Royal Mile, standing behind elegant wrought iron gates in a spacious courtyard, is the Queen's official residence in Scotland. Built for James IV in 1498, it was extensively renovated in the 1670s. The palace is normally open to the

public and the tour includes Mary, Queen of Scots' apartments. Holyroodhouse sits within the vast **Royal Park,** where you can take a gentle stroll by the pond to watch the swans, climb the hill paths to the top of **Arthur's Seat** or cycle through to nearby Duddingston to enjoy a drink in the quaint Sheep's Heid Inn.

🔲 199 F4 ✉ Canongate ☎ 0131 5561096 ⏰ Daily 9:30–6, Apr–Oct; 9:30–4:30, Nov–Mar (Palace may occasionally close at other times) 🚌 Guide Friday tour bus 🚉 Waverley 💷 Expensive

🔟 Royal Yacht *Britannia*

Now docked at the Port of Leith, the Royal Yacht *Britannia* is a magnet for royalists but has a much wider appeal. A tour of the yacht gives a fascinating insight into the private lives of the British royal family, who often took holidays on board. Countless royal couples, including the Prince and Princess of Wales, honeymooned here. You can peep into the bedrooms of the Queen and her family, as well as her office, and also walk through the informal lounge. In complete contrast are the state rooms and formal dining room where politicians, diplomats and world leaders were entertained. You can also see the crew's quarters. Don't miss the engine, a gleaming antique but still in perfect working order.

🔲 199, off E5 ✉ Ocean Drive, Leith ☎ 0131 5555566 ⏰ Daily 10:30–4:30 🍴 Café (£) 🚌 Bus from Waverley Station 💷 Expensive

4 Great Viewpoints

Calton Hill
From here you get a superb view along Princes Street to the castle, particularly impressive as the sun sets over the city. There are also fine views of the New Town, the Port of Leith, the Forth River and the Kingdom of Fife.

The Old Observatory, Calton Hill
Every Friday evening you can look through the great telescope here for a magnificent view of the night sky.

The Camera Obscura
On the Royal Mile just down from the castle, this is a great place to spy on the shoppers in Princes Street. Using a Victorian lens and mirror, an image of the surrounding city is projected onto a table in front of you. There are also good views from the roof.

Salisbury Crags
These rocky crags in Holyrood Park, just in front of Arthur's Seat, offer panoramic views of the city, particularly the Old Town and the countryside to the south.

Where to...
Eat and Drink

Prices

The £ amounts indicate what you can expect to pay for a three-course meal for one person, including coffee and service.

£ = under £15   **££** = £15–25   **£££** = over £25

RESTAURANTS

The Atrium £££

Atrium is as cutting edge as Edinburgh gets. A cool minimalist design is lent a rustic air with tables made of railway sleepers and twisted willow decorations. The kitchen's heart lies in the Mediterranean, and offers a sunny, upbeat and popular menu. Study the lengthy and knowledgeable wine list – over 20 wines are sold by the glass.

198 A3 10 Cambridge Street 0131 2288882 Lunch Mon–Fri; dinner Mon–Sat; closed Dec 24–Jan 2

Iggs £££

Ignacio Campos (Igg) runs his elegant, but informal Victorian-style restaurant with panache, aided by a likeable team dressed in 'Iggs'-emblazoned pink polo shirts. Located in the heart of Edinburgh's Old Town, just off the Royal Mile, it's deservedly popular. Menus are full of contemporary ideas but with the emphasis on simplicity, exemplified by well-sourced raw ingredients giving impact to fresh flavours.

199 D4 15 Jeffrey Street 0131 5578184 Lunch and dinner Mon–Sat

Kalpna £

This long-established vegetarian Indian restaurant is regarded by many as one of the best in the country. Freshly ground spices are used to produce interesting dishes. *Thalis* (set meals) give a good snapshot of what's on offer, and the Wednesday buffet, which specialises in regional cuisine, is a bargain. The service is helpful and charming.

199 D2 2–3 St Patrick Square 0131 6679890 Lunch Mon–Fri; dinner Mon–Sat

The Marque ££

Yellow walls and a black-and-white chequered floor form a perfect backdrop to lively contemporary cooking. There's the occasional church pew and a cosy alcove – it's a great place to see and be seen. The light, modern food is offset by a carefully sourced wine list, with plenty of half-bottles and wines by the glass.

199 E1 19–21 Causewayside 0131 4666660 Lunch and dinner Tue–Sun

Restaurant Martin Wishart £££

Confident cooking from a chef who has worked with some of the greats. The menu is small – two choices per course for lunch, slightly more at dinner – but ranges from classic French to salsa-infused modernism. Set by the water in Leith, it's a bright, intimate restaurant that's perhaps best saved for a special occasion rather than a casual meal.

199, off E5 54 The Shore, Leith 0131 5533557 Lunch Tue–Fri; dinner Tue–Sat

Tower Restaurant ££

Take the lift to level 5, the rooftop floor of the Museum of Scotland, to try this spacious, sophisticated brasserie-style restaurant. Its design takes advantage of the setting and there is a superb view of the castle. Dishes echo the menus of the Mediterranean with seafood, sushi and salads.

199 D3 Museum of Scotland, Chambers Street 0131 2253003 Daily noon–11; closed Dec 25

Winter Glen ££

This comfortable, stylish and spacious basement restaurant offers the best of Scotland's larder: first-class ingredients drawn from glen, loch, bay and river. Dishes such as game terrine, roast salmon or Aberdeen Angus beef are presented with a simple, light touch.

➕ 198 B5 ⊠ 3A1 Dundas Street ☎ 0131 4777060 ⓦ Lunch and dinner Wed–Sun; closed 1st week in Jan and Dec 25–26

Witchery by the Castle ££

Set in a 16th-century building near the gates of Edinburgh Castle, the atmosphere is indeed bewitching. Both dining-rooms are candlelit, adorned with gilded heraldic ceilings, tapestries, and leather and wood panels. Confident cooking brings modern ideas from around the world. The extensive wine list offers consistent quality.

➕ 198 C3 ⊠ Castle Hill ☎ 0131 2255613 ⓦ Lunch and dinner daily; closed Dec 25–26

CAFÉS

The Bookstop Café £

Located opposite Edinburgh University, this bookshop and café is popular with students, academics and families. If you buy a book, the coffee is on the house, but the extensive selection of keenly priced sandwiches, salads and light snacks is not included in the deal.

➕ 199 D2 ⊠ 4 Teviot Place ☎ 0131 2255298 ⓦ Mon–Sat 10–8, Sun noon–8

Café Florentin £

It may be a well-established Edinburgh institution, but you could almost believe you were in Paris. This authentic French café is a magnet for those searching for just one more almond croissant or heavenly pastry. It's open early until late, and the simple décor, rich coffee smells and richer cakes make a perfect treat at any time.

➕ 198 C3 ⊠ 8 St Giles Street ☎ 0131 2256267 ⓦ Daily 7am–11pm

Cornerstone Café £

The undercroft of St John's Church has been converted into a pleasant, inexpensive self-service café – a welcome refuelling stop. It is renowned for its carefully prepared vegetarian menu and for an excellent selection of home-made cakes. It is noted for being child friendly. No credit cards are taken.

➕ 198 A3 ⊠ St John's Church, Princes Street and Lothian Road ☎ 0131 2290212 ⓦ Mon–Sat 9:30–4

Valvona & Crolla Caffe Bar ££-£££

The Continis import produce from Italy for sale in their delicatessen, and to supplement the prime Scottish beef, west-coast seafood and organic vegetables that appear on the menu of their bright, firstfloor cafe-bar. With a menu that runs until 5pm, queues can build up, with pasta and pizza always popular choices.

➕ 199 E5 ⊠ 19 Elm Row ☎ 0131 5566066 ⓦ Mon–Sat 8–5

PUBS/BARS

Café Royal £-££

This bustling pub has a Victorian-baroque elegance, summed up by its showy central bar counter. There's a stylish, if expensive, oyster bar that also offers caviar, lobster and champagne, but the lunchtime carvery with hot sandwiches made to order is a popular alternative.

➕ 199 D4 ⊠ West Register Street ☎ 0131 5564124 ⓦ Mon–Wed 11–11, Thu 11am–midnight, Fri–Sat 11am–1am, Sun 12:30–11

Traverse Theatre Bar £

This spacious, modern bar, with its extensive selection of draught beers, draws a wide clientele. The reasonably priced lunch menu is popular during the day while a trendier crowd arrives in the evening.

➕ 198 A3 ⊠ 14 Cambridge Street ☎ 0131 2285383 ⓦ Mon 10:30am–11pm, Tue–Thu 10:30am–midnight, Fri–Sat 10:30am–1am, Sun 6:30–midnight

Where to... Stay

Prices

Price categories are per person, including English breakfast.

£ = under £30 per night ££ = £30–60 per night £££ = over £60 per night

Balmoral £££

The clock in this endearingly imposing classic Edwardian building is two minutes fast (except at Hogmanay) to ensure that no one misses their train at Waverley Station next door. The Balmoral is expensive, central and offers every facility, ranging from an indoor swimming-pool and gym to a beauty salon. Bedrooms are luxurious with some superb views over the city. Afternoon tea in the Palm Court is a must, and there's acclaimed cooking at No 1 The Restaurant, plus a less formal brasserie.

🕂 199D4 ⊠ 1 Princes Street
☎ 0131 5562414 E-mail: reservations@balmoral-rf.demon.co.uk

The Bonham £££

Occupying an elegant and discreet Georgian town house in a fine West End crescent on the edge of the New Town, the Bonham is one of the smartest places to stay in Edinburgh. It's a converted university residence, but you'd never know. All 48 bedrooms are imaginatively designed and have high-tech communications systems and splendid bathrooms. Its striking, brasserie-style restaurant offers a catchy menu with adventurous dishes.

🕂 198, off A3 ⊠ 35 Drumsheugh Gardens ☎ 0131 2266050/6036060; fax: 0131 2266080 ⓒ Closed Dec 24–28
E-mail: reserve@thebonham.com

Caledonian Hotel £££

Built in the 1900s, the 'Cally' is virtually a national monument. Set at the end of Princes Street, it has fabulous views of the castle. Public areas are elegant, but bedrooms vary in size and style. Of the two restaurants, Chisholms offers contemporary surroundings, while the Pompadour is formal and luxurious.

🕂 198A3 ⊠ Princes Street
☎ 0131 4599988; fax: 0131 2256632
E-mail: reservations_caledonian@hilton.com;
www.caledonianhotel.co.uk

Carlton Hotel £££

This large hotel is in a prime position between Princes Street and the Royal Mile. The bedrooms are traditionally styled but well-equipped. There is also a leisure centre and nightclub. Quills Restaurant offers an intimate library setting in which to enjoy fine Scottish produce.

🕂 199 D4 ⊠ North Bridge ☎ 0131 4723000 E-mail: chh@scottishhighlandhotels. co.uk

Elmview ££

Proprietors Marny and Richard Hill offer a unique, highly individual bed and breakfast of just three *en suite* rooms. The standard of accommodation is superb: the tasteful furnishings, stylish bathrooms and thoughtful extras, such as fridges with fresh milk, add up to a high level of comfort. Breakfasts are excellent, served at a large, elegantly appointed table, and will set you up for the day. No children under 15.

🕂 19881 ⊠ 15 Glengyle Terrace
☎ 0131 281973; fax: 0131 2297296

George Inter-Continental £££

The classical facade of the George conceals a grand lobby with elegant fluted Corinthian columns and polished marble floors, as well as a superb bar sporting clan mementoes and curios from the whisky trade. Luxurious bedrooms vary in size, but have comfortable armchairs or sofas and quality fittings. The restaurant, Le Chambertin, reflects the grand scale of the hotel, but manages to balance this with an intimate, comfortable atmosphere. The location is also very convenient for shopping on Princes Street.

✚ 198C4 ⊠ 19–21 George Street
☎ 0131 2251251
E-mail: edinburgh@ interconti.com

Hotel Ibis ££

There's been a scramble in Edinburgh to build hotels that cater for the boom caused by the new Parliament and Ibis was among the first. This warehouse conversion offers 99 practical, modern rooms (all *en suite*) and a simple dinner menu. It also offers one of the best locations in Edinburgh (close to the Royal Mile) at a reasonable price.

✚ 199D3 ⊠ Hunter Square
☎ 0131 2407000
E-mail: H2039@acor-hotels.com

The Howard £££

Created from three linked town houses in the New Town area, the Howard's austere exterior conceals a hotel of comfort and discreet luxury. The Edwardian drawing room is filled with sumptuous furnishings and ornate chandeliers. The bedrooms boast antiques, while the bathrooms have shower cubicles or old-fashioned, free-standing tubs. By contrast, the highly regarded restaurant is minimalist with abstract canvases and jewel-coloured chairs.

✚ 198 B5 ⊠ 36 Great King Street
☎ 0131 3363636
E-mail: reserve@thehoward.com

Malmaison Hotel et Brasserie ££

This upbeat designer hotel is part of an acclaimed and rapidly expanding chain. It occupies a fine period building that was formerly a seaman's mission, next to Leith dock gates. The bedrooms are minimalist, but manage the right degree of comfort, and facilities such as CD players are standard. The brasserie and all-day café are also fashionable.

✚ 199, off E5 ⊠ 1 Tower Place
☎ 0131 4685000
E-mail: edinburgh@malmaison.com

Norton House Hotel ££

This extended Victorian mansion is peacefully set amid 20 hectares of parkland, yet is convenient for the city centre and Edinburgh Airport. All 47 rooms are very comfortably furnished, but the most spacious are those in the original house. The Gathering, set in the grounds, is, as its name suggests, a popular meeting place for an informal meal, but the Conservatory restaurant is the flagship, serving good modern Scottish cooking.

✚ 198, off A3 ⊠ Ingliston ☎ 0131 3331275 E-mail:
hotel.reservations@virgin.co.uk

Sheraton Grand Hotel £££

This striking, modern building forms part of an evolving development to be known as Exchange Square. Attention to small detail extends to the hotel's own, specially-commissioned tartan. The best bedrooms have castle views, and all rooms are comfortable, well proportioned and pleasantly styled. A leisure centre with swimming pool and gym adds to the attractions. The conservatory-style Terrace Restaurant overlooks the square, Usher Hall and the castle beyond, while the Grill Room is elegant and discreet, best suited to executive lunches.

✚ 198A3 ⊠ 1 Festival Square
☎ 0131 2216422 (Grill Room), 2216423 (Terrace); E-mail:
rachel_williamson@sheraton.com

Travel Inn (City Centre) £

Although hardly luxurious, the Travel Inn concept is highly competitive, with an honest, no-frills approach and an impressive pricing structure. Modern, comfortable, well-equipped bedrooms (all with *en-suite* facilities) can accommodate two adults and two children for an inexpensive flat rate. The hotel serves continental breakfast, and there is also a relaxed family restaurant called Slice.

✚ 198, off A2 ⊠ 1 Morrison Link
☎ 0131 2289819

Where to... Shop

SHOPPING HOURS

Usual shopping hours are 9am to 6pm, with late opening until 8 or 9pm on Thursdays. Many shops open on Sunday afternoons, particularly during the summer.

Edinburgh's main shopping areas are Princes and George Streets in the New Town and the Royal Mile and Grassmarket in the Old Town.

DEPARTMENT STORES

Often called the Scottish Harrods, **Jenners** (founded c1830), opposite the Scott Monument in Princes Street, is the oldest independent department store in the world. It's worth a visit just to wander round the old-fashioned tiered wooden balconies, take afternoon tea in the tea room, stock up on Scottish fare in the food hall and get lost in the labyrinthine departments. Other trusty choices are **Marks and Spencer** (several branches in Princes Street) and **John Lewis** in St James shopping centre.

SCOTTISH GOODIES

The Royal Mile has enough gift-shops to keep the most enthusiastic souvenir hunter occupied for days, and even if you avoid the tackier options there are plenty of quality outlets to explore to everything from cashmere to whisky. **Scottish Gems** (24 High Street) has a wide range of Celtic jewellery. **Geoffrey (Tailor)** at 57–9 High Street is the best place in town to buy a traditional kilt outfit, either made-to-measure or off-the-peg. But if it's tartan you're after, try **Scottish Crafts** at 328 Lawnmarket, near the top of the Royal Mile.

FOOD AND DRINK

Valvona and Crolla in Elm Row, at the top of Leith Walk, is where Edinburgh's Italian community shops for food (▶ 62). Strings of garlic and chillies hang over shelves packed with cooking oils, olives, bread and pasta. For whisky try the **Scotch Whisky Heritage Centre** on Castlehill, **Royal Mile Whiskies**, opposite St Giles Cathedral and **William Cadenhead** (172 Canongate), or **The Scotch Malt Whisky Society** (87 Giles Street, Leith) for rare and unusual malts.

BOOKS

Edinburgh is a splendid city for buying books. Places to head for include the excellent **Bauermeister Bookshop** (George IV Bridge), **James Thin** (53 South Bridge) and **Waterstone's** on Princes Street and George Street. Second-hand shops can be found along the Westport from the Grassmarket. Particularly tempting is **West Port Books**, an Aladdin's cave of old and remaindered books.

THE QUIRKY AND UNUSUAL

Edinburgh has a fine selection of individual, offbeat and oddball shops – for example, **Mr Wood's Fossils** in the Grassmarket is the only place in Britain where you can buy petrified dinosaur droppings. A few doors along, **Wm Armstrong and Son** is the capital's coolest second-hand clothes shop, while on the opposite corner TV cook Clarissa Dickson-Wright sells new and second-hand cookery books in the **Cook's Book Shop**. In Victoria Street look out for **Cresser's Brush Shop**, **Mellis the Cheesemonger**, a genuine French baker and **Byzantium**, an eccentric flea market in an old church. For other memorable shops wander down **Cockburn** Street from the Royal Mile or along **Rose Street**, between George Street and Princes Street.

Where to...
Be Entertained

The most comprehensive 'what's on' guide is *The List*, a fortnightly publication available from newsagents throughout the city. Detailed listings covering theatre, cinema, live music, sporting events, readings and festivals are also carried daily in the *Edinburgh Evening News*, the weekend section of the *Scotsman* and in *Scotland on Sunday*. The *Scotsman's* website (www.scotsman.com) also has a fairly comprehensive list of events for the week ahead.

THEATRES AND CONCERT HALLS

The **Royal Lyceum** on Grindlay Street stages plays and comedies, while in contrast, the **Traverse Theatre** on Cambridge Street is known for its experimental performances. Head for the **Playhouse** or the **Kings Theatre** for lightweight or musical entertainment. The **Festival Theatre** and the **Usher Hall** are prestigious concert venues throughout the year or, for a more intimate concert setting, go to the **Queen's Hall** on Clerk Street.

CINEMAS

Excellent independent cinemas include the **Dominion** in Morningside and the well-loved **Cameo** in the West End. The **Filmhouse** on Lothian Road is another venue for less commercial and foreign language films.

BEST PUBS

Starting at the **Ensign Ewart** at the castle end of the Royal Mile, you could go on a pub crawl all the way to **Jenny Ha's** near Holyrood, but there are so many pubs and bars, it's difficult to tell the good from the bad. But don't miss **Deacon Brodie's** on the corner of George IV Bridge, or the **Mound**, a busy traditional bar that's a great place for spotting politicians when the Parliament is in session. **The Tass** (Jeffrey Street) has real ale, cheap food and folk music, not to mention a life-size papier-mâché model of Robert Burns. Opposite, the **World's End** is famed for its grub. Elsewhere in Old Town, **Sandy Bell's** (Forrest Road) is one of the most atmospheric pubs in the capital. The tiny bar of the **Royal Oak** (Infirmary Street) is the hang-out of some interesting characters, attracted by the ambience and the selection of fine malts and cask ales. There are music sessions downstairs every night. **Bannerman's** in the Cowgate is formed by a cosy collection of vaulted rooms offering regular live rock, soul and jazz.

In the New Town, **Mather's Bar** (1 Queensferry Street) features its original Victorian fittings. The **Oxford Bar** in Young Street, a lane between George Street and Queen Street, is the regular watering hole of the fictitious Inspector Rebus (▶10–11), but you may find real off-duty cops in for a wee bevvy.

NIGHT-LIFE

Take your pick from a selection of venues covering the musical spectrum from hip hop and house to reggae. Youngsters gravitate towards the **Grassmarket**, along the **Cowgate**, **Lothian Road** and in the **West End**, while the sophisticated and trendy tend to hang out in the area around **Broughton Street** in the growing collection of café-bars such as the **Outhouse** or **Po-Na-Na** in nearby Frederick Street. At 11pm these bars turn into night-clubs and are open until the small hours. Fashions change so make sure you consult *The List* before heading out.

Glasgow

The coat of arms bears the motto:

LET GLASGOW FLOURISH

Glasgow in a Day 70 – 71
Don't Miss 72 – 73
At Your Leisure 84 – 88
Where to... 89 – 94

Getting Your Bearings

From its Victorian position as second city of the British Empire to UK City of Architecture and Design at the end of the 20th century, Glasgow has continually reinvented itself while preserving the best of its past. At its heart is the River Clyde, with the remnants of a once mighty shipbuilding industry. Close by, in the Merchant City, the refurbished mansions of the Industrial Revolution barons and the opulent Victorian public buildings recall the city's prosperous trading past in tobacco, sugar and cotton. Nowadays trendy bars, pavement cafés and restaurants buzz with Glasgow's stylish young as they take a break from shopping in the 'Golden Z', the best three shopping streets in Britain outside London.

If your shopping style is more flea market than upmarket, then Glasgow's famous Barras Market in the East End is the place to rummage for bargains. Enjoy the noisy sales pitches of the stallholders, known locally as 'patter merchants', and their lively repartee as they trade insults with hecklers in the crowd. The West End, with parks and museums around the university, is more refined. But wherever you go in this friendliest of cities, you'll never be alone – sit on a park bench at Kelvingrove, in Glasgow Green or in George Square and watch the world bustle by.

Glasgow is a large city but it has an excellent public transport system, so buy a Roundabout Ticket for the local rail network, which includes access to Glasgow's Underground, the famous 'Clockwork Orange'.

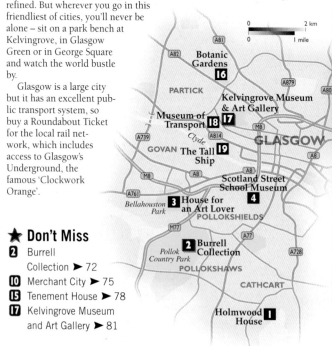

★ Don't Miss

2 Burrell
   Collection ➤ 72
10 Merchant City ➤ 75
15 Tenement House ➤ 78
17 Kelvingrove Museum
   and Art Gallery ➤ 81

At Your Leisure

1 Holmwood House ➤ 84

3 House for an Art Lover ➤ 84

4 Scotland Street School Museum ➤ 85

5 Glasgow Green ➤ 85

6 The Barras ➤ 85

7 Provand's Lordship ➤ 86

8 Glasgow Cathedral ➤ 86

9 Wellpark Brewery ➤ 86

11 Gallery of Modern Art ➤ 87

12 The Lighthouse ➤ 87

13 Willow Tea Room ➤ 87

14 Glasgow School of Art ➤ 87

16 Botanic Gardens ➤ 88

18 Museum of Transport ➤ 88

19 The Tall Ship ➤ 88

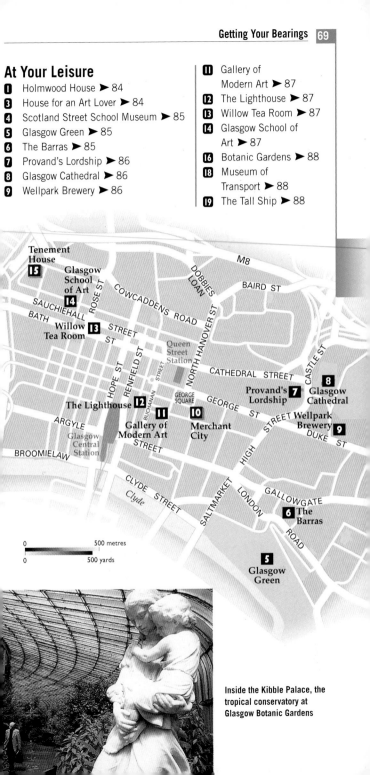

Inside the Kibble Palace, the tropical conservatory at Glasgow Botanic Gardens

View one man's amazing art collection, explore Kelvingrove, the most popular free attraction in Scotland, and enter a time warp in the tiny Tenement House. In between, stroll through some of Glasgow's many parks and the historic Merchant City.

Glasgow in a Day

9:30am

Start in George Square in the **Merchant City** (▶ 75), then pop into the City Chambers to see the marvellous marble staircase (pictured right). Head along Ingram Street to the Italian Centre, then turn left up Montrose Street, left into Cochrane Street and back to George Square. Continue along St Vincent Street to Buchanan Street, the heart of Glasgow's shopping area. Turn left for the Princes Square shopping centre which is on the left-hand side. To your right, at the top of the street, is Buchanan Galleries, Glasgow's newest shopping mall.

10:30am

Come back down Buchanan Street and at Royal Exchange Square spend some time browsing in the **Gallery of Modern Art** (▶ 87). Stop for a drink at the top-floor café, which has interesting views across the Glasgow rooftops.

11:30am

To continue the theme of art, take a local train from Glasgow Central station to Pollokshaws West to visit the award-winning **Burrell Collection.** This specially built museum houses more than 8,000 *objets d'art* collected by shipping magnate Sir William Burrell (including several sculptures by Rodin, left, ▶ 72).

1:00pm

By now you'll be in need of lunch, so return to Glasgow Central station and head right from the exit, along Gordon Street, turn right and right again into Drury Street. Here you'll find Glasgow's famous pub, The Horseshoe, containing the longest bar in the UK, its Victorian style virtually unchanged since 1884 and full of Glasgow character. On offer are delicious inexpensive lunches and the cheapest beer in town. From here visit **The Lighthouse** centre for Architecture, Design and the City at the bottom of Mitchell Street (left, ► 87). Then cross Argyle Street to St Enoch Square and the underground station, and take the train to Cowcaddens Station. You could walk or take a bus, but the underground is the most convenient way to travel and is an attraction in its own right.

3:00pm

At Cowcaddens cross Garscube Road, turn left into West Graham Street, then left down Scott Street and right into Buccleuch Street to the **Tenement House** (pictured right, ► 78). Then return to the underground and take a train to Kelvinhall. Leave the station and turn left past Glasgow University to reach **Kelvingrove Museum and Art Gallery** (► 81), with the **Museum of Transport** (► 88) just across the street.

5:00pm

Unwind and get some fresh air with a stroll left along the river walkway through **Kelvingrove Park,** behind the museum, to Kelvinbridge station then catch the underground back to the city centre.

6:00pm

From St Enoch's head up Buchanan Street, turn right through Royal Exchange Square and along Ingram Street to the Corinthian at No 191, where you can enjoy some pre-dinner drinks in one of Glasgow's finest Victorian interiors. For dinner there's nowhere better than the Buttery at 652 Argyle Street (► 89). Entertainment's next, so try a show at the Citizens' Theatre, music at the Royal Concert Hall, dance the night away at Victoria's nightclub, Sauchiehall Street, or enjoy a traditional music session in the Scotia Bar in Stockwell Street.

The Burrell Collection

This collection of sculptures, paintings, ceramics, metalwork, tapestries, stained glass and much more spans all periods of history across three continents, and is probably the most diverse art collection ever assembled by a private individual.

The collection is housed in a building specially created by the architect Barry Gasson between 1971 and 1983. His brief – to design a modern gallery, incorporating Burrell's collection of porticos and doorways and re-creating several rooms from Sir William's home – has resulted in a work of art in its own right. Pink Dumfriesshire sandstone, wood and glass have been used to produce a series of long external galleries combining light and space, while light-sensitive objects are displayed in the window-less core. Trees surrounding the gallery allow dappled light to fall on precious Ming vases and pottery from ancient civilisations. The ancient doors and windows are built into the fabric of the building so that you approach a richly carved, 14th-century stone doorway down a long corridor of light, glimpse trees and greenery through another or find an exquisite religious icon framed in an arched window.

Medieval stone windows have been incorporated in the fabric of the building

Rodin's most famous work, The Thinker, at the Burrell Collection

Late-15th century stained glass panel of the Adoration of the Magi incorporated in the re-creation of the Hall of Hutton Castle

Sir William Burrell (1861–1958)

Burrell was a Glasgow shipping magnate, who amassed his fortune by ordering ships during times of depression and selling them when demand exceeded supply. As a youth with a passion for art and plenty of money, he started collecting artefacts at the age of 16, and would devote the rest of his long life to acquiring the very best.

In 1944 Sir William and Lady Burrell gave the collection to the City of Glasgow along with the money to build a home for it, and continued adding to the hoard until his death at the age of 96. After 80 years of collecting he had acquired around 8,000 objects, which equates to two a week, though it's difficult to comprehend that this incredible collection could be the lifetime achievement of just one man. Unfortunately, Sir William didn't live to see his collection displayed in such worthy surroundings.

The Highlights

Pass through the medieval stone entrance to find **bronzes by Rodin** lining the light inner courtyard, and in the centre a massive **vase from the villa of the Emperor Hadrian** at Tivoli. Through the windows you can see a room from a 16th-century castle, part of the reconstruction of Burrell's home at Hutton Castle near Berwick-upon-Tweed. The rooms are arranged round the courtyard to allow light to shine through the windows. The **dining room, hall and drawing room,** which contained the main display of tapestries, are reproduced complete with the original furniture and 16th-century panelling, and are undoubtedly among the highlights of the collection. The windows are inset with precious stained glass, sculptures are arranged on the 16th-century oak buffet cupboards and the great refectory table sits on a Persian flowered carpet.

From the courtyard you can walk clockwise round the building, passing through the **Ancient Civilisations collection,** with its pottery, carvings and statues from Mesopotamia, Egypt, ancient Greece and Rome, including a mosaic of a cockerel from the 1st century BC.

Continue into the **Oriental collection,** which includes Chinese bronzes as well as vases and ceramics from the Ming dynasty and an interesting pair of green-glazed, armoured guardian figures from the same period. The **Medieval and Post-Medieval European Art collection** houses Burrell's prized tapestries and stained glass, examples surpassed only by the national collection at the Victoria and Albert Museum in London. Among the stained glass in the long galleries at the front and side of the building is an exquisite 15th-century small panel portrait of Edward IV's daughter Princess Cecily, and a German window of the Ten Commandments from the same period. The panel depicting the prophet Jeremiah, made for the abbey of St Denis outside Paris in around 1140, is one of the oldest surviving pieces of stained glass.

Gallery No 3 contains one of the finest tapestry collections in Europe: 150 examples from the 15th and 16th centuries. They hang on great expanses of wall protected from sunlight that streams through the stained-glass panels.

Behind the tapestries are the entrances to three period galleries: an Elizabethan room, a 17th- and 18th-century room and a Gothic domestic room.

TAKING A BREAK

When your feet begin to ache, head along the outer gallery housing the stained glass collection and go downstairs to the Burrell's **tea room** . Or, if you're going to spend the whole day here, take a lunch break in the excellent restaurant.

This tapestry of peasants hunting rabbits with ferrets is one of the finest examples from the 15th century

🕂 200, off A1 ✉ Pollok Country Park ☎ 0141 2872550
🕐 Mon–Thu and Sat 10–5, Fri and Sun 11–5 🍴 Café and restaurant (£–££)
🚌 Regular service from town centre, half-hourly park bus from park gates
🚆 Pollokshaws West or Shawlands 💷 Free

THE BURRELL COLLECTION: INSIDE INFO

Top tip On a hot summer's day the temperature in the outer galleries can become high, so visit them early in the morning, then retreat to the cooler windowless interior.

Hidden gem Stairs lead up from the tapestries' gallery to a collection of paintings that includes masterpieces such as a Rembrandt self-portrait, the *Rehearsal* by Degas and Manet's *Women Drinking Beer*.

Merchant City

Trendy Merchant City, once just containing warehouses and the homes of Glasgow's tobacco, sugar and cotton barons, is now the place to eat, drink and be entertained in fashionable bars, restaurants and clubs. Wander idly through the streets absorbing the architecture and the ambience and you'll understand why. Then finish your tour indulgently along Argyle Street, Buchanan Street and Sauchiehall Street – the shopping area collectively known as Glasgow's 'Golden Z'.

The Merchant City spreads west from the old High Street in a grid pattern, but the best place to start a tour is George Square, the centre of Glasgow. It's right beside Queen Street Station, so it's easily accessible from outside the city too.

Glasgow goes continental with pavement cafés in the Italian Centre

After the Act of Union in 1707 (➤ 29) Scotland was allowed to trade with the colonies for the first time. Glasgow's merchants took full advantage, importing tobacco, sugar and cotton and amassing huge fortunes, which they ploughed back into the city, building warehouses, docks and sumptuous mansions. By the 19th century Glasgow was the second city of the British Empire, and from then on its fortune fluctuated with that of the Empire.

The Heart of Glasgow

Glasgow City Chambers, an opulent display of Victorian self-importance wrought in gold and marble, dominates **George Square.** Queen Victoria was certainly impressed when she opened it in 1888, and modern film-makers have cast its impressive Italian Renaissance façade, its high ceilings and massive marble staircases as law courts, embassies, palaces and even the Kremlin. It's still the administrative centre of Glasgow and the council are so proud of it that they offer free tours, so take advantage of this if you can.

To the right of the City Chambers, between Cochrane and Ingram Streets, is the **Italian Centre,** an eclectic mix of pavement cafés, shops, wine bars and bistros and the place to see and be seen. Stylish Versace- and Armani-clad citizens mingle with their equally stylish counterfeit counterparts, fresh from the Barras.

At the corner of the next block, at 158 Ingram Street, is **Hutcheson's Hall,** one of the most elegant buildings in the area. Tall and with a church-like spire, it was built in 1802 to replace a 17th-century hospice, and statues from the original building were incorporated into the frontage. Inside is a National Trust for Scotland shop and visitor centre with a superb audio-visual presentation on the Merchant City and a Glasgow Style exhibition. The Hall, with its impressive staircase and portraits of Glasgow worthies, is often used for functions, but you can have a look round at other times.

Past the Italian Centre, at 191 Ingram Street, you'll find the finest Victorian interior in Glasgow. **The Corinthian** started life in 1842 as Virginia Mansion, housing a bank. By 1929 the building became the High Court, but the unfortunately, conversion concealed most of the ornate features behind false walls and ceilings. It's now a fashionable eating place and watering hole and the trendiest of nightclubs, complete with free-standing classical figures and a Doric balustrade.

Glassford Street is dominated by the green dome and classical façade of **Trades House** at No 85. It's the second-oldest building in the city and was built between 1791 and 1794 by Robert Adam and his brothers James and William, although most of the interior is Victorian. Still occupied by the original owners, the Glasgow Trades Guild, its main attraction is the arms of the original guilds of hammer men, weavers, tailors and others carved on the furniture and walls and visible in the stained-glass windows. Entrance is free, but you will need to call for an appointment (tel: 0141 5522418; www.bbnet.demon.co.uk/thall).

Statue of the founder of Hutcheson's Hall hospice, George Hutcheson

---

🗺 201 D3
✉ Area west of High Street
🚇 Queen Street

Glasgow City Chambers
☎ 0141 2872000
🕐 Tours Mon–Fri 10–2
💷 Free

Hutcheson's Hall
☎ 0141 5528391
💷 Free

The Corinthian
☎ 0141 5521101
💷 Free

MERCHANT CITY: INSIDE INFO

Top tip In Buchanan Street look out for **Princes Square shopping centre** on the east side. This is Glasgow's finest shopping experience: shops selling designer labels, expensive jewellery and fine crafts stand around an enclosed Victorian courtyard on several tiered galleries interspersed with restaurants, cafés, bars and entertainment.

Hidden gem At 16–18 Blackfriars Street is **Babbity Bowster**, a late 20th-century conversion of an 18th-century Adam building on the site of a medieval monastery (► 90). Babbity Bowster was an 18th-century Scottish dance and, appropriately, this is one of the best places for impromptu sessions of Celtic music. It's a great place to stay (there are a few bedrooms) or to eat, drink and relax in the bar, restaurant, café or garden (tel: 0141 5525055).

The Tenement House

Tenement living was the norm for most Glaswegians from the mid-19th century right up to the 1950s, and here you can really get under the skin of Glasgow. Agnes Toward and her mother moved into 145 Buccleuch Street in 1911, where they stayed until the late 1960s. As a result, this tenement flat has never been altered since it was built in 1892. During her long life Agnes Toward never threw anything away, and her legacy is a fascinating social history of Glasgow.

No 19th-century middle-class parlour would be complete without a piano

When Agnes died her house was crammed with the ephemera of a lifetime: letters, personal treasures and mementoes, including postcards and theatre programmes. She'd hoarded bills, receipts, bus and rail tickets and, tied in neat bundles piled high on the kitchen table were old newspapers. When the National Trust for Scotland acquired the property they were able to reconstruct the history of Agnes Toward's life in detail.

Visit the **kitchen** first, which is typical of Glasgow life at the end of the 19th century. Large families lived, slept, ate and socialised in such rooms, but Agnes had this room to herself after the death of her mother. The bed was concealed behind curtains by day and heated by an earthenware hot-water bottle at night. The large, black coal range was used for cooking and provided hot water and heating. In its day this range, with its regulated oven, hotplates and cast-iron pots and kettles, was at the leading edge of domestic technology. In the 1960s Agnes was still cooking on it and cleaning it daily with black liquid polish. The coal was stored in a large wooden bunker beside the food preparation area.

On the shelves are baking implements, a brass preserve pan and earthenware pots of plum jam made in 1929. The old-fashioned zinc washboard sits in the white sink and the laundry hangs on the pulley as if still waiting for the irons to heat up on the range.

In Edwardian Glasgow this was an affluent middle-class home. Miss Toward and her widowed mother lived on what her mother earned as a dressmaker, the income from taking in

Agnes Toward's collection of potions and lotions remain on the window sill in her bathroom

lodgers and Miss Toward's wages as a clerk. But the lovely 18th-century grandfather clock in the hall and the set of silver plate covers, incongruous in the kitchen of a Glasgow tenement, suggest that her family was once more comfortably off.

In the **parlour** the oval mahogany table, draped with red chenille, is set for afternoon tea with the best china. The fire is lit and teacakes, scones and shortbread are piled high on the plates. Windows draped in white lace curtains, the rosewood piano with brass candle-holders and mother Toward's sewing machine complete the picture of respectable gentlewomen

The front room, or parlour, would only be used on special occasions

keeping up appearances. In the **lodger's bedroom,** a traditional iron bedstead, high wardrobe and marble washstand with basin and jug are part of the original furnishings. Hot water for a morning wash and shave was brought from the bathroom.

The **bathroom,** with its deep bath and hot water on tap, was a rare luxury in late 19th-century Glasgow tenements, as most had only a draughty stairhead toilet shared by all the families in the block.

On your way out look for the brass plate at the entrance to the close advertising Mrs Toward's business.

> By never throwing anything away, Agnes Toward created a fascinating and nostalgic legacy

🔁 200 A5 ✉ 145 Buccleuch Street ☎ 0141 333018; www.nts.org.uk
🕐 Daily 2–4:30, Mar–Oct 🚇 Cowcaddens 🎟 Moderate

THE TENEMENT HOUSE: INSIDE INFO

Top tip Try out one of the chairs – typical of the period, they are made of mahogany and stuffed with scratchy horsehair that pokes through the cover.

Hidden gem Check out the box bed behind the door in the corner of the parlour. This provided extra sleeping accommodation, but was rather unhealthy and was banned after 1900.

One to miss There's an exhibition of some of Miss Toward's treasures in the National Trust for Scotland's rooms on the ground floor and a display telling the story of the Tenement House. If you're in a hurry you can skip this or come back to it later.

Kelvingrove Museum and Art Gallery

This diverse museum collection is the top free attraction in Scotland and features everything from natural history, through industrial exhibits to Egyptian mummies and African relics. The collection of armour is one of the finest in Europe and the art collection, featuring works by the Glasgow Boys, is the best in the UK outside of London.

Kelvingrove is one of Glasgow's finest buildings

The museum building, a magnificent turreted, red sandstone fantasy, is an exuberant expression of late-Victorian confidence and aplomb. It's worth a visit just to admire the huge main hall, with its high vaulted ceiling and galleries, black-and-white tiled marble floor and the massive pipe organ set in an ornate arched recess.

Museum Highlights

You could spend hours exploring, but if time is short here are some highlights. From the entrance hall turn left into the gallery holding the armour collection. You'll immediately see a huge **warhorse and rider in 16th-century field armour** made for the 1st Earl of Pembroke by the Greenwich Armoury. Gilded and decorated in the fashion of the day, it's thought to be the only surviving man and horse set, and was probably worn at the battle of St Quentin in France in 1557. In contrast to this ancient battledress is the white armoured spacesuit of an **Imperial Stormtrooper** from the Star Wars films.

Free Admission – Pay on Exit

Kelvingrove is a collection of national importance but is funded entirely by the generosity of Glasgow taxpayers. Spare them a thought as you leave and deposit your small change, or better still some paper money, in the donations box.

The huge vaulted entrance hall is the focal point of the museum

This set of 19th-century Ting Kia armour can be found beside the main hall

Across the main hall, through the museum shop, is the natural history collection, including dinosaurs and fossils. Here in a glass case, under a magnifying glass and a bright light, is a **block of amber with a mosquito trapped within.** The notes tell of how Michael Crichton, author of *Jurassic Park*, got the idea of using DNA from dinosaur blood sucked up by the insect before it was trapped and preserved. The notes suggest that 'such a technique is, in reality, well beyond present capabilities.'

Major Renovations

Kelvingrove is set for a £25-million facelift: the display area will increase by 35 per cent, enabling many fine pieces to emerge from dusty basements. The building will be closed for about a year from late 2001, so phone first if you're visiting around this time.

One interesting exhibit in this hall is the skeleton of the **Baron of Buchlyvie,** a horse with an extraordinary story. His ownership was disputed in court and the judge ruled that the beast be sold at auction, where one of the disputing owners paid £9,500 for him, a record in the early-20th century. Two years later the Baron broke a leg and was put down. The break is still visible on the skeleton.

Rossetti's painting of Alice Wilding as Regina Cordium is part of the Pre-Raphaelite art collection

On the upper floors is Glasgow's **art collection,** covering Flemish, Italian, Dutch and British works, from the early Italian masters through Impressionists and Pre-Raphaelites to modern classics. Wander clockwise through each gallery or use the free map to guide you. Look particularly for works by **Charles Rennie Mackintosh** (► 18–20) and his contemporaries, including **the Glasgow Boys** – a group of artists who came together in the 1880s and spent their summers capturing the essence of the Scottish countryside. For examples of their work look for the paintings by James Guthrie, John Lavery, George Henry, E A Hornel and James Patterson. You'll also find many examples of the **Glasgow Style** (► 18–20) in the form of paintings, sculpture and furniture.

✚ 200, off A5 ✉ Kelvingrove ☎ 0141 2872700 🕐 Mon–Thu and Sat 10–5, Fri and Sun 11–5 🍴 Café in museum (£) 🚇 Kelvinhall 🚌 Regular service from city centre 🚉 Partick 💷 Free, donations welcome

KELVINGROVE ART GALLERY: INSIDE INFO

Hidden gem In a small gallery you can see a fascinating film about the Native American Ghost Dance religion and the massacre of the Sioux people at Wounded Knee Creek in 1890. The **Ghost Dance Shirt**, an important religious talisman, was taken from one of the fallen at the massacre, exhibited in Buffalo Bill's Wild West Show, and finally donated to Kelvingrove. But it was returned to the Wounded Knee Survivors Association in 1998 and is now back in South Dakota. The shirt here is a replica presented to Kelvingrove by Marcella Le Beau, a Two Kettle Lakota Indian.

At Your Leisure

🚺 Holmwood House

This is the finest example of domestic architecture by Alexander 'Greek' Thomson, the architect whose designs helped to give Glasgow its distinctive look. Holmwood was built in 1857 for the wealthy paper manufacturer James Couper, who gave Thomson a free hand in the design and got this gem in return. Thomson made the house asymmetrical, with the flat gable and large windows of the dining room on one side of the door. On the other side he created the appearance of a circular bay window by placing the free-standing columns of a Greek temple in front of the windows. The interior continues the classical theme, with original wallpaper in shades of russet depicting scenes from the Trojan War.

➕ 200, off C1 ✉ 61–63 Netherlee Road, Cathcart ☎ 0141 6372129; www.nts.org.uk ⏰ Daily 1:30–5:30, Apr–Oct 🚌 Frequent from city centre 🚉 Cathcart Station 💷 Moderate

🚺 House for an Art Lover

In 1901 when Charles Rennie Mackintosh and his wife Margaret (▶ 18–20) entered a competition to

Alexander 'Greek' Thomson's ornate cupola at Holmwood House

design a 'House for an Art Lover', they were unrestricted by finance or client specifications, and so let their imaginations run riot. The perfect proportions, the use of space, the careful balancing of dark and light, of lines and curves in the resulting House for an Art Lover represent the ultimate in Mackintosh design. Herman Muthesius, a contemporary critic said 'It exhibits an absolutely original character unlike anything else known.' However, the designs lay untouched for over 90 years until Graham Roxburgh, a Glasgow engineer and Mackintosh enthusiast, came across them and initiated the idea of building the house, in collaboration with Glasgow City Council and Glasgow School of Art.

So at the end of the 20th century modern artists and craftspeople from Scotland and beyond had the opportunity to work with one of Scotland's greatest architects to produce the furniture, stencilling, gesso panels and decorative metalwork displayed in the house. Completed in 1996, it has an exhibition space and visitor centre, and also serves as a postgraduate study facility for Glasgow School of Art.

➕ 200, off A1 ✉ Bellahouston Park, Dumbreck Road ☎ 0141 3534770 🕐 Sun–Thu 10–4, Sat 10–3, Apr–Sep; Sat–Sun 10–4, Oct–Mar; weekdays vary, phone for info 🍽 Art Lovers' Café (£) 🚇 Ibrox Station 🚌 17, 39, 53, 54, 55, 91 🚉 Dumbreck Station 💷 Moderate

4 Scotland Street School Museum

Mackintosh's Scotland Street is a great place for kids and adults alike. Built in 1904, it was a school until 1979, and inside you'll find reconstructed classrooms from the Victorian and Edwardian periods, World War II and 1960s, some with pupils and teachers in period costume during term time. For a real nostalgia trip, try out the playground toys, supposedly for children, but grown-ups love them too.

➕ 200 A1 ✉ 225 Scotland Street ☎ 0141 2870500 🕐 Mon–Thu and Sat 10–5, Fri and Sun 11–5 🍽 Museum café (£) 🚇 Shields Road 💷 Free

5 The People's Palace and Glasgow Green

Established as common land since 1178, Glasgow Green is the oldest public park in Britain, and has been the scene of many political meetings and demonstrations through the ages. Don't miss the People's Palace in the centre. This museum of social and working-class history is one of the city's gems, particularly the wonderful Winter Gardens, where you can listen to live music as you sit and have tea amid the greenery. The multicoloured, richly patterned building at the end of the green, modelled on the Palazzo Ducale (Doge's Palace) in Venice, was formerly Templeton's Carpet Factory.

Stained-glass panel in the collection at the People's Palace

➕ 201 E1 ✉ Glasgow Green ☎ 0141 5540223 🕐 Mon–Thu and Sat 10–5, Fri and Sun 11–5 🍽 Tea room in Winter Gardens (£) 🚉 Argyle Street or Bridgeton 💷 Free

6 The Barras

This combination of market and flea market is spread over several streets in a variety of buildings, sheds and halls, not to mention on the pavements and in doorways. You'll find everything here from antique furniture, strange musical instruments and pirated computer software, to for-tune-tellers and counterfeit designer clothing. Even snake-charmers have been known to make an appearance. Don't miss the oldest pub in town, the Saracen's Head, near the Barrowland Ballroom on the Gallowgate. Dr Samuel Johnson (1709–84), the English lexicographer and essayist, and his Scottish biographer James Boswell (1740–95) stopped here for refreshments on the way home from their Highland tour in 1773.

🚏 201 E2 ✉ Gallowgate and London Road between Ross Street and Bain Street 🕐 Sat–Sun all day 🍴 Various cafés, tea stalls and snack bars (£) 🚇 Argyle Street, High Street or Bellgrove 💷 Free

Glasgow for the Children

- Scotland Street School Museum (➤ 84)
- Museum of Transport (➤ 88)
- Kelvingrove Museum (➤ 81)
- Botanic Gardens (➤ 88)
- The Tall Ship (➤ 88)

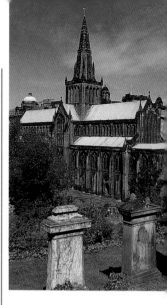

Glasgow Cathedral and Necropolis offer a peaceful break from frenetic city life

🔟 Provand's Lordship

Opposite 12th-century Glasgow Cathedral is the city's oldest house, built in 1471. The low-ceilinged, dark wood medieval interior and the re-created medieval garden contrast vividly with the rest of Victorian Glasgow and recall that the original Glasgow was this East End strip from the cathedral to the Clyde.

🚏 201 F3 ✉ High Street opposite the cathedral ☎ 0141 5528819 🕐 Mon–Sat 9:30–6:30, Sun 2–6:30, Apr–Sep; Mon–Sat 9:30–4:30, Sun 2–4:30, Oct–Mar 🍴 Several nearby in Merchant City (£) 🚇 High Street 💷 Free

🔟 Glasgow Cathedral

This awesome medieval cathedral is reputedly built over the grave of Glasgow's founder, St Mungo (also known as St Kentigern), near the site of his 7th-century church. This is the only mainland pre-Reformation Scottish cathedral to have survived

the Reformation, and its main features are the 15th-century stone screen, the vaulted crypt and the Blackadder aisle. The St Mungo Museum of Religious Life and Art and the Cathedral Visitors' Centre next door are worth a visit just to see Salvador Dali's *Christ of St John of the Cross*, purchased by the city in 1952.

🚏 201 F3 ✉ Cathedral Square ☎ 0141 5526891; www.historic-scotland.gov.uk 🕐 Mon–Sat 9:30–6, Sun 2–5, Apr–Sep; Mon–Sat 9:30–4, Sun 2–4, Oct–Mar 🍴 Several in Merchant City (£) 🚇 High Street 💷 Free

🔟 Wellpark Brewery

Lager was first brewed in Britain on this very site in 1885 after a member of the Tennent family returned with a recipe from Germany. You can learn all about the history of brewing here in the 200-year-old vaults. There's lots of restored brewing equipment and memorabilia from the last century of Tennent's brewing, plus a chance to sample the product in a neat wee bar.

🚏 201 F3 ✉ St Mungo Heritage Centre, 161 Duke Street ☎ 0141 5526552 🕐 Mon–Thu 2:30–5, 7–9 (pre-booking essential) 🍴 Several nearby in Merchant City (£) 🚇 High Street 💷 Inexpensive

11 Gallery of Modern Art

Four floors of modern art from around the world display the witty, dark, clever and surprising. This is one of the most consistently interesting modern art galleries in Britain. The mirror mosaic work on the pediment of this classical building is a perfect statement of Glasgow Style and a prelude to the varied collection inside. Look out for the papier-mâché statue of Her Majesty the Queen as a council-house tenant, complete with dressing gown, hairnet and curlers. Also worth seeing are the contemporary paintings on the ground floor, including works by Scottish playwright John Byrne, and sculpture by Andy Goldsworthy.

➕ 200 C3 ✉ Queen Street ☎ 0141 2291996; www.glasgow.gov.uk
🕐 Mon–Thu and Sat 10–5, Fri and Sun 11–5 🍴 Café and restaurant (£) 🚇 St Enoch, Buchanan Street 🚉 Queen Street, Argyle Street, Central 💷 Free

12 The Lighthouse

Scotland's centre for Architecture, Design and the City is a lasting legacy from the Year of Architecture in 1999. The building, which used to house the *Herald* newspaper, was designed by Charles Rennie Mackintosh and now houses the **Mackintosh Interpretation Centre** (➤ 18–20) as well as an area of changing displays and exhibitions.

➕ 200 C3 ✉ 11 Mitchell Lane
☎ 0141 2216362;
www.thelighthouse.co.uk 🕐 Mon, Wed, Fri–Sat 10:30–5:30, Tue 11–5:30, Thu 10:30–7, Sun 2–4 🍴 Café (£) 🚇 St Enoch 🚉 Argyle Street, Central
💷 The Lighthouse and Mackintosh Interpretation Centre inexpensive

13 The Willow Tea Room

If you have time for just one cup of tea in Glasgow, have it here.

Mackintosh designed this, along with several others, in 1904 for caterer Kate Cranston, the pioneer of Glasgow tea rooms. There's no better way to imagine yourself back in the city's Victorian heyday than to have afternoon tea in the mauve-and-silver high-backed chairs of the Salon de Luxe (➤ 90).

➕ 200 B4 ✉ 217 Sauchiehall Street, through a jeweller's shop and upstairs
☎ 0141 3320521 🕐 Mon–Sat 10–5
🍴 (£) 🚇 Cowcaddens, Buchanan Street 🚉 Charing Cross
💷 Free

The Salon de Luxe in the Willow Tea Room

14 Glasgow School of Art

This is the earliest example of a complete art-nouveau building in the UK. Mackintosh won the competition to design a new school in 1896 and everything, right down to the furnishings and fittings, is his work. Students still sit in Mackintosh chairs in the library and use his original bookcases. It's not open to the public, so the only way to see this is by taking the tour.

➕ 200 B4 ✉ 167 Renfrew Street
☎ 0141 3534526 🕐 Guided tours
Mon–Fri 11 and 2, Sat 10:30 and 11:30
(booking advisable) 🍴 Willow Tea
Room (£) 🚇 Cowcaddens 🚉 Charing
Cross 🚶 Moderate

16 Botanic Gardens

These have been a peaceful oasis in Glasgow's West End since 1842. In bad weather head for the Kibble Palace, the massive glass conservatory at the centre, dating from 1873. It's a great steamy jungle that provides a wonderful escape from a cold, wet Glasgow day.

➕ 200, off A5 ✉ Great Western Road
☎ 0141 3342422 🕐 Daily 7am–dusk
🍴 Café in Kibble Palace (£)
🚇 Kelvinbridge 🚶 Free

18 Museum of Transport

A re-created Glasgow street from the 1930s, complete with shops, cinema and Victorian underground station, is the highlight of this museum. For transport enthusiasts, there are also early bicycles, motorbikes, steam trains, Glasgow tramcars and some fine examples from the Scottish motor industry that flourished in the early 20th century. These range from early

Glasgow School of Art, Charles Rennie Mackintosh's masterpiece

Arrol Johnstone cars – made in the same Dumfries factory that built Donald Campbell's record-breaking *Bluebird* – to the little 1960s Hillman Imp.

➕ 200, off A5 ✉ Kelvin Hall, 1
Bunhouse Road ☎ 0141 2872700
🕐 Mon–Thu and Sat 10–5, Fri and Sun
11–5 🍴 Museum and Art Gallery
across the road (£) 🚇 Kelvinbridge
🚶 Free

19 The Tall Ship

The *SV Glenlee* (1886) in Glasgow Harbour is one of the last Clyde-built sailing ships still afloat. Rescued from the scrap heap and restored to exhibition standard, it shows life aboard a cargo vessel, and the holds have been re-created with all the original sounds and smells. The Pumphouse Visitor Centre has changing displays, a restaurant and café-bar.

➕ 200, off A3 ✉ Yorkhill Quay, 100
Stobcross Road ☎ 0141 3390631;
www.glenlee.co.uk 🕐 Daily 10–5
(phone first in Jan) 🍴 Pumphouse
Visitor Centre (£) 🚇 Kelvinhall 🚌 First
Bus No 3 🚉 Finnieston 🚶 Moderate;
one child enters free with each adult

Where to...
Eat and Drink

Prices

The £ amounts indicate what you can expect to pay for a three-course meal for one person, including coffee and service.

£ = under £15 ££ = £15–25 £££ = over £25

RESTAURANTS

Buttery Restaurant ££–£££

This popular, long-established, old-fashioned restaurant is set in the one remaining tenement block in a redeveloped area. The cooking looks at traditional Scottish food through a surprisingly modern eye. Make sure to leave room for the superb desserts. The Belfry Bistro below offers lighter meals.

✚ 200 A3 ✉ 652 Argyle Street
☎ 0141 2218188 ◉ Lunch Mon–Fri; dinner Mon–Sat; closed Jan 1–2 and Christmas

Fratelli Sarti £

Glasgow has long had a love of Italian food and the '100 percent authentic Italian' motto sums up the philosophy of this mini chain of family-run restaurants. Tucked away at the quieter end of Bath Street is Café Sarti, informal, busy and pitched somewhere between a restaurant and a deli, which offers something for everyone – whether a quick snack or a relaxed, three-course blow-out.

✚ 200 C4 ✉ 121 Bath Street
☎ 0141 2040440 ◉ Mon–Sat
8am–10:30pm, Sun noon–10:30

Gamba £–££

A stylish setting and upbeat service mark out this award-winning basement restaurant. The striking fish mural and the strong Mediterranean look set the theme – this is a seafood restaurant serving the best Scottish fish cooked in an unfussy manner. The wine list is excellent.

✚ 200 B4 ✉ 225a West George Street ☎ 0141 5720899 ◉ Lunch and dinner Mon–Sat; closed Christmas and New Year

Nairns ££

This is one of the best-value restaurants in Glasgow. TV chef Nick Nairn offers sharp cooking and equally sharp service. Set-price menus have about six choices for each course, with a spin on familiar Mediterranean fare. The en-suite bedrooms above the restaurant are recommended.

✚ 200 A5 ✉ 13 Woodside Crescent
☎ 0141 3530707 ◉ Lunch and dinner daily ; closed Jan 1–2 and Dec 25–26

La Parmigiana £–££

One of the best of Glasgow's many Italian restaurants, with a cool Milanese-style interior and warm, enthusiastic service in true family-run tradition. The menu has a few contemporary touches, but old favourites, with lashings of cream and alcohol in the sauces, reign supreme. Good value set lunch.

✚ 200, off A5 ✉ 447 Great Western Road ☎ 0141 3340686 ◉ Lunch and dinner Mon–Sat

Rogano ££–£££

The 1930s art deco interior is authentic, built when the Queen Mary ship was being constructed on the Clyde. The seafaring connection is reflected in the classic fish soups, smoked salmon, oysters, lobster Thermidor and grilled halibut fillet. The traditional approach ensures a loyal following, drawn by generous portions and impeccable freshness.

✚ 200 C3 ✉ 11 Exchange Place
☎ 0141 2484055 ◉ Daily lunch and dinner; closed Jan 1 and Dec 25

Two Fat Ladies ££

The name comes from the bingo-caller's jargon for 88, and not the British TV cooks. One of Glasgow's best options for fish, it's also one of the most relaxed and informal – there are only nine tables – and there is an emphasis on quality and freshness. The set lunch and pre-theatre menus are very good value. Reservations are essential.

✚ 200, off A3 ⊠ 88 Dumbarton Road ☎ 0141 3391944 ⓖ Lunch Tue–Sat; dinner Fri–Sat

Ubiquitous Chip ££–£££

After 30 years, The Chip is a Glasgow landmark that still has a good buzz with a plant-strewn, covered courtyard at its heart. An innovative dedication to the best Scottish produce ranges from haggis 'n' neeps to Troon-landed cod and Ayrshire bacon. Upstairs, a brasserie offers food at more modest prices.

✚ 200, off A5 ⊠ 12 Ashton Lane ☎ 0141 3345007 ⓖ Lunch and dinner daily; closed 1 Jan and 25 Dec

Yes ££–£££

This spacious restaurant exudes cosmopolitan style and swagger, with glass doors, bold colours and modern art. There's a feel for the Mediterranean, but also the Pacific, with coconut, coriander and mango found in the risottos, pesto butters and dressings.

✚ 200 C3 ⊠ 22 West Nile Street ☎ 0141 2218044 ⓖ Lunch / dinner Mon–Sat; closed 1–2 Jan and Christmas

CAFÉS/TEA ROOMS

Café Gandolfi £

Established over 20 years ago, Café Gandolfi has always been noted for its lively atmosphere and unstuffy attitude. Stained-glass windows and wooden furniture contrast with the light, imaginative modern food. With a flexible all day menu, it's also one of the best tea rooms in the city.

✚ 201 E3 ⊠ 64 Albion Street ☎ 0141 5526813 ⓖ 9am–11:30pm (Sun noon–11:30)

Stravaigin £–££

This basement café has wooden tables and benches, raffia chairs and eye-catching murals on the walls. A lively crowd is attracted by modern cooking and low prices. The kitchen transforms Scotland's produce into global dishes.

✚ 201 F2 ⊠ 30 Gibson Street ☎ 0141 3342665 ⓖ Lunch Mon–Sat; dinner daily; 1–2 closed Jan and Dec 25–26

Willow Tea Room £

Sauchiehall means valley of willows, hence Willow Tea Room (▶ 87), once one of several quirky tea rooms designed by Charles Rennie Mackintosh (▶ 18–20) in the 1900s. The restored Salon de Luxe sparkles with mirrors, coloured glass, and mauve and silver furniture. Enjoy the 30 blends of loose-leaf tea, cakes, muffins, scones and sandwiches, as well as daily specials.

✚ 200 B4 ⊠ 217 Sauchiehall Street ☎ 0141 3320521 ⓖ Mon–Sat 9:30–4:30

PUBS

Auctioneers £

Former auction rooms have been cleverly transformed into a pub, although the windows look more like a shop front, filled with bric-a-brac. Inside, the valuation booths are now intimate tables and the pub is full of antiques. There's a great buzz, with excellent beers and single-malts. Food, such as soup, haggis and fish and chips, is served all day.

✚ 200 C3 ⊠ 6 North Court, St Vincent Place ☎ 0141 2295851 ⓖ Daily 11–8:45 (Fri–Sat 9:45)

The Babbity Bowster £

This famous pub is in a stylish 18th-century town house, giving it the look of a mid-European café. Food is served all day: after breakfast, hearty home-made soups, snacks and filling haggis, neeps and tatties are good choices.

✚ 201 E3 ⊠ 16–18 Blackfriars Street ☎ 0141 5525055 ⓖ Daily 11am–midnight

Where to... Stay

Prices

Price categories are per person, including English breakfast.

£ = under £30 per night ££ = £30–60 per night £££ = over £60 per night

Beardmore Hotel ££

This impressive modern hotel is on the banks of the Clyde near Erskine Bridge. It is well placed for business travellers and tourists heading for Loch Lomond and Argyllshire. The Beardmore boasts tremendous facilities such as a leisure centre with an indoor swimming pool, gym and a full range of beauty treatments, while the bedrooms are attractive and comfortable. As a further bonus, the well-regarded restaurant offers a great line in modern British cooking with a strong Mediterranean bias.

➕ 200, off A5 ✉ Beardmore Street, Clydebank ☎ 0141 9516000
E-mail: beardmore.hotel@hci.co.uk

The Brunswick Hotel ££

This chic, minimalist and very modern hotel is located in Glasgow's trendy Merchant City area (▶ 75), beneath the distinctive copper roof of the award-winning Primavera building. It's intriguingly designed to make the best possible use of a tight space, offering 22 light, bright, air-conditioned rooms with low, Japanese-style beds. There is also a café bar and basement bistro. For a particularly memorable stay, the two-level penthouse apartment comes complete with sauna and kitchen and can sleep six.

➕ 201 D3 ✉ 106–108 Brunswick Street ☎ 0141 5520001
E-mail: brunhotel@aol.com

Carrick ££

Opposite Cadogan Square at the west end of one of Glasgow's best-known streets is this pleasant, modern hotel. Although the 121 bedrooms are compact, they are very well equipped with the essential facilities. Over half are non-smoking. There's a restaurant and lounge bar, and parking is available near by.

➕ 200 B3 ✉ 377 Argyle Street ☎ 0141 2482355

The Devonshire Hotel of Glasgow £££

The Devonshire Hotel is found at the end of the same terrace as One Devonshire Gardens (listed below) so make sure you're going to the right place. With just 14 individually designed rooms, The Devonshire is a stylish hotel with an emphasis on traditional comforts. Public areas, including a drawing room, exude charm and elegance.

➕ 200, off A5 ✉ 5 Devonshire Gardens ☎ 0141 3397878; fax: 0141 3393980 E-mail: devonshire@aol.com

Ewington ££

A classic hotel, carefully developed from a former Victorian residential terrace, the Ewington lies on the south side of Glasgow, opposite Queens Park, and is just six minutes by rail link to Glasgow city centre. The standard of service here is second to none, with dedicated staff creating a warm, welcoming atmosphere. Public areas include a pretty foyer/lounge and a cocktail lounge. The 44 bedrooms come in a mix of sizes and styles, including spacious executive rooms.

➕ 200, off B1 ✉ Balmoral Terrace,132 Queens Drive, Queens Park ☎ 0141 4231152

Glasgow Marriott £££

Close to the city centre (by junction 19 of the M8), the Marriott offers a high standard of facilities, including a smart ground-floor bar/lounge, informal café and attractive restaurant. It also has its own leisure club with gym and swimming pool, as well as offering beauty treatments

and hairdressing. Standard bedrooms are all good-sized, with generous beds, breakfast table, ample desk and storage space and air-conditioning. If your budget allows, book one of the suites.

🚹 200 A3 🏠 500 Argyle Street, Anderston ☎ 0141 2265577

Glasgow Moat House ££

Instantly recognisable from its mirrored glass exterior, the Moat House is one of the tallest buildings in Scotland. Built on the old Queens Docks, it's adjacent to the Scottish Exhibition Centre and has fine views of the Clyde. A huge mural of the Clyde's shipbuilding past is a feature of both of its restaurants. It also houses the Waterside health and leisure club. Spacious bedrooms are identically equipped, most enjoy panoramic views over the river and city, and there are also various family facilities. Ample parking space is an added bonus.

🚹 200 off A3 🏠 Congress Road ☎ 0141 3069988

Holiday Inn Express £

The location is great, near Merchant City with its restaurants and nightlife, the price is one of the best deals in town, and it's close to the river – on the corner of Stockwell and Clyde streets (but no river views). The Holiday Inn Express is essentially just somewhere to sleep, but all 120 rooms are en suite, modern and well designed.

🚹 201 D2 🏠 122 Stockwell Street ☎ 0141 5485000

The Malmaison ££

A sister hotel of its namesake in Edinburgh, this is part of an outstanding mini-chain of design-led hotels. All 72 bedrooms (20 of which are non-smoking) ooze stylish excellence, and come equipped with extras such as CD players and cable TV. The food is highly regarded: the basement brasserie has an energetic club-like appeal, and next door is the equally fashionable Café Mal. After eating, you can work out in the gym.

🚹 200 B4 🏠 278 West George Street ☎ 0141 5721000; fax: 0141 5721002
E-mail: glasgow@malmaison.com

Kelvin Park Lorne ££

This popular hotel is just 10 minutes from the city centre and a few minutes' walk from the Scottish Exhibition Centre and art galleries. The largest bedrooms are n the Apsley Wing and, although the other bedrooms can be quite small, they are smart and attractively designed. A private underground car-park is a plus for a hotel so close to the city centre.

🚹 200 off A5 🏠 923 Sauchiehall Street ☎ 0141 3149955

One Devonshire Gardens £££

Without doubt this unique hotel is one of the most notable in Scotland. Three splendid Victorian town houses were combined to make a complete design statement, one where the golden rule has been to keep it simple, and where every detail has been carefully considered. Each of the 27 rooms has its own individual style with extras such as CD players, big beds, deep baths, fresh flowers, books, magazines and bathrobes. The small restaurant offers some of Glasgow's finest food.

🚹 200, off A5 🏠 1 Devonshire Gardens ☎ 0141 3392001; fax: 0141 3371663
E-mail: onedevonshire@btconnect.com

The Tinto Firs ££

A modern, if modest, hotel in the suburbs (6km south of the city centre), the Tinto is convenient for the airport and the Burrell Collection (▶ 72–4). But the great attraction of this 27-room hotel is its small size – it has more personality than many of its kind, and the friendliness of the staff is enhanced by the relaxed atmosphere they create. Bedrooms are mostly cosy studio singles, but they are very well equipped; there are also some family rooms. Public areas include a choice of bars.

🚹 200, off B1 🏠 470 Kilmarnock Road ☎ 0141 6372353

Where to... Shop

Most shops open from 9 or 9:30am until 5:30 or 6pm, and many stores now regularly open until 7 or 8pm. You'll find **Tower Records** open till midnight every night. Not all shops open on Sundays but many do, often just in the afternoon – however, you could always try the **Barras** (▶ 85).

Shaped like a Z, **Argyle Street, Buchanan Street** and **Sauchiehall Street** form Glasgow's main shopping area, known by locals as the 'Golden Z'. This is without question Scotland's premier shopping area, the best selection of stores in the UK outside London. Buchanan Street and the near end of Sauchiehall Street have been pedestrianised, so there's only minimal traffic-dodging to spoil your day.

MAIN MALLS AND CENTRES

The **Buchanan Galleries** is a classy new shopping centre, bringing the excellent John Lewis department store to Glasgow for the first time. The **Sauchiehall Street Centre** has a good number of High Street chains, as has the slightly downmarket **St Enoch Centre**. Retro clothes and audacious young designs can be found in **Virginia Galleries** (33 Virginia Street), a 19th-century former tobacco and sugar trading house, while more exclusive shops can be found at **Princes Square** in Buchanan Street. The **Victorian Village** (57 West Regent Street) features a collection of antiques shops.

CLOTHING

Designer clothes abound in the expensive boutiques of the **Italian Centre** (Renfield Street) has a huge range of designer gear for men and women. In the basement of the Sauchiehall Street Centre you'll find **TK Maxx**, a discount shop selling a whole range of designer labels at affordable prices. **Diesel**, the Italian label, has a two-floor outlet in Buchanan Street. Meanwhile, big girls and boys can get kitted out in **Long Tall Sally's** and **High and Mighty**, both in West Nile Street. For cut-price denims the best place in town is **Bankrupt** (Queen Street), selling well-known and obscure labels. And **Slater Menswear** (165 Howard Street) has been described as the largest of its kind in the world, stocking over 17,000 suits.

BOOKS

For new books **Waterstone's** in Sauchiehall Street has five floors, an internet café and reading areas. **Ottokar's** in the Buchanan Galleries has a more comfortable feel, with cosy seats for browsers and a coffee bar while **Borders** in Buchanan Street is always popular. **Adam's Books** (Parnie Street) is one of the best and friendliest places for second-hand gems, particularly Scottish books, and **Voltaire & Rousseau** (18 Otago Lane) is another rich seam.

FOOD AND DRINK

For whisky try the **Ubiquitous Chip Wine Shop** in Ashton Lane in the West End (▶ 90), the **Wine and Whisky Shop** (116 Saltmarket) or the **Whisky Shop** in Princes Square. **Peckham's** in Central Station and Byres Road is a great deli.

JEWELLERY

Many independent and gift shops stock distinctively Scottish jewellery. The **Argyle Arcade**, which links Argyle Street to Buchanan Street, is wall to wall jewellers' shops. **Henderson The Jeweller**, through which you have to walk to get to the **Willow Tea Room** (▶ 87 and 90), has the best collection of silver jewellery in Mackintosh designs.

Where to...
Be Entertained

Like Edinburgh, the best source of information on what's currently on in Glasgow is *The List*, available every two weeks from newsagents. *The Glasgow Evening Times* has listings each day, and the weekend supplement of the *Saturday Herald* covers events nationwide for the next seven days.

CINEMA

The **Odeon** in Renfield Street, with its renovated art deco facade, is a six-screen facility showing all the latest releases. The **Glasgow Film Theatre** in Rose Street (just off Sauchiehall Street) is another art deco building, where you can see a selection of independent, foreign-language and art films.

THEATRE AND MUSIC

Many of Glasgow's fine old theatre buildings have been closed or torn down, but there are still enough left to attract the serious theatregoer. The **Citizens'** in Gorbals Street is simply the best in Scotland, covering everything from revamped Restoration comedies to the latest thing by 21st-century playwrights. The **Tron** regularly puts on productions of small touring companies as well as in-house shows, live music and occasional comedy. For traditional performances the **Theatre Royal**, home of Scottish Opera, is the venue for opera, ballet and all things highbrow, while the **King's** tends to present musicals, both by touring companies and amateur

productions. It stages a great pantomime during the winter months. Classical music concerts can be heard in the **Royal Concert Hall**, headquarters of the Royal Scottish National Orchestra. The venue also hosts gigs by visiting rock and pop stars as well as the successful Celtic Connections traditional music festival every January (▶ 12–13, 42).

PUBS AND CLUBS

The Glasgow pub scene is fantastic and world-renowned – from trendy Merchant City bars packed with Armani-clad yuppies to West End student hang-outs and the traditional haunts of working-class Glasgow. Try a mixture, and make sure not to miss the **Saracen's Head** (London Road near the Barras) for the best slice of old Glasgow life. Best of the rest are the **Scotia Bar** (Stockwell Street), **Barga** and the **Babbity Bowster** (▶ 90) in the Merchant City and **The Curlers** (Byers Road) in the West End.

The rock and pop scene is vibrant, with great live music. **King Tut's Wah Wah Hut** (St Vincent Street) features the best of bands on the circuit plus a few top names popping in from time to time. The **Cat House** in Union Street is the favoured rock venue, while the **Scotia** and the **Babbity Bowster** are best for folk and Celtic sounds.

Dancing has been big in Glasgow since the days of the Plaza Ballroom and the famed Denistoun Palais. Nowadays it's not just hip hop and house – there's a thriving ceilidh dance scene, and if you watch the queues outside the **Riverside** club on a Saturday night you'll realise that this is part of a very young and vibrant movement. Elsewhere, try the **Sub Club** in Jamaica Street, the **Velvet Room** (520 Sauchiehall Street) and the **Arches** underneath Central Station in Midland Street for the latest in dance music. As always, clubs disappear, so check *The List* before getting all dressed up and finding nowhere to go.

South of
Scotland

In Three Days 98 – 99
Don't Miss 100 – 107
At Your Leisure 108 – 111
Where to… 112 – 116

Getting Your Bearings

This is one of the prettiest but least visited parts of Scotland, with castles, towers and ruined abbeys nestling among rolling hills and pastoral lowlands. Rocky coves and sandy beaches are enhanced further by the glorious sunsets that gild the islands to the west. Inland, the wilderness of the Galloway Hills and the vast woodlands are a hillwalker's paradise, particularly beautiful when the fresh spring foliage sprouts in dazzling greens or woodland trails are canopied in autumn flame and gold. Visitors speed past, heading for Edinburgh, Glasgow and the Highlands, and miss out on this secret land beyond the motorway.

From the Middle Ages until the 17th century the border country was a wild frontier, subject to continual cross-border raids and clan feuds. The many strong stone towers, still in evidence, provided defences and an early-warning system. Some are ruined, some have been incorporated into later mansions, while others have been restored. The great Border Abbeys, now picturesque ruins, are all that remain of the splendour and power of the pre-Reformation Church.

Greenock A82 A80 Cumbernauld
A78 MB GLASGOW Summerlee MB Livir
Paisley Coatbridge A71
Largs M77 Hamilton Motherwell
A737 East New
Lochranza Kilbride Lanark
Ardrossan A77 Strathaven Lanark 2
Arran Irvine Kilmarnock M74 Bigga
4 Brodick A78 A77 A76 Museum
Firth of Mauchline
Clyde Ayr A70
Dunure Burns New Leadhills
Culzean Castle Country Cumnock 7
& Country Park 6 A77 Maybole A76 A
Girvan Dalmellington Nith M
Southern Thornhill
Moniaive A76 Lo
A75 Dun
Castle
Douglas

Solway Firth

Exquisite Rosslyn Chapel, on the outskirts of Edinburgh

This area was Robert the Bruce's home territory and where he harried the English in a series of guerrilla raids during the Wars of Independence which raged from 1296 until the English defeat at Bannockburn in 1314 (➤ 27–30).

There are traces here too of Industrial Scotland. Kilmarnock, for example, which was once filled with factories, now produces little more than the whisky that Johnny Walker first blended in the back shop of his grocery business. Near by in the Irvine valley, the towns of Darvel and Newmilns are the remnants of Britain's once flourishing lace industry, which survives by producing high-quality traditional products on 19th-century machinery. Dunaskin, at Patna near Ayr, has a museum in an old Industrial Revolution ironworks, while at New Lanark an entire industrial complex is preserved.

Loading the twine at Robert Owen's mills, New Lanark

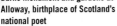

Burns Monument and gardens at Alloway, birthplace of Scotland's national poet

★ Don't Miss

2 New Lanark ➤ 100
5 Burns Country ➤ 104

At Your Leisure

1 Summerlee Heritage Park ➤ 108
3 Biggar Museums ➤ 108
4 Arran ➤ 109
6 Culzean Castle & Country Park ➤ 109
7 Gold Panning in the Leadhills ➤ 109
8 Border Abbeys ➤ 110
9 Traquair ➤ 110
10 Rosslyn Chapel ➤ 111
11 Haddington ➤ 111

Enjoy the rolling hills and majestic abbeys of the Borders,
the lush lowland pastures and rugged coastline of
Ayrshire, Burns' heritage country, ancient castles, a preserved
gasworks and the fascinating mysteries of Rosslyn Chapel.

The South in Three Days

Day 1

Morning

Leave Glasgow or Edinburgh by the M8 motorway, exiting for Coatbridge at J8 or J6 and spend an hour or so at **Summerlee Heritage Park** (➤ 108). Then drive south via the M74 to **New Lanark** (➤ 100–3) and spend a couple of hours exploring the old mills and houses of industrialist Robert Owen's Utopian dream. Take the riverside walk up to the Falls of Clyde if the weather's fine.

Afternoon

After a late lunch in the tea room at New Lanark, take the A72 to **Biggar,** home to an amazing number of museums (➤ 108): there's even a museum of the local gasworks. The Victorian Puppet Theatre Museum is a must, particularly if you can manage to see a performance. And if you have time, the Moat Park Heritage Centre and the Gladstone Court Museum (with its re-creation of an historic pharmacy, below) are also worth visiting. Return on the A72 and head west on the A70 for the town of Ayr and your overnight stop. In Ayr try Fouter's Bistro in Academy Street for a friendly welcome and a superb evening meal.

Day 2

Morning
Just south of Ayr is the **Burns National Park** (➤ 104–7) in Alloway. Spend a couple of hours exploring the Tam o' Shanter Experience, Burns' Cottage, the Auld Haunted Kirk and the Brig o' Doon before heading south on the A719 for the scenic route along the coast road to Culzean. Stop to enjoy the views to the isle of Arran and the Kintyre peninsula. If there's time, take a detour to the pretty little fishing harbour at Dunure. On the coast road near Croy look out for the 'Electric Brae', an optical illusion where your car seems to roll uphill. Continue on to **Culzean Castle and Country Park** (pictured left, ➤ 109), where you can spend the rest of the morning.

Afternoon
Head south on the A70 and A76 to Dumfries, via Ellisland Farm. Here you can visit the Robert Burns Centre, Burns' House and the Mausoleum in St Michael's churchyard. Have a coffee at Gracefield Arts Centre on Edinburgh Road, where you can enjoy their current exhibits and browse in the excellent little craft shop selling work by local artists.

Day 3

Morning
Take the winding route of the A709, B7068, A7 and A698 through pleasant pastureland, by rivers and hills via Lockerbie, Langholm and Hawick, to Jedburgh and its stunning abbey (➤ 110). Lunch at Simply Scottish in the High Street.

Afternoon
Head north on the A68 to Melrose for a look at the abbey and the town's quirky little shops. Then take the A72 west to Innerleithen and Scotland's oldest continually inhabited house at **Traquair** (➤ 110). Finally, if you have time, head north on the A703 and A701 to the mysterious **Rosslyn Chapel** (the famous 'Apprentice Pillar' is pictured right ➤ 111) and a welcome cup of tea in the visitors' centre.

New Lanark

The merchant David Dale built his cotton mills at New Lanark in 1785 to take advantage of the narrow gorge in the River Clyde to power the mills. The elegant sandstone buildings were a welcome contrast to the usual working-people's slums. And for the large number of Highlanders, cleared from the north, this rural location must have seemed closer to home than the industrial heart of Glasgow.

As you descend the hill from the car-park, the arresting panoramas of New Lanark's idyllic setting on the banks of the Clyde will stop you in your tracks. Almost unchanged since it was completed in the early-19th century, the beautiful buildings show a classical simplicity. Yet there's no mistaking their industrial purpose. The massive mill buildings ranged along the river, the channel carrying the water to drive the mills and the rows of workers' tenements couldn't be further from a rural village scene. As you explore the village, the combination of industrial efficiency and clear sense of community is evident.

From Apprentice to Merchant

David Dale (1739–1806) started as an apprentice weaver in Paisley before becoming a weaver's agent and eventually a merchant in Glasgow. He went into partnership with inventor Richard Arkwright (1732–92), and together they built the mills at New Lanark.

Dale's mill initially employed around 400 adults and 800 children, some of whom were only five or six years old, supplied by local orphanages. Child labour was the norm, but Dale actually provided well for the children in terms of hygiene, clothing, education and food in that Dickensian world.

New Lanark's **Visitor Centre** is housed in the **Institute for the Formation of Character,** which was built 30 years later by David Dale's son-in-law, the Welsh industrialist and social reformer Robert Owen (1771–1858) as part of 'the most important experiment for the happiness of the human race that has yet been instituted at any time in any part of the world.' This was the social hub of New Lanark, at the centre of a community of 2,500 people. It had a library and reading room and was used for adult education, concerts, carpet bowls, dances and

Robert Owen, the industrialist and idealist who tried to create a Utopia at New Lanark

Ride into the
future with
Harmony on
the new
Millennium
Experience

weddings. It even served as a works canteen and a religious
meeting place. It now houses the audio-visual **Millennium
Experience,** guided by Harmony, a young girl from the future
explaining how Robert Owen's ideas and aspirations for a better
future led him to develop his ideas at New Lanark.

Owen refused to employ children below the age of ten, but
he enabled their mothers to work by providing a nursery for
their babies. Children continued in full-time education until 10
or 12. Dancing and singing were regarded as central to their
education, and both punishments and rewards were banned.

Prices were
kept low at
New Lanark's
local stores, to
the benefit of
the workforce

Thousands visited New Lanark in the years that followed to
observe Owen's experiment. His competitors were scornful,
expecting his business to collapse and were astonished when it
flourished. His belief that decent conditions would produce a
more contented and efficient workforce, which would in turn
improve business, was vindicated.

In the **village store,** where Owen's prices undercut the inflated rates of the grocers and butchers, you can buy everyday 1920s goods such as enamel cookware or *soor plooms* (sour plums), and in the adjoining section see how different the choice would have been 100 years earlier. The nearby **mill-workers' house** shows living conditions in the early 19th and 20th centuries, including the shared stairhead toilet and the communal wash-house.

The **mill** itself has working machinery that once filled all these massive buildings. The great 19th-century spinning mule clatters noisily as one person controls countless spinning threads – a task that would once have been the work of hundreds of spinners.

When the mill closed in 1968, New Lanark quickly became derelict and the whole complex was very close to demolition when the New Lanark Conservation Trust was set up in 1973. The buildings were all listed as Category A and a long restoration programme began. The tenements have been transformed

Robert Owen's main mill at New Lanark is set idyllically on the river

into comfortable modern flats, and the preserved shell of Mill No 1 is now a luxury hotel, while the Waterhouses (formerly used to store the raw cotton) are rented as holiday apartments.

TAKING A BREAK

The **tea room in the mill** serves snacks and light lunches at very reasonable prices.

New Lanark
➕ 203 D3
✉ Lanark
☎ 01555 661345
🕐 Daily 11–5; closed 1 Jan and 25 Dec
🍴 Café (£)
💷 Moderate

Falls of Clyde Wildlife Reserve
➕ 203 D3
✉ Scottish Wildlife Trust's Visitor Centre, The Old Dyeworks, New Lanark
☎ 01555 665262
🕐 Daily Apr–Sep; closed Oct–March
💷 Donations

NEW LANARK: INSIDE INFO

One to miss Robert Owen's house is not as interesting as the rest of the complex, so if you're pushed for time this is the one to skip.

In more depth If you have time, visit the Scottish Wildlife Trust's **Falls of Clyde** wildlife reserve, where the river flows through the gorge over a series of waterfalls, including the spectacular 26m cascade of Corra Linn. There's a wide range of wildlife here, including badgers, foxes and roe deer. A treat during the spring and summer months is peregrine falcon-watching from a viewing area across the gorge from their nest. You can get close enough to watch the birds with the naked eye, but remain far enough away not to disturb them.

The Falls of Clyde provided Owen's mills with power

Burns Country

Robert Burns (1759–96), Scotland's national poet, was born in an 'auld clay biggin' near the banks of the River Doon, with thatched roof, thick walls and tiny windows to protect against the grim Scottish winters. You can see hundreds of similar long, low cottages across the southwest of Scotland, slated now rather than thatched. Restored to its original condition, Burns' cottage is now part of the Burns National Park at Alloway, where he spent the first six years of his life. In the cottage is the original manuscript of 'Auld Lang Syne'. Burns would recognise the cottages, but the boggy moorland from which he scratched a living has been transformed into a fertile farming landscape.

Start your tour at the visitors' centre in **Alloway**. After a video about Burns' life and an excellent audio-visual presentation of his greatest poem, *Tam o' Shanter*, you can follow in Tam's footsteps to 'Alloway's Auld Haunted Kirk', where he chanced

upon a coven of witches and was chased for his life to the ancient **Brig o' Doon**. Burns' parents are buried in the auld kirk yard, and he often took the narrow road over the Brig o' Doon to Carrick shore.

Burns was brought up on tales of legend and superstition told by his mother Agnes Broun. She was from Kirkoswald village, 23km south of Ayr on the A77, where Robert went to school, and where he met the local characters who were later immor-

Tam O' Shanter's statue sits drinking

talised in his poems. Their gravestones are in the yard of the ruined pre-Reformation village church. Look out for Douglas Graham of Shanter Farm, the original Tam. Buried near by is 'his ancient, trusty, drouthy, crony' Soutar Johnnie – the village cobbler John Davidson. His cottage and workshop, opposite the churchyard, have been restored, complete with tools and stone statues of Tam and the Soutar.

Follow the trail north from here to **Kilmarnock**, where John Wilson's printing shop produced the first volume of

Burns' poems in 1786. At the Dean Castle in the town is a rare original copy of the 'Kilmarnock Edition'. A year later Burns moved a short distance down what is now the A76 to the farm at Mossgiel near **Mauchline**, where he wrote one of his best-loved poems, 'To a Mouse', after ploughing up the nest of a fieldmouse.

Burns met his future wife Jean Armour in Mauchline and regularly fell foul of the Kirk Session, which com-

Robert Burns was born in this cottage in Alloway

prised the elders of the church who judged the morals of their fellow parishioners and decided appropriate penalties. Burns retaliated against their hypocrisy with satirical verse. In the churchyard here is the grave of Willie Fisher, a particularly vicious church elder, ridiculed by Burns in 'Holy Willie's Prayer' following his death in a ditch after a drinking session. Willie drank in **Poosie Nancie's Tavern** at Mauchline, and it's still a grand place to stop for a dram before continuing to **Dumfries,** where Burns spent his last years.

The Auld Brig O' Doon which Tam O' Shanter crossed to escape the witches in Burns' poem

Burns worked as an exciseman in Dumfries, and he would still recognise the broad sweep of the River Nith, Devorgilla's Bridge, the lade or weir feeding the watermill and the observatory. The poet's statue stands in front of Greyfriars Church,

looking down the High Street to the Midsteeple, the former town house where his body lay the night before his funeral. In his last home, now Burns' House Museum, you can see his desk and the bed in which he died on 21 July, 1796, aged 37, his health broken by years of unrelenting toil and poor diet.

TAKING A BREAK

In the Burns' Centre is **Hullabaloo**, a café run by lively and imaginative young people. Whether you choose a sandwich, home-made soup or a light lunch or eat there at night, the food is superb and cheap.

Robert Burns National Heritage Park
🕂 202 C2 ✉ Alloway, near Ayr ☎ 01292 443700
🕐 Daily 9–6, Apr–Oct ; daily 9–5, Nov–Mar 🍴 Café and restaurant in visitors' centre (££) 🚌 From Ayr bus station, Sandgate 🚉 Ayr 💷 Moderate

Burns House
🕂 203 D2 ✉ Burns Street, Dumfries ☎ 01387 255297
🕐 Mon–Sat 10–5, Sun 2–5, Apr–Sep; Tue–Sat 10–1, 2–5, Oct–Mar
🍴 Globe Inn nearby (£) 🚉 Dumfries 💷 Free

Above: Devorgilla's Bridge across the River Nith, the ancient entry to the county town of Dumfries
Right: Pub sign for The Globe, where Burns was a regular customer

Left: Burns' Monument at Mauchline. The poet farmed near here at Mossgiel

BURNS COUNTRY: INSIDE INFO

Top tip Visit the eerie ruin of the **Auld Haunted Kirk o' Alloway** if not, like Tam o' Shanter, at midnight, then in the long, atmospheric twilight shadows.

Hidden gems In Burns' favourite *howff* (an old Scots word for pub), **The Globe Inn in Dumfries**, his chair is still by the fireside and you can see his bedroom and the verses he scratched on the windowpanes with a diamond.

At Your Leisure

① Summerlee Heritage Park

Based in the old Summerlee Ironworks, which was dug out from under 6m of slag and industrial waste, this museum preserves and interprets the history of the steel and heavy-engineering industry that was once the lifeblood of the surrounding communities. It's certainly Scotland's noisiest museum, with engineers giving daily demonstrations of historic machines and making parts to restore others. In the exhibition hall you'll find a reconstructed tinsmith's shop, brass foundry and a spade forge, as well as an Edwardian photographer's studio and the interior of an old Co-op grocery shop. Even the tea room was built in 1880 but moved here from Coatbridge in the 1980s. But pride of place goes to the large-scale reproduction of the ironworks as they were in 1880, contained in a blast furnace structure with a viewing gallery.

For sheer nostalgia though, there's nothing to beat a ride in an old tram-car along 1.2km of relaid track.

✚ 203 D3 ✉ Heritage Way, Coatbridge
☎ 01236 431261 ◷ Daily 10–5,
Apr–Oct; 10–4, Nov–Mar 🍴 Tea room at
museum (£) 🚉 Coatbridge 🎫 Free

② Biggar Museums

The town of Biggar, on the A701 road just west of Peebles, has more museums per head of population than anywhere in Scotland. Moat Park, the headquarters of the Trust, deals with the history of the area. The reconstructed Victorian street at Gladstone Court includes an ironmonger's store, a bank, photographer, chemist, dressmaker, watchmaker, milliner, printer and bootmaker. Albion Motors, once the largest truck manufacturer in the

On the moors at Machrie, on Arran, are the remains of an ancient civilisation

British Empire,
started here in
1899 and the entire
Albion Motors archive
is housed in Gladstone Court.

Greenhill Covenanters Museum
comprehensively covers the religious
strife of the 17th century when the
Scottish Presbyterian Covenanters
fiercely resisted the imposition of an
Episcopalian system on them in a
particularly turbulent period of history. And Biggar Gasworks Museum
tells of the works that supplied the
town until the advent of North Sea
gas in 1970.

Another attraction near by is Biggar
Puppet Theatre, home of the
International Purves Puppets, with
seating for 100. Enjoy a guided tour
of the Victorian theatre and museum,
but also try to catch a performance.
Times vary, however, so check in
advance for details.

➕ 203 D3 ✉ Moat Park Heritage
Centre, Kirkstyle ☎ 01899 221050
🕐 Mon–Sat 10–5, Sun 2–5, Easter–Oct
🍴 Cafés and restaurants (£) 🚌 bus
from Peebles 🎟 Free

Biggar Puppet Theatre
➕ 203 D3 ✉ Puppet Tree House,
Broughton Road ☎ 01899 220631;
www.puppets.freeserve.co.uk
🕐 Mon–Sat 10–5, Sun 2–5 🍴 Cafés in
Biggar (£) 🎟 Inexpensive

❹ Arran

The most southerly of the islands is
sometimes called Scotland in miniature because of its mountainous,
underpopulated north and lush, fertile south. The Arran glens are as varied as the mainland's, attracting
climbers and walkers to easy pastoral
rambles in Glen Rosa, or the more
strenuous climbs of
Glen Sannox and
Goat Fell. Highlights
include Holy Isle
(reached by boat from
Lamlash), with its
Buddhist meditation
centre, Brodick Castle
and Gardens and the mas-
sive standing stone circles on
Machrie Moor.

➕ 202 B3 ✉ Brodick Tourist Office, by
the Calmac Pier ☎ 01770 302140
🕐 Mon–Sat 9–7:30, May–Sep; Mon–Sat
9–5, Oct–Apr 🚢 Ferry from Ardrossan

❻ Culzean Castle and Country Park

This spectacular clifftop castle, built
by the renowned architect Robert
Adam in the late-18th century, is the
National Trust for Scotland's most
visited property. Wandering through
the extensive grounds, which forms
Scotland's first country park, you'll
find shore walks with caves to
explore, delightful woodland paths
and mature parkland. In the house
itself the magnificent central oval
staircase and the circular saloon overlooking the Firth of Clyde are
considered among Adam's most
daring and brilliant designs. The
Eisenhower exhibition recalls the
former US president's role as Supreme
Commander of the Allied Forces in
Europe during World War II, after
which he was given the use of an
apartment within the building for life.
The rooms here, including
Eisenhower's suite, are now rented to
guests for the night.

➕ 202 C2 ✉ Maybole (on A719, 6.4km
west) ☎ 01655 884455; www.nts.org.uk
🕐 Castle, walled garden, Visitor
Centre: daily 10:30–5:30, Apr–Oct; park:
daily 9:30–dusk 🍴 Restaurants and
snack bars (£–££) 🚌 Ayr–Girvan via
Maidens 🚉 Maybole 🎟 Castle and
park expensive; park only moderate

❼ Leadhills Gold Panning

At Wanlockhead, Scotland's highest
village, you can still pan for gold in
the streams that produced the precious metal for the Scottish Crown.

The Museum of Lead Mining has demonstrations and will supply all the necessary kit.

✚ 203 D2 ✉ Wanlockhead ☎ 01659 74387 🕐 Daily 10–5, Jul–Aug 🍽 Tea room and restaurant (£) 🚌 Infrequent service from Sanquhar 🎫 Moderate

8 Border Abbeys

These magnificent abbeys were founded during the reign of Scotland's King David I (c1085–1153) and destroyed by Henry VIII in 1545. The friars were essentially the king's men in the borders and their abbeys became great centres of power and wealth. The heart of Robert the Bruce (► 27–30) is buried at Melrose Abbey, and Sir Walter Scott is buried at Dryburgh. Kelso Abbey is the most romantically ruinous, but if you only have time to visit one, make it Jedburgh, which remains closest to its original medieval splendour.

✚ Kelso 203 F3; Jedburgh 203 F2; Dryburgh and Melrose 203 E3 ☎ Jedburgh 01835 863925; Dryburgh 01835 822381; Melrose 01896 822562 🕐 Daily 9:30–6:30, Apr–Sep; Mon–Sat 9:30–4:30, Sun 2–4:30, Oct–Mar 🍽 Visitors' centre at Jedburgh (£) 🚌 Service from Edinburgh to Melrose; also from Melrose to Kelso and Jedburgh; postbus to Dryburgh one-way only, Mon–Fri 🎫 Jedburgh, Melrose and Dryburgh inexpensive; Kelso free

9 Traquair

Dating from the early-12th century, Traquair is the oldest continually inhabited house in Scotland. Built as a hunting lodge for the Scottish kings, it was then fortified to defend against border raiders. Since 1700, it has been a family home, and has changed very little since then. Within the massive stone walls the house is a fascinating maze of corridors, tiny windows and

The magnificent remnants of Jedburgh's once mighty abbey

secret passages. But above all it's a welcoming and comfortable home, and the Maxwell Stuart family has lived here since the 15th century.

When Bonnie Prince Charlie left on his way to Derby in 1745 the Laird locked the famous Bear Gates and vowed that they would never be opened again until the Stuarts were restored to the throne of Scotland. The gates have now been chained for over 250 years.

Also at Traquair, you can see the

Traquair's Bear Gates take their name from the carved bears on top of the posts

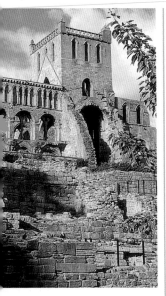

old brewhouse, which makes Traquair House ale in original 200-year-old oak casks.

to conceal the Holy Grail. If you ask, a guide will point out the death mask of King Robert the Bruce (▶ 27–30) carved into the stone and tell you about the treasures of King Solomon's Temple and the Knights Templar, buried in full battle armour in the vault below. In addition to these mysterious associations, Scott's romantic poem, 'The Lay of the Last Minstrel', is also connected with the chapel.

🔲 203 E3 ✉ Rosslyn, Midlothian
☎ 0131 4402159; www.rosslynchapel.org.uk ⏰ Mon–Sat 10–5; Sun noon–4:45 🍴 Tea room in visitor centre (£) 🚌 C70 and 315 from Edinburgh 💷 Moderate; under 12s free

⑪ Haddington

This picturesque country town played a central part in 'The Rough Wooing', when the English army besieged it in 1548 as part of Henry VIII's campaign to persuade the Scots to marry the infant Queen Mary to the heir to the English throne. St Mary's parish church was almost destroyed during the siege and still bears the cannonball marks. The church has one of the most interesting interiors in Scotland, including the alabaster tombs in the tiny side chapel, the Lauderdale Aisle and a window by the English Pre-Raphaelite artist and designer Sir Edward Burne-Jones (1833–98).

🔲 203 E3 ✉ Church Street ☎ 01620 825111; htttp://ourworld.compuserve.com/homepages/Russell_Darling/ ⏰ Mon–Sat 11–4, Sun 1–4:30 🍴 Tea room in church (£) 🚌 106, Edinburgh–Dunbar 💷 Free

🔲 203 E3 ✉ South of Innerleithen on the B709 ☎ 01896 830323 ⏰ Daily 12:30–5:30, Apr–May and Sep–Oct; 10:30–5.30, Jun–Aug 🍴 Café and restaurant (£) 🚌 From Peebles 💷 Inexpensive

⑩ Rosslyn Chapel

Founded in 1446 by the 3rd Earl of Orkney, this has all the grace and splendour of the great French cathedrals, but in miniature, and the richly carved interior features the finest collection of masonic carvings anywhere in the world. Look particularly for the remarkable Apprentice Pillar, reputed

For the children
- Biggar Puppet Theatre (▶ 109)
- Culzean Country Park (▶ 109)
- Falls of Clyde Wildlife Reserve (▶ 103)
- Gold panning (▶ 109)
- Teddy Melrose Museum, Melrose

Where to…
Eat and Drink

Prices

The £ amounts indicate what you can expect to pay for a three-course meal for one person, including coffee and service.

£ = under £15 **££** = £15–25 **£££** = over £25

Fouters Bistro ££

It's a tribute to the quality of the cooking that Fran and Laurie Black's simple bistro has been going strong since 1975. Made up of a series of cellar rooms connected by arched doorways, it offers much in the art of serving unfussy food with the minimum of pretence. Organic and regional produce form the likes of fisherman's soup piled high with mussels, salmon, mullet, haddock and cod, and chargrilled steaks.

➕ 202 C2 🗺 2a Academy Street, Ayr
☎ 01292 261391 🕑 Lunch and dinner Tue– Sat; closed Jan 1–3 and Dec 25–27

Harold's Restaurant £–££

You'll find this contemporary all-day eatery in the Visitor Centre at the Island Distillery. During the day Harold's offers morning coffee, light lunches and afternoon teas. But in the evening, the mood changes – out come the white tablecloths and there's a more serious approach to the food, with a short menu based on fresh ingredients sourced from across the island.

➕ 202 B3 🗺 Isle of Arran Distillery, Lochranza, Isle of Arran ☎ 01770 830264 🕑 Lunch daily; dinner Thu–Tue; closed Jan–Mar

Kailzie Gardens Tearoom £

A handy pitstop after visiting Traquair House (➤ 110), this cottagey restaurant in converted stables offers some really good food. The atmosphere is relaxed and informal, and examples of the very best home-baking include fine cakes and superlative bread. Lunch-time brings soups, sandwiches, pies and salads, but afternoon tea is a treat – it's hard to choose which cake to have.

➕ 203 E3 🗺 Kailzie Gardens, Peebles ☎ 01721 722807 🕑 Daily 11–6

Knockinaam Lodge £££

This former Victorian lodge, now a small hotel with an outstanding restaurant, is surrounded by wooded hills, and lawns rolling down to a private beach. Although the four-course menu offers no choice until dessert, it brings a modern approach to prime Scottish produce. The huge wine list includes some vintages, and you can retire to the bar for a single-malt whisky from a choice of over 100 (➤ 114).

➕ 202 B1 🗺 Stranraer, Portpatrick ☎ 01776 810471 🕑 Lunch and dinner daily

Plumed Horse Restaurant £–££

Proprietor and chef Tony Borthwick chose a small village in which to open his elegant restaurant. Quality is the keynote here, from the warm yellow décor and fine table arrangements, to the modern menu that has roots in classical French cooking and makes good use of luxury ingredients such as foie gras, sweetbreads and wild mushrooms. There's excellent fresh bread, as well as a short, well-balanced wine list.

➕ 203 D1 🗺 Main Street, by Castle Douglas, Dumfries & Galloway ☎ 01556 670333 🕑 Tue–Sun 12:30–1:30, 7–9:30

La Potinière £££–£££

A small, enduring restaurant, this is noted for consistently accomplished food and high standards. The menu is written in French, uncompromisingly with no translation. No-choice four-course lunches are served on Thursday and Sunday, and five-course dinners on Friday and Saturday. Booking essential.

🚩 203 E3 ⊠ Main Street, Gullane ☎ 01620 843214 ⏰ Lunch at 1, Sun and Thu; dinner at 8, Fri and Sat; closed 1 week in Jun and all Oct

Wheatsheaf Restaurant with Rooms £

At heart the Wheatsheaf is a village pub – it overlooks the green and the bar offers a warm welcome. But such is the restaurant's reputation that it's essential to book in advance. Scottish beef, duck, game and fish appear on a lengthy menu that is further extended with daily specials, and there's a certain experimental streak to the style that works well. Desserts are worth trying, the beer is good and there's a comprehensive wine list.

🚩 203 F3 ⊠ Main Street, Swinton ☎ 01890 860257 ⏰ Lunch Tue–Sun; dinner Tue–Sat; closed 2 weeks in Jan and last week in Oct

PUBS/BARS

The Anchor £

This is a waterfront inn with a bustling summer trade. The location is splendid, overlooking the natural harbour and the hills beyond. The traditional-style back bar is warmed by a coal fire, but the non-smoking lounge is where food is served. On offer is good, hearty, home-cooked fare along the lines of soup, sandwiches, steak pies and fresh, breaded haddock. The large collection of malt whisky is worth exploring.

🚩 203 D1 ⊠ Kippford ☎ 01556 620205 ⏰ Daily noon–2:30, 5–9:30

Creebridge House Hotel £

This pretty country house hotel makes a fine stop-off for light refreshment or a substantial meal. In fine weather, tables on the front terrace look out over the lawn, otherwise the bar is welcoming. Real ales, over 50 malt whiskies and a good wine list complement carefully prepared bar/bistro choices such as home-made soup, sandwiches, Cullen skink and steaks. The Sunday lunch-time carvery is popular. Staff are friendly and helpful.

🚩 202 C1 ⊠ Minnigaff, Creebridge, near Newton Stewart ☎ 01671 402121 ⏰ Lunch and dinner daily

The Crown £–££

The rambling bars, an open fire and heavy furniture conjure up images of an old smugglers' haunt and contribute towards the popularity of this harbourside inn. Afternoon tea in the bar is good. The more modern-looking bistro is the place to eat: the menu is imaginative and slightly more expensive, but the quality of the cooking is high, with fish featuring strongly.

🚩 202 B1 ⊠ 9 North Crescent, Portpatrick ☎ 01776 810261 ⏰ Daily 12:30–10

Riverside Inn ££

Across the road from the River Esk, this traditional, 17th-century village inn has been run with enthusiasm by Susan and Robert Phillips for 25 years. Much of the produce on the daily-changing menu is local, and the basic philosophy of the kitchen is simplicity. Soups are a speciality and fish is always very fresh.

🚩 203 E2 ⊠ Canonbie ☎ 01387 371295 ⏰ Lunch and dinner daily; closed Feb

Traquair Arms £

The Bear Ale served in the bar of this Victorian, town-centre hotel is brewed just a few hundred metres away in the Traquair House Brewery. The bar menu makes good use of local ingredients and has the added attraction of serving food all day. Soups, Aberdeen Angus beef, fish and game are backed up by a wide selection of vegetarian dishes. There's a splendid range of desserts and the cheeses are Scottish.

🚩 203 E3 ⊠ Traquair Road, Innerleithen, Borders ☎ 01896 830229 ⏰ Daily noon–9; closed 2 Jan and 25 Dec

Where to... Stay

Prices

Price categories are per person, including English breakfast.
£ = under £30 per night ££ = £30–60 per night £££ = over £60 per night

Auchrannie Hotel £££

Genuine hospitality, together with extensive leisure facilities (heated indoor swimming-pool, sauna, solarium and gym) and sound cooking are all part of the appeal of this renovated Victorian mansion set in extensive landscaped grounds. The 28 bedrooms are well equipped, and those in the new wing are particularly spacious. There's a range of lounges to choose from as well as the Garden Restaurant, which showcases the best Scottish produce; Bramble Bistro offers a more informal atmosphere.

➕ 202 B3 ✉ Brodick, Isle of Arran
☎ 01770 302234; fax: 01770 302812
E-mail: info@auchrannie.co.uk

Burts Hotel ££

Burts was originally built in 1722 for a local dignitary, but over the years it has been transformed into this likeable, family-run former coaching inn. The setting, in the centre of a pretty market square in an historic town, has real picture-postcard charm, and the bar (well stocked with single-malt whiskies) is a popular meeting place. The 20 en-suite rooms vary in size, but are comfortably modern, and the restaurant has a good reputation. The hotel has a wide appeal, catering for most types of visitors.

➕ 203 E3 ✉ The Square, Melrose
☎ 01896 822285; fax: 01896 822870
E-mail: burtshotel@aol.com

Creggans Inn ££

Sir Fitzroy and Lady Maclean's lovingly tended inn offers spectacular views over Loch Fyne, from the pretty bedrooms and the candlelit restaurant. There are burgers in the bar, cream teas in the coffee shop and a cluster of inviting lounges. Fishing, clay-pigeon shooting and archery are also options.

➕ 202 B4 ✉ Strachur ☎ 01369
860279; fax: 01369 860637
E-mail: info@creggans-inn.co.uk

Cringletie House Hotel £££

This 19th-century, turreted baronial mansion is set in 11ha of wooded grounds. Lunches and afternoon teas are served in the conservatory, and the walled garden provides fruit and vegetables. The 13 bedrooms are individually designed and come with sweeping views. Hard-court tennis, croquet and a putting green complete the genteel picture.

➕ 203 E3 ✉ Eddleston, Peebles
☎ 01721 730233; fax: 01721 730244
www.cringletie.com

Crutherland House Hotel £££

This is a much-renovated mansion, and behind the Georgian façade is a modern hotel set in 15ha of landscaped grounds. All 76 rooms are spacious and comfortably furnished. The extensive leisure facilities include a heated indoor swimming-pool, gym, sauna and steam room.

➕ 202 C3 ✉ Strathaven Road, East
Kilbride ☎ 01355 577000; fax: 01355
220855 E-mail:
info@crutherland.macdonald.co.uk

Knockinaam Lodge £££

On a quiet winding road, this welcoming Victorian lodge has an air of contentment. An eclectic clock collection is an interesting feature. The morning room overlooks the sea, and the panelled bar offers over 100 single-malt whiskies. Bedrooms vary in size, but are prettily decorated without being fussy. The acclaimed restaurant offers a modern approach to prime Scottish produce (▶ 112).

➕ 202 B1 ✉ Stranraer, Portpatrick
☎ 01776 810471

Lochgreen House Hotel £££

Bill and Catherine Costley have developed this splendid country house into one of Scotland's finest hotels. Its position beside Royal Troon Golf Course provides fine views over the fairways, expanses of woodland and immaculate gardens. The 15 rooms, in the main house and converted stables, show meticulous attention to detail. The restaurant is highly regarded, with its combination of French techniques and Scottish ingredients.

+ 202 C2 ✉ **Monktonhill Road, Southwood, Troon** ☎ **01292 313343; fax: 01292 318661 E-mail: lochgreen@costley-hotels.co.uk**

The Roxburghe Hotel & Golf Course £££

Built in 1853, this imposing Jacobean-style mansion near the River Teviot is popular with shooting parties, anglers and golfers (it has its own 18-hole course). The hotel is owned by the Duke of Roxburghe, whose estate provides much of the game and salmon served in the classically styled dining-room. The 22 bedrooms are luxurious, and several have four-posters and open fires.

+ 203 F3 ✉ **Heiton, Kelso** ☎ **01573 450331; fax: 01573 450611**

Selkirk Arms Hotel ££

Stay in the delightful town of Kirkcudbright (pronounced 'kur-koo-bree') and enjoy the Robert Burns connection at the 200-year-old Selkirk Arms. The 16 en-suite rooms are comfortable, and there are several lounges and a pretty garden. The conservatory dining-room has a deserved reputation and there's also a less formal bistro.

+ 202 C1 ✉ **Old High Street, Kirkcudbright** ☎ **01557 330402; fax: 01557 331639 E-mail: reception@selkirkarmshotel.co.uk**

Shieldhill Hotel £££

This fortified mansion is surrounded by lawns and woodlands and has parts dating from the 12th century. At its heart is the oak-panelled lounge, warmed in winter by a blazing fire, and the grounds provide opportunities for clay-pigeon shooting, croquet and hot-air ballooning. The Gun Room is best for casual meals – pies, casseroles, steaks and burgers – while the Chancellor Restaurant is grandly furnished with a menu to suit. The 16 bedrooms offer every comfort.

+ 203 D3 ✉ **Quothquan, Biggar** ☎ **01899 220035; fax: 01899 221092 E-mail: enquiries@shieldhill.co.uk**

Tibbie Shiels Inn £

Just off the A708 between Moffat and Selkirk stands this historic drovers' inn with strong literary connections: Robert Louis Stevenson and Sir Walter Scott were both drawn by its romantic setting between two lochs. Despite modernisation, parts of the inn retain a lot of character, but contemporary bedrooms ensure a comfortable stay.

+ 203 E2 ✉ **Tibbie Shiels** ☎ **01750 42231**

Turnberry Hotel £££

This is a world-class hotel with tremendous views over the Isle of Arran, the Mull of Kintyre and Ailsa Craig. Guests can play on the two golf courses, which have staged the Open Championship. The spa offers a range of health treatments, and there is a 20m pool. The 100-plus bedrooms and suites are second to none. Eat either in the traditional dining-room, the Mediterranean-style Bay Restaurant or the grill.

+ 202 B2 ✉ **Turnberry** ☎ **01655 331000; fax: 01655 331706 E-mail: turnberry@westin.com**

Well View Hotel ££

Just south of Glasgow and Edinburgh on the M74/M6, the Well View makes a splendid stopover or base for touring. The delightful Victorian house has just six bedrooms, all individually furnished, and the dining-room serves good food based on local ingredients.

+ 203 D2 ✉ **Ballplay Road, Moffat** ☎ **01683 220184**

Where to... Shop

Many artists and artisans are inspired by this area, so you'll find interesting gifts everywhere. The Borders are also the centre of the Scottish textile industry, with Selkirk, Hawick and Galashiels specialising in knitwear and tweeds. In Peebles you'll find the **Edinburgh Crystal Visitor Centre** (tel: 01968 672244), whose shop stocks vases, glasses, bowls, candlesticks and ornaments, as well as a selection of seconds at greatly reduced prices.

DUMFRIES AND THE SOUTHWEST

In Dumfries, visit **Greyfriars Crafts** (Buccleuch Street) and **Gracefield Arts Centre** (Edinburgh Road). **Drumlanrig Castle** near Thornhill (tel: 01848 330248) has a craft centre featuring jewellery, leatherwork and ceramics, and the **Art Garden** (tel: 01848 200466) at **Moniaive**, west of Drumlanrig, sells works by local artists at low prices. Moniaive also has Britain's only **poetry shop**, where the resident poet will write you a personalised memento. **Galloway Gems** in the market town of Castle Douglas stocks gem-set jewellery and will create variations to order.

THE BORDERS

Mill factory shops are great sources of bargains. Start at Chas N Whillan's **Teviotdale Mills** in Hawick (tel: 01450 373128) for cashmere and lambswool sweaters. **Peter Scott** in Buccleuch Street, Dumfries (tel: 01450 372311) specialises in knitwear and coats. Caps, rugs and skirts in tweed and wool are found at **Wrights** of Trowmill (tel: 01450 372555). **Selkirk Glass** (tel: 01750 20954) produces paperweights, pottery and glass animals.

Where to... Be Entertained

ACTIVITIES

The **Ice Bowl** in Dumfries (tel: 01387 251200) offers curling, ice skating and indoor bowling, while the **Magnum Leisure Centre** in Irvine (tel: 01294 278381) is one of the largest in Europe. **West Pelton Activity Centre** (tel: 01873 75768) offers abseiling, archery, canoeing, paintball and rock climbing. The Borders area is popular with anglers – contact the **Tweed Foundation** (tel: 01896 848271) or Galashiels tourist office (tel: 01896 755551).

SPECTATOR SPORTS

Football is played everywhere and Kilmarnock, Ayr, Dumfries and Stranraer have national league teams, but look elsewhere for the freshness of Saturday afternoon junior matches. Rugby union is so popular in the Borders that every small town has a rugby ground.

MUSIC AND THEATRE

Most towns will have a night-club of sorts, but don't expect sophistication. Concerts are held in the **Magnum** at Irvine, the **Ryan Centre** in Stranraer and in town halls; check locally for details.
The **Theatre Royal** in Dumfries is Scotland's oldest theatre. Run by an amateur dramatic society, it stages in-house and visiting productions.
The **Gaiety Theatre** in Ayr continues the music-hall tradition with its summer variety show, Gaiety Whirl.

Central
Scotland

In Three Days 120 – 121
Don't Miss 122 – 129
At Your Leisure 130 – 133
Where to… 134 – 138

Getting Your Bearings

From Loch Lomond to the Angus Glens, the broad sweep of Central Scotland is a land of sharp contrasts. It offers rich farmland and industrial heartlands, a rugged coastline dotted with tiny fishing villages, bustling towns, ancient castles and sweeping battlegrounds, and a wild mixture of moor, mountain and loch.

Central Scotland has long been the playground of Glaswegians, drawn to the beauty of Loch Lomond or the hills around Arrochar. Queen Elizabeth Forest Park is a great spot for mountain biking, and is within an easy bus or train ride from Glasgow city centre.

Here, past and present, and fact and fiction, merge. From the Queen Elizabeth Forest Park, the Trossachs stretch east to Stirling, Scotland's ancient capital in the central plain. They extend north to the Braes of Balquhidder, haunt of Rob Roy MacGregor, Scotland's infamous outlaw immortalised by Sir Walter Scott's eponymous novel in the 19th century and more recently by Hollywood.

To the north is industrial Dundee, once famed for jam, jute and journalism but recently rejuvenated as a conference and tourist centre. South across the long bridges of the River Tay in the Kingdom of Fife is St Andrews, which has been a university town and the home of golf since the 15th century. Fife is ideal walking and cycling country, with probably more signposted cycling trails than anywhere else in Scotland.

To the north of Dundee, at Kirriemuir, you can visit the birthplace of author J M Barrie, and from Kirriemuir the Glens of Angus fan north into the arresting highland landscape of the Grampian Mountains.

Lobster fishing is still an important part of the economy in Crail

★ Don't Miss

1 Loch Lomond and its
Islands ➤ 122

2 Stirling and the
Trossachs ➤ 126

0   20 km

0   10 miles

Clova

Glen Slee

6 Angus Glens

achry

Kirriemuir   A90

Blairgowrie   Forfar

3 Dunkeld

A9   Coupar Angus

Carnoustie   A92

Dundee

7 8 RRS *Discovery*

Scone Palace **5**   A90   *Firth of Tay*

4

Perth   A92

chterarder   A91   A91   Cupar

Hills   St Andrews

9 Secret Bunker

East Neuk of Fife **10** **11**

Kinross   **12** Crail

Glenrothes   Scottish Fisheries Museum

M90   A92

Kirkcaldy   *Forth*

A985   **Dunfermline**   *Firth of Forth*

A90   **EDINBURGH**

lithgow

M8

The frosted peaks of the Arrochar Alps are reflected on the clear water of Loch Arklet

At Your Leisure

3 Dunkeld ➤ 130

4 Perth ➤ 130

5 Scone Palace ➤ 130

6 The Angus
Glens ➤ 131

7 Dundee ➤ 131

8 RRS *Discovery* ➤ 132

9 St Andrews ➤ 132

10 East Neuk of
Fife ➤ 132

11 The Secret
Bunker ➤ 133

12 Scottish Fisheries
Museum ➤ 133

The fair city of Perth on the
River Tay

This fascinating trip takes you through a range of landscapes, from romantic Loch Lomond, through the wild beauty of the Trossachs, to the splendour of the Angus Glens and picturesque fishing villages.

Central Scotland in Three Days

Day 1

Morning

Drive up the western side of **Loch Lomond** (➤ 122–5) along the A82 West Highland Way north to Crianlarich. Take the A85 to Lochearnhead then the A84 to Kingshouse. From here detour to the hamlet of Balquhidder, where **Rob Roy MacGregor** (➤ 127) lies buried in the tiny churchyard (pictured right). Return to the A84 and head for Callander and a bar lunch at the Bridgend House Hotel.

Afternoon

In Callander visit the **Rob Roy and the Trossachs Visitor Centre** on the main street for an overview of the life and times of Scotland's most famous cattle rustler. Then drive through the Queen Elizabeth Forest Park on the meandering A821 to Brig o'Turk, Loch Katrine (left) and Aberfoyle. Take the A81 to **Stirling** (➤ 126–9), where you can spend the rest of the day visiting the castle, the atmospheric Old Town Jail, the Wallace Monument, the battlefields at nearby Bannockburn or just wandering the town's historic streets.

Day 2

Morning

Spend the morning finishing your tour of Stirling, then head for Perth on the A9. If you have time, carry on to the Caithness Glass Factory at Inveralmond before returning to Perth for a short stroll through the streets. The highlight of the area is **Scone Palace** (left, ➤ 130), about 3km north of town on the A93, so allow at least an hour here and stop for lunch in the excellent restaurant.

Afternoon

Head north on the A93 towards Glenshee and spend the rest of the afternoon driving round the Glens. Use a local map to pick any combination of roads you like. Or simply turn right on to the B951 through Glenisla to Kirriemuir and from there follow the B955 around Glen Clova, or take the local road, from Dykehead, to Glen Prossen. When you've overdosed on scenery return to Kirriemuir for an overnight stop.

Day 3

Morning

Head south to **Dundee** (➤ 131) on the A928 and visit Scott's ship **RRS Discovery** (pictured left, ➤ 132) before crossing the Tay Bridge to Fife. Then follow the signs to **St Andrews** (➤ 132), where you can stroll through the streets and visit the cathedral and castle before lunching in Littlejohn's in Market Street.

Afternoon

Leave St Andrews on the A917 and enjoy the scenic drive round the coastline of the **East Neuk of Fife** (➤ 132). Don't miss the quiet picture-postcard harbours at Crail, Pittenweem (the village sign is pictured right) and St Monans and the **Scottish Fisheries Museum** at Anstruther (➤ 133). On your way back, take the B9131 to the **Secret Bunker** (➤ 133) before heading back to St Andrews.

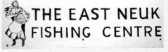

THE EAST NEUK FISHING CENTRE

0

Loch Lomond and its Islands

One of the first acts of the new Scottish Parliament was to
protect the landscape by establishing national parks, and
Loch Lomond and the Trossachs is scheduled to become
Scotland's first. Not only is it an area of outstanding beauty,
but it's accessible to all. A popular leisure choice for locals
and tourists alike, it's still possible to find serene, isolated
spots overlooking the waters.

Take the A811 from Balloch towards Stirling but
turn off after 11km on to the B837 to Drymen,
Balmaha and then on to Rowardennan. The road
stops at this point so it's much quieter than the
busy A82 along the west side. From here you
can climb **Ben Lomond** (974m), the highest
mountain in the area and Scotland's most
southerly Munro (see panel ► 124). From its
peak, there is a superb view back over the
loch. Or you can continue walking from
Rowardennan on the **West Highland Way**, a
157km long-distance footpath which follows
the banks of the loch as it winds its way via
Inversnaid, to the top of the loch and on to
Crianlarich. Wildlife thrives in this clean and
tranquil area – waders, geese, capercaillie,
golden eagles and sometimes white fallow deer
all thrive in the vicinity of the loch. A quarter
of all known British wild plant species are also
found here.

If you prefer the busier areas with more
facilities, try
the villages of
Luss and **Tarbet** on the west side of Lomond.
Although they get busy, especially in summer,
they don't usually feel crowded and offer an
array of hotels, tea rooms and picnic spots,
many with peaceful views of the loch and the
surrounding mountains.

Just west of Tarbet is the village of
Arrochar, whose nearby hills have long been a
popular haunt of climbers. Take to the hills
and the open spaces are so vast that the countryside feels almost deserted despite the hundreds of climbers out Munro-bagging. Shade
and shadow change with the seasons, making
the lure of the lovely scenery around the loch
hard to resist.

Climbing Safety

It's important to be well prepared if you're climbing in
the Scottish hills and mountains. Make sure you have
the proper footwear and
equipment. Even in the
height of summer don't venture into the hills without
warm clothing, maps and a
compass and make sure that
someone knows your route
and expected return time.

Island Highlights

If you really want to get away from it all, explore some of Loch Lomond's 30-plus small islands. Some are inhabited, while others are nature reserves or Sites of Special Scientific Interest (SSSI). Inchcailloch belongs to Scottish Natural Heritage and Bucinch and Ceardach are National Trust for Scotland properties. The other islands are privately owned.

The largest is **Inchmurrin**, which was reputedly visited by Robert the Bruce, King James VI and Mary, Queen of Scots, as well as St Mirren, after whom it is named. You can explore the ruins of a 7th-century monastery as you undertake the various walks along the island's 2.4km length. It's even got a hotel (tel: 01389 850245), some self-catering flats and a holiday cottage.

Inchgalbraith island is an ancient 'crannog', a loch dwelling built by Iron-Age people as a safe haven. The name means

The bonnie banks of Loch Lomond with Ben Lomond in the background

'Island of the Galbraiths' and in medieval times it was the base of their castle, now in ruins but visible through the trees as you approach by boat.

Inchfad was the site of an ancient illicit whisky still which did a brisk trade until a government cutter appeared on the loch in the mid-19th century. The still became legitimate and the island acquired a registered distillery, but only its ruins remain. If you take a trip on the mail boat, the boatman will tell you all about it, as it was run by his ancestor.

A nature trail covers the whole island of **Inchcailloch**, which takes about an hour and a half to stroll round and features the ruins of a 14th-century chapel and burial ground. There are great views over the loch from the rest area at the highest point on the island and at Port Bawn on the south side are picnic tables, barbecue facilities and a superb beach. The

Munro-bagging

Munros are the (currently) 284 Scottish peaks over 914m (3,000ft), first classified by Sir Hugh Munro, president of the Scottish Mountaineering Club, in 1891. Munro-baggers will try to climb them all, ticking each off the list as it's conquered. There are four Munros in the Arrochar Alps.

Fishing in the tranquil waters of Loch Lomond at Luss Bay

ferry service runs on demand from the boatyard at nearby Balmaha, which also hires out various boats and fishing tackle, and sells fishing permits as well as running daily cruises round the nature reserve islands.

TAKING A BREAK

There are numerous tea rooms and pubs around Loch Lomond, but try the 18th-century **Drover's Inn** at Inverarnan for hearty, traditional Scottish food in friendly surroundings. There's also a fine selection of malt whiskies (▶ 135).

✚ 202 C4
✉ The Loch Lomond Visitor Centre, Balmaha
☎ 01360 870470
🕐 Daily 10–5:45, Easter–Oct

The loch from the RSPB reserve at Inversnaid

LOCH LOMOND AND ITS ISLANDS: INSIDE INFO

Top tip To explore the islands, **take the Balmaha mail boat** from Sandy MacFarlane's boatyard, which his great-grandfather started 150 years ago. The boat serves the islands of Inchtavannich, Inchmurrin, Inchcruin and Inchfad Monday to Saturday in July and August, leaving Balmaha at 11:30am and returning at 2pm. The one-hour stop on Inchmurrin is just long enough to explore a little and enjoy a bar lunch at the hotel. A restricted service operates at all other times, so you should check with the boatyard in advance (tel: 01360 870214).
• You can also take a pleasant boat trip on the loch from Balloch, or if you're feeling adventurous hire a speedboat, jet ski or canoe.

Hidden gem From the car-park at Balmaha take one of the short **woodland walks** with wonderful views over the islands and Loch Lomond. Details and maps are available from the visitor centre.

Stirling and the Trossachs

Stirling Castle at the eastern edge of the Trossachs has been perched on its plug of volcanic rock for centuries, a lone sentinel overseeing Scotland's central lowland plain as far as the eye can see and guarding the gateway to the Highlands. Its strategic significance has made it the scene of many battles from the 12th century onwards, as successive waves of English forces swept north and were repelled.

The current **castle**, with its chapel and palace, dates mainly from the 16th century and is dominated by the recently renovated Great Hall. The main feature, however, is the spectacular view from the esplanade, and if you take the **Back Walk** around the castle you can enjoy a full panorama of the surrounding countryside. For an explanation of the principal hills and battlesites, there's a viewfinder on Ladies' Rock in the cemetery below the castle. This vast historic burial ground beside the Church of the Holy Rude is an attraction in its own right, containing the remains of Stirling's most prominent citizens, and an assortment of ancient gravestones, both fascinating and odd. A little down the hill is the **Old Town Jail**, where actors re-create the once horrifying conditions of this 19th-century prison.

The cemetery and Church of the Holy Rude lie beneath the battlements of Stirling Castle

Old Stirling Bridge dates from the 15th century and replaces the even older wooden one, where William Wallace defeated the English in 1297 when he cut off the English forces at the narrow bridge while the Scots army annihilated the vanguard. This local success is commemorated at the **Wallace Monument**, a striking tower just outside the town, set, like the castle, on a rocky outcrop (▶ 28 for picture).

Another important battle on the outskirts of Stirling was the decisive Scottish victory at **Bannockburn** in 1314 where the boggy ground decimated the English cavalry, while the Bannock Burn prevented easy withdrawal. The site now boasts exhibitions and an audio-visual representation of the battle,

Old Stirling Bridge, site of William Wallace's famous victory

and you can wander round the field and imagine the scene 700 years ago. At the centre is a majestic statue of Bruce on horseback, looking every bit the royal hero.

The Trossachs Trail

From Stirling, the Trossachs stretch out to Loch Lomond and Crianlarich in the west, to Loch Tay in the north and through Callander, Aberfoyle and Loch Katrine. Pick up a **Trossachs Trail** leaflet and map from the tourist office in Stirling's Dumbarton Road and head for **Callander**, an essential first stop because of the Rob Roy and the Trossachs Visitor Centre. Here you'll learn all about the real character behind the novels and films and decide for yourself whether he was a daring hero or a notorious cattle thief. Robert MacGregor, (the 'Roy' was from the Gaelic *rua*, meaning 'red', because of the colour of his hair), was a cattle drover. He ran a protection racket, extorting money from other drovers so that their cattle came to no harm while travelling through MacGregor land. Despite his turbulent life, he died at a ripe old age in his cottage and you can visit his grave in the old churchyard at Balquhidder. Go north along the A84 and then turn right at Kingshouse.

Port of Menteith church overlooks the calm waters of the lake

Area Highlights

There's plenty to see and do in the Trossachs. Visit Scotland's only lake, the **Lake of Menteith**, and take a boat trip out to the island in the middle, to explore **Inchmahome**, a ruined Augustine priory founded in 1238. The infant Mary, Queen of Scots, was hidden here in 1547 before she was exiled to France. Look for the effigy of Walter, Steward of Menteith and his wife, carved in an eternal embrace, in the choir of the church.

Rob Roy MacGregor is immortalised at Stirling

The paddle steamer SS *Sir Walter Scott* on Loch Katrine

Nearby **Aberfoyle** is the home of the Scottish Wool Centre, with displays of spinning, sheepdogs and presentations explaining how different breeds of sheep played a part in building the Scottish wool industry.

From Aberfoyle, meander over the hills to the Duke's Pass for spectacular views over the whole area. You'll also find the visitors' centre for the **Queen Elizabeth Forest Park**. Covering an immense 30,300ha, this apparent wilderness stretches from the eastern shores of Loch Lomond to rugged Strathyre. It's home to red and roe deer, wild goats and smaller creatures. There are forest trails, woodland walks, mountains to climb and bike trails to work up a sweat on, and a forest drive for the exhausted.

TAKING A BREAK

The **King's House Hotel** near Balquhidder on the A84 serves grand bar lunches.

Balquhidder church where Rob Roy MacGregor and his family are buried

---

✚ 203 D4
✉ Stirling Tourist Office, 41 Dumbarton Road
☎ 01786 475019 🕐 Mon–Sat 10–5, Oct–May; Mon–Sat 9–6, Sun 10–4, Jun; Mon–Sat 9–7:30, Sun 9:30–6:30, Jul–Aug; Mon–Sat 9–6, Sun 10–4, Sep
🍴 Darnley Coffee House, Bow Street (£)
🚌 Regular service from Glasgow and Edinburgh 🚆 Stirling

✚ 202 C4
✉ Rob Roy and the Trossachs Visitor Centre, Ancaster Square, Callander
☎ 01877 330342 🕐 Daily 10–5, Mar–May & Oct–Dec; Sat–Sun 10–5, Jan–Feb; daily 9:30–6, Jun and Sep; daily 9–7, Jul–Aug 🍴 Murtle Inn (£)
🚌 From Stirling 🎫 Inexpensive

STIRLING AND THE TROSSACHS: INSIDE INFO

Top tip Take a trip around Loch Katrine on the Victorian steamer *Sir Walter Scott*. Scott's novel *Rob Roy* and his romantic poem 'The Lady of the Lake', which was set on the loch, have long drawn visitors to this area. When the parts for the boat were shipped overland from Glasgow and assembled here at the end of the 19th century, practically every inland waterway had a steamer service. A century later, only the *Sir Walter Scott* remains. As Loch Katrine supplies Glasgow with much of its water, the West of Scotland Water Authority, which owns and runs the boat, allows no other craft on the Loch.

Hidden gem Behind the church at Balquhidder you'll find a stile leading to a forest road. Go along this until the first junction on the right, and that will take you to a small hill above the church with views to the steep Braes of Balquhidder and secluded Balquhidder Glen. Along the road is Iverlochlarig, where Rob Roy died, and it was along the 24km of this glen that his funeral procession marched on New Year's Day, 1735.

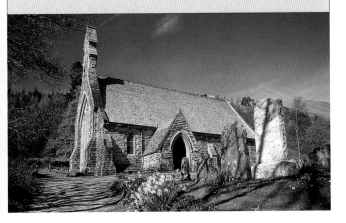

At Your Leisure

❸ Dunkeld

Rebuilt after the Battle of Dunkeld in 1689, at the heart of this delightful village is a square of 17th-century whitewashed cottages. From here it's a short stroll along the river to the partially ruined cathedral where services are still held. There are many wonderful riverside and woodland walks around Dunkeld, for example along the Tay and across Thomas Telford's bridge to the neighbouring village of Birnam. The last ancient oak from Birnam Wood – as featured in the prophecy of Macbeth's death in Shakespeare's play – stands beside the river. The Hermitage Woodland Walk takes in many exotic trees and Britain's tallest – a Douglas fir of over 61m – stands close to the curious Ossian's Hall, an elegant 18th-century folly on a rocky outcrop over a dramatic waterfall. In contrast, nearby Ossian's Cave is a primitive roofed cell built from natural rock formations.

You can pick up trail leaflets and more information at the National Trust for Scotland (NTS) shop in the Ell House, named after the brass measure on the wall, which medieval merchants used to measure cloth.

Ossian's Hall or the Hermitage Folly overlooking the Falls of Braan at Dunkeld

🚹 203 D4 ✉ NTS The Ell Shop
☎ 01350 727460 🕙 Mon–Sat 10–5:30, Apr–Sep (also Sun 1:30–5:30 in Jun–Aug); Mon–Sat 10–4:30, Oct–Dec 25
🍴 Cafés and tea rooms in village (£)

❹ Perth

Scotland's former capital is now a prosperous market town and makes a good base for exploring the area. While in town visit the restored Victorian oatmeal mill at Lower City Mills (tel: 01738 627958) and the Black Watch Museum (tel: 0131 3108530) in Balhousie Castle. Bell's Cherrybank Garden on the edge of town has one of the best collections of heathers in Britain, and there's also an aviary and a children's play area. Popular Branklyn Garden (NTS) on the Dundee Road covers just less than 1ha of hillside with a superb collection of alpine plants, rhododendrons and other trees and shrubs.

🚹 203 D4 ✉ Tourist Information Centre, West Mill Street ☎ 01738 450600 🕙 Daily 9–5, Jan–Dec (also 9–7 in summer) 🍴 Various (£)

❺ Scone Palace

Scotland's monarchs were crowned here on the Stone of Destiny (also known as the Stone of Scone) until it was stolen by Edward I of England in 1296 (► 48). The present building dates from the 16th century but was restored and extended in the 19th century. The grand rooms, with magnificent ornate ceilings and French period furniture, contain an amazing collection of porcelain, clocks and 16th-century needlework, yet still manage to retain the feel of a family house. The grounds are a delight, with parklands, peacocks and a children's playground among the attractions.

➕ 203 D4 ✉ A93, 3.2km northeast of Perth ☎ 01738 552300 🕒 Daily 9:30–4:45, Easter–Oct 🍴 Restaurant and tea room (£–££) 🚌 Limited service from Perth 🚉 Perth 💷 Moderate

🎜 The Angus Glens

The glens of Angus are atmospheric even in torrential rain, but when the sun shines a blue vista stretches out before you. Hillsides thick with heather are dotted with sheep and deer, while numerous burns tumble to the winding rivers far below. This is walking country at its very best: there are ten Munros. The area's abundant wildlife attracts naturalists and birdwatchers, while botanists come for the unusual plants.

The glens fan out over 48km from Kirriemuir and Blairgowrie to Braemar and Balmoral, with the Highlands beyond. Drive up Glenshee from Blairgowrie on the A93 to view the majestic scenery as the road rises to over 600m past the Devil's Elbow, a double hairpin bend now bypassed by the road. Quiet B-roads meander up through the glens from the pleasant low-lying towns of Alyth, Kirriemuir and Edzell. You can leave your car at one of the car-parks and explore on foot if the weather is up to it.

➕ 203 E5 ✉ North of Blairgowrie and Kirriemuir

🎜 Dundee

The ancient city of Dundee is a fun, down-to-earth place with many fine buildings and a thriving theatre scene. It is a far more attractive and modern city than its reputation as the centre of 'jute, jam and journalism' would suggest. Highlights include the McManus Galleries featuring the oldest-known astrolabe (an instrument used to make astrological measurements), dating from 1555; Mills Observatory; Barrack Street Museum of natural history and 16th-century St Mary's Tower. In 1999, the innovative Dundee Contemporary Arts centre was opened, a modern gallery with a

The 19th-century Scone Palace is one of the grandest buildings in Scotland

lively programme of events, experimental films and exhibitions.

The old jute industry is recalled in the restored mill at the Verdant Works, with its noisy textile machines. At 1pm the wailing of the 'bummer', the factory whistle that once regulated the lives of Dundee's families, is achingly evocative for some. The industry once employed 50,000 people in the city. Today, however, Dundee is better known as a centre for high technology, in the fields of science and electronics.

➕ 203E4 ✉ Verdant Works, 27 West Henderson's Wynd ☎ 01382 225282 🕐 Mon–Sat 10–5, Sun 11–5, Apr–Oct; Mon–Sat 10–4, Sun 11–4, Nov–Mar 🎟 Moderate

🎱 RRS *Discovery*

Built in Dundee's Panmure shipyard in 1901, the Royal Research Ship *Discovery* carried Captain Robert Falcon Scott's (1868–1912) expedition team to the Antarctic in 1900–4. Fully restored after years spent rotting on the Thames embankment in London, it is Dundee's main attraction and a fascinating glimpse into the life of the intrepid explorer, who eventually perished in his polar attempts.

➕ 203 E4 ✉ Discovery Point, near the Tay Road Bridge ☎ 01382 201245 🕐 Mon–Sat 10–5, Sun 11–5, Mar–Oct; Mon–Sat 10–4, Sun 11–4, Nov–Feb 🍴 Café in visitor centre (£) 🚆 Dundee 🎟 Moderate

🎱 St Andrews

St Andrews is home to Scotland's oldest existing university, founded in 1411. Students wander the medieval cobbled streets and narrow alleys just as their predecessors did nearly 600 years earlier. Guided tours of the ancient buildings include the eerie ruins of the 12th-century cathedral where Robert the Bruce worshipped. Details are available from the International Office in Butts Wynd.

The Royal and Ancient Golf Club is another venerable institution. The oldest golf club in the world, it is also the headquarters of the game and attracts golfers from all over the world. The British Open has been played here many times. If you have a handicap certificate you can play a round on the famous Old Course (► 138 for booking details) either by booking far in advance or by entering the daily lottery for a place. Near by is the British Golf Museum with all manner of memorabilia from ancient to modern.

➕ 203 E4 ✉ Tourist Office, 70 Market Street ☎ 01334 472021, 🕐 Mon–Sat 9:30–5, Nov–Mar; Mon–Sat 9:30–6, Sun 11–4, Apr–May; Mon–Sat 9:30–7, Sun 11–6, Jun; Mon–Sat 9:30–8, Sun 11–6, Jul–Aug; Mon–Sat 9:30–7, Sun 11–6, Sep–Oct 🍴 Numerous cafés, restaurants and tea rooms (£) 🚆 Regular service from Leuchars, Dundee or Edinburgh 🚆 Leuchars

🔟 The East Neuk of Fife

The coastline of this small corner of Scotland is best seen at a walking or cycling pace, or you could take an afternoon drive down the coast from St Andrews. Highlights are the fishing villages of Crail, Anstruther, Pittenweem and St Monans, where

cottages with red-tiled roofs and crow-stepped gables crowd around picturesque harbours littered with nets and lobster pots. There are coastal walks to view the massed seabirds nesting on the rocks, or you can go diving in the clear waters below, which are swarming with different species of sea life.

➕ 203 E4 ✉ Fife coast, south of St Andrews

🕦 The Secret Bunker

This underground command post, which would have become the administrative centre of Scotland in the event of a nuclear attack, was one of Scotland's best kept secrets – it was only removed from the Official Secrets List in 1995. But now sign-posts everywhere point to it. The entrance, through a small, nonde-script building, intended to resemble a traditional Scottish farmhouse, doesn't prepare you for the labyrinth below. Once through the massive steel bomb doors, built to withstand the full force of a nuclear explosion, you can wander round a subterranean maze of dormitories, communications equipment and control rooms, and even have a cup of tea in the NAAFI. Tunnels cover over 150m in all. This was to become the base of important people from all over Scotland, such as government ministers, scientists and computer operators.

Part of the bunker is still opera-tional, so if the doors suddenly slam shut behind you, it's time to panic.

🕂 203 E4 ✉ 5km north of Anstruther
☎ 01333 310301 🕐 Daily 10–5,
Apr–Oct 🍴 Café in bunker (£)
🚻 Moderate

Typical East Neuk crow-stepped gables and red pan-tiled roofs, in Pittenweem

Something for the Children

If you're in St Andrews with children, then the **Sea Life Centre** on The Scores is a must. With its under-ground walkways, pools, shark displays and all manner of other marine creatures, it's a great place for all the family.

🕦 Scottish Fisheries Museum

Contained in a number of harbour-front buildings dating from the 16th to the 19th centuries, this museum recounts Scotland's long fishing tradition in displays that include a reconstruction of the interior of a fisherman's cottage. Opposite, in the harbour, you'll find a Zulu and a Fifie, traditional fishing boats of a bygone age.

🕂 203 E4 ✉ Harbourhead, Anstruther
☎ 01333 310628 🕐 Mon–Sat 10–5:30,
Sun 11–5, Apr–Oct; Mon–Sat 10–4:30,
Sun 11–4:30, Nov–Mar 🍴 Tea room (£)
🚌 From St Andrews to Leven
🚻 Moderate

Where to...
Eat and Drink

Prices

The £ amounts indicate what you can expect to pay for a three-course meal for one person, including coffee and service.

£ = under £15   ££ = £15–25   £££ = over £25

RESTAURANTS

Cellar Restaurant ££

This old merchant's house, named after the moody look created from candles, rough stone walls, tiled floor, heavy oak furniture and open fire, is considered one of the best seafood restaurants in Scotland. Chef/proprietor Peter Jukes keeps it simple, using prime ingredients, and new season's crab is especially good.

➕ 203 E4 ✉ 24 East Green, Anstruther ☎ 01333 310378 🕐 Lunch Fri–Sat; dinner Mon–Sat

Creagan House ££

This is a welcoming 17th-century farmhouse restaurant-with-rooms in the heart of Queen Elizabeth Forest Park. The tiny dining-room, in faux baronial style with an open fireplace, serves fresh produce that is grown on organic smallholdings and cooked in a bold innovative style. Five en-suite bedrooms are thoughtfully equipped with extra touches.

➕ 202 C4 ✉ Callander, Strathyre ☎ 01877 384638 🕐 Daily 7.30pm–8.30pm; closed Feb and 1 week in Oct

Kind Kyttock's Kitchen £

Kind Kyttock is the heroine of an early Scots poem, who served good food and drink to weary travellers. This long-established tea room follows faithfully in her footsteps, drawing folk from afar to enjoy substantial snacks of omelettes, baked potatoes, salads and some impressive baking. Afternoon tea is excellent, the scones perfect. That Scottish treat, cloutie dumpling, also gets the thumbs up.

➕ 203 E4 ✉ Cross Wynd, Falkland, Fife ☎ 01337 857477 🕐 Tue–Sun 10.30–5.30

Let's Eat, Let's Eat Again £–££

Honest meals with lots of flavour and innovative twists is the hallmark of Tony Heath's bistro-style menus. It's all extremely good value for money, with very fresh fish the mainstay of the repertoire (check the daily blackboard specials), but meat-eaters are catered for with the likes of chargrilled Scotch ribeye steak. Leave plenty of room for dessert. Tony Heath's sister bistro, Let's Eat Again, at 33 George Street (tel: 01738 633771), is a more informal, slightly cheaper establishment with a Mediterranean bias.

➕ 203 D4 ✉ 77-79 Kinnoull Street, Perth ☎ 01738 643377 🕐 Lunch and dinner Tue–Sat; closed 2 weeks in Jan and 2 weeks in Jul

Monachyle Mhor ££–£££

The Lewis's converted farmhouse is full of rustic charm and character, set amid some 800ha of tranquil farmland at the loch-head of a beautiful glen. The view from the dining-room alone is beyond compare, looking out over Loch Voile and Loch Doine. The kitchen offers some exemplary cooking with simple dishes that rely on natural flavours enhanced by a careful blend of herbs, fruits and vegetables. Snacks are served in the bar at lunchtime.

➕ 202 C4 ✉ Lochearnhead, Balquhidder ☎ 01877 384622 🕐 Lunch and dinner daily

Ostlers Close Restaurant ££

The series of small rooms that form this tiny restaurant, tucked away in an alley, show that it was converted from ancient cottages. Ingredients are impeccably sourced – vegetables, salad leaves and herbs from an organic farm, game from local estates, lobsters and crabs delivered according to the tides. Flower displays, from the first snowdrops to autumnal foliage, come from the owners' garden. There's an informal atmosphere but serious cooking.

🚹 203 E4 ⊠ Bonnygate, Cupar
☎ 01334 655574 ⓦ Lunch Tue,
Fri–Sat; dinner Mon–Sat

PUBS

The Byre Inn £

Converted from an 18th-century stone byre (cowshed), this cosy, spotless little inn edging a network of forest and loch-side tracks in the Queen Elizabeth Forest Park is remote, but it makes a peaceful spot for some sound home-cooking.

reflects classical French techniques. Staff here are genuinely hospitable, and the eight luxurious bedrooms come highly recommended.

🚹 203 E4 ⊠ Peat Inn, Cupar
☎ 01334 840206 ⓦ Tue–Sat 12:30
for 1, 7–9:30; closed Jan 1 and Dec 25

Unicorn Inn £–££

In a back street of a small, unassuming town, the Unicorn is an unlikely place in which to find a laid-back Mediterranean-style atmosphere and an imaginative choice of dishes featuring plenty of olive oil, garlic, herbs and tomato. The kitchen's repertoire encompasses substantial tapas dishes at lunchtime, alongside a good-value two-course menu; the dinner menu is more extensive. Service is as informal as the décor, and both the wine list and the daily-changing blackboard listings are strongly influenced by the warmer European countries.

🚹 203 D4 ⊠ 15 Excise Street,
Kincardine-on-Forth ☎ 01259
730704 ⓦ Lunch and dinner Tue–Sat

Food in the bar, which is full of traditional features such as beams, log fire, rugs and old pews, is based on fresh local produce. Dishes include soups, local sausages, neeps and tatties, and game casseroles. It's best to book the restaurant, which offers more elaborate dishes in the evening.

🚹 202 C4 ⊠ Brig o' Turk ☎ 01877
376292 ⓦ Lunch and dinner Wed–
Mon in summer; Fri–Sun in winter

The Drover's Inn £

At the head of Loch Lomond stands this famous drover's inn in which many swear hasn't changed much since it opened in 1705 – with bare boards, open ranges, smoky, low-ceilinged rooms, lots of tartan, stuffed animals and whisky galore (over 100 malts). The food is good, plain country cooking featuring rich broth, steak pies and toasted sandwiches, served in generous portions. The atmosphere is friendly.

🚹 202 C4 ⊠ Inverarnan ☎ 01301
704234 ⓦ Daily noon–8:15; closed
Dec 25

Fisherman's Tavern £

A boat will drop you at the nearby jetty for this charmingly unspoilt 17th-century fisherman's cottage. The owners maintain a solid reputation for good food and superb real ales; they also offer some cask-strength malt whiskies. The bar menu is strong on the local staple catch – haddock – as well as soups, pasta and game. Barbecues are popular in the summer.

🚹 203 E4 ⊠ 10–14 Fort Street,
Broughty Ferry ☎ 01382 775941
ⓦ Daily 11am–midnight

The Peat Inn £££

Created from the original coaching inn, the beautifully located Peat Inn is considered one of the most charming restaurants-with-rooms in Scotland. Over the years David and Patricia Wilson have painstakingly built up an enviable reputation for the excellence of their kitchen, with David's name legendary in modern Scottish cooking. His menus draw on regional produce, but the style

Where to... Stay

Prices

Price categories are per person, including English breakfast.

£ = under £30 per night **££** = £30–60 per night **£££** = over £60 per night

Arden House £

Guests over 50 years old might experience a sense of *déjà vu* on seeing Arden House for the first time. Arden had a starring role as the doctors' house in the popular 1960s British TV series *Dr Finlay's Casebook*. Now a well-run, very comfortable bed and breakfast, the Dr Finlay associations are worked into a theme, but are not overdone. The substantial, stone-built house stands in a quiet location, just a short walk uphill from the main street of Callander. There are just six *en-suite* bedrooms.

➕ 202C4 ✉ Bracklinn Road, Callander ☎ 01877 330235 www.smoothHound.co.uk/hotels/arden.html

Cromlix House Hotel £££

A long drive winding through a vast 1,200ha estate is a magnificent prelude to the charms of this outstanding Victorian mansion with a great reputation. In winter roaring log fires ensure that the impressive public rooms are kept warm, while in the summer months you can enjoy a game of croquet or tennis, or perhaps a spot of trout and salmon fishing. Of the 14 bedrooms, most have private sitting rooms, and the restaurant is noted for some innovative cooking.

➕ 203D4 ✉ Kinbuck by Dunblane ☎ 01786 822125, Fax: 01786 825450 E-mail: reservations@cromlixhouse-hotel.co.uk

The Gleneagles Hotel £££

Acclaimed internationally, this top-class hotel is set in beautiful countryside surrounded by its famous golf courses, leisure facilities including a country club and health spa, and well-tended grounds. Children are made very welcome. Sumptuous afternoon teas are served in the drawing room, but for dinner, go to the Strathearn Restaurant. Luxurious suites have every imaginable comfort, and standard rooms are well designed and equipped.

➕ 203D4 ✉ Auchterarder ☎ 01764 662231; fax: 01764 662134 E-mail: resort.sales@gleneagles.com

Isle of Eriska Hotel £££

On a private island with vehicular access from the mainland via an iron bridge, Eriska is a nature-lover's dream, with beaches, woodlands and moors. The comfortable baronial house is furnished with style, and excels in standards of service and hospitality. There's a 9-hole golf course, swimming pool and gym, as well as putting, clay-pigeon shooting and tennis. All 17 bedrooms are spacious and thoughtfully equipped, and seafood features strongly in the renowned restaurant.

➕ 202B4 ✉ Ledaig by Oban, Isle of Eriska ☎ 01631 720371; fax: 01631 720531 E-mail: office@eriska-hotel.co.uk

Kinnaird £££

High in the wooded Tay Valley, surrounded by a 3,600ha estate, stands this imposing Edwardian mansion, one of the finest country-house hotels in Scotland. It's furnished almost entirely with antiques, paintings and fine china, yet still exudes a lived-in feel, aided by deep sofas, armchairs, open fires and family mementoes. All nine bedrooms are spacious and luxurious. In the dining-room glimpses of the gardens create a soothing setting for menus featuring the best Scottish produce.

➕ 203D4 ✉ Kinnaird Estate, Dunkeld ☎ 01796 482440 E-mail: enquiry@kinnairdestate.demon.co.uk

Lake of Menteith Hotel ££

Deep in the heart of the Trossachs lies this charming hotel with magnificent views. The hotel makes an ideal base for touring and walking, and the Inchmahone ferry leaves for the island monastery from close by. Unfortunately, only a few of the 16 rooms directly overlook the lake, so it's worth paying the extra required to snap these up. But as compensation, the splendid conservatory restaurant is the setting for magnificent sunset dinners.

🚹 2O2C4 ☒ Port of Menteith, near Stirling ☎ 01877 385258; fax: 01877 385671

The Lodge on Loch Lomond ££

The setting is idyllic and the panoramic views are taken for granted in this low-slung, modern building that hugs the shore of Loch Lomond. The hotel is entirely pine clad, including its 29 bedrooms, which range from suites to executive and standard rooms, and all but two overlooking the loch. Uniquely,

each room has its own sauna, although those in standard rooms are single size only. Fishing and boating pursuits that the hotel can arrange.

🚹 2O2C4 ☒ Luss ☎ 01436 860201; fax: 01436 860203
E-mail: lusslomond@aol.com

The Old Course Hotel £££

The setting, beside the 17th hole of St Andrews' famous championship course, is a great attraction for golfers from all over the world. But non-golfers are also well catered for with an indoor heated swimming pool and extensive leisure facilities that include a gym, steam room and health spa. The fourth-floor cocktail bar offers an excellent selection of single-malts, and the Road Hole Grill provides some impressive cooking. With over 100 rooms, this large hotel offers high standards in every respect.

🚹 2O3E4 ☒ St Andrews ☎ 01334 477668
☎ 01334 477371; fax: 01334 477668
E-mail: sales@oldcoursehotel.co.uk

Old Mansion House Hotel £££

Although this sturdy castellated house dates from the 16th century, it stands on the site of an earlier dwelling associated with Scottish freedom fighter William Wallace (▶ 28–9). Fine Jacobean ceilings, plenty of open fires and comfortable lounges set the scene, with just eight spacious and traditionally furnished bedrooms providing every modern comfort.

🚹 2O3E4 ☒ Auchterhouse
☎ 01382 320366; fax: 01382 320400
E-mail: oldmansionhouse@netscape-online.co.uk

Sandford Country House Hotel ££

This fine, if austere, country house (built around 1900) is set in glorious grounds that include a wild, romantic tennis court. It backs on to extensive farmland and yet is less than 7km south of the Tay bridge. All 16 rooms are individually styled and have wonderful views, while public areas boast a minstrels'

gallery and oak bar. Pittenweem and Neuk o' Fife fish feature in the restaurant's menu, along with sirloin of Angus beef.

🚹 2O3E4 ☒ Newport Hill, Wormit, Dundee ☎ 01382 541802; fax: 01382 542136 E-mail: sandford.hotel@btinternet.com

Stirling Highland £££–£££

The Highland is in a great location, just a few hundred metres from Stirling Castle and beside the historic Church of the Holy Rude. This unusual hotel was created from a former high school and still retains many original features. Meeting rooms, for example, are named after classrooms, drinks are served in the Headmaster's Study and meals are served in the high-ceilinged Scholars' Restaurant. There's also a leisure club with a good-sized swimming pool, and some 94 bedrooms.

🚹 2O3D4 ☒ Spittal Street, Stirling
☎ 01786 475444; fax: 01786 462929
E-mail: andrews@scottish
highlandhotels.co.uk

Where to... Shop

ARTS AND CRAFTS

In Fife, don't miss the excellent **Crail Pottery** which you'll find down Rose Wynd, just off the main street. Also in Fife, the **Balbirnie Craft Centre**, near Balbirnie House Hotel at Markinch, has a collection of individual shops selling ceramics, jewellery, glass and leatherwork. **Crieff Visitors Centre** on Muthill Road (tel: 01764 654014) has a good selection of mugs, plates and coffee pots, while just along the road **Stuart Crystal** is the place to head for if you want fine lead crystal, as it stocks both factory seconds and perfect products.

If you venture as far as Dunoon pop into **Dunoon Ceramics** (Hamilton Street), which produces the tartan and Mackintosh design mugs you'll come across in all the gift shops. Naturally they're much less expensive here, and you can pick up bargains in factory seconds.

GOLF GEAR & CLOTHING

St Andrews is the home of golf and **Auchterlonies**, in North Street near the Old Course, stocks all that distinctive gear that golfers love to wear. **Heritage Golf** on the Argyll Business Park, Largo Road, has enough clubs, bags, carts and sweaters to kit out the entire Open Golf Championship. They also make a range of reproduction 19th-century golf clubs.

The **St Andrews Woollen Mill** (North Street) boasts a huge variety of woollen items: piles of scarves, gloves, mittens and bobble hats compete for space with sweaters of all descriptions, and you'll also find a range of tartan and tweeds.

Where to... Be Entertained

Local newspapers usually carry a 'what's on' section. Notice boards in village halls are also useful, as are local tourist offices. Look out for fly-posters, often the only source of information on a ceilidh or event.

GOLF

There's hardly a small town in Scotland without a golf course. Most are municipally owned and not very expensive. Ask at the local tourist office for details. **Rosemount** at Blairgowrie (tel: 01250 872622) is a fine course, or you could try the **King James VI** course in the middle of the River Tay at Moncrief Island (tel: 01738 625170), or the more expensive and famous **Gleneagles** (tel: 01764 694469, ▶ 17, 136). The **Old Course** at St Andrews (▶ 132; tel: 01334 466666) is every golfer's dream, but you have to take part in a draw the day before to get a place and you'll need a handicap certificate. Or you could opt for the tree-lined course at **Ladybank** (tel: 01337 830814), designed by Old Tom Morris (▶ 17).

THEATRE

Perth Theatre (tel: 01738 621031) is one of the best in the region and the place to see up-and-coming young stars. The **MacRobert Arts Centre** (tel: 01786 461081) on Stirling University campus is another highlight of the region.

Highlands & Islands

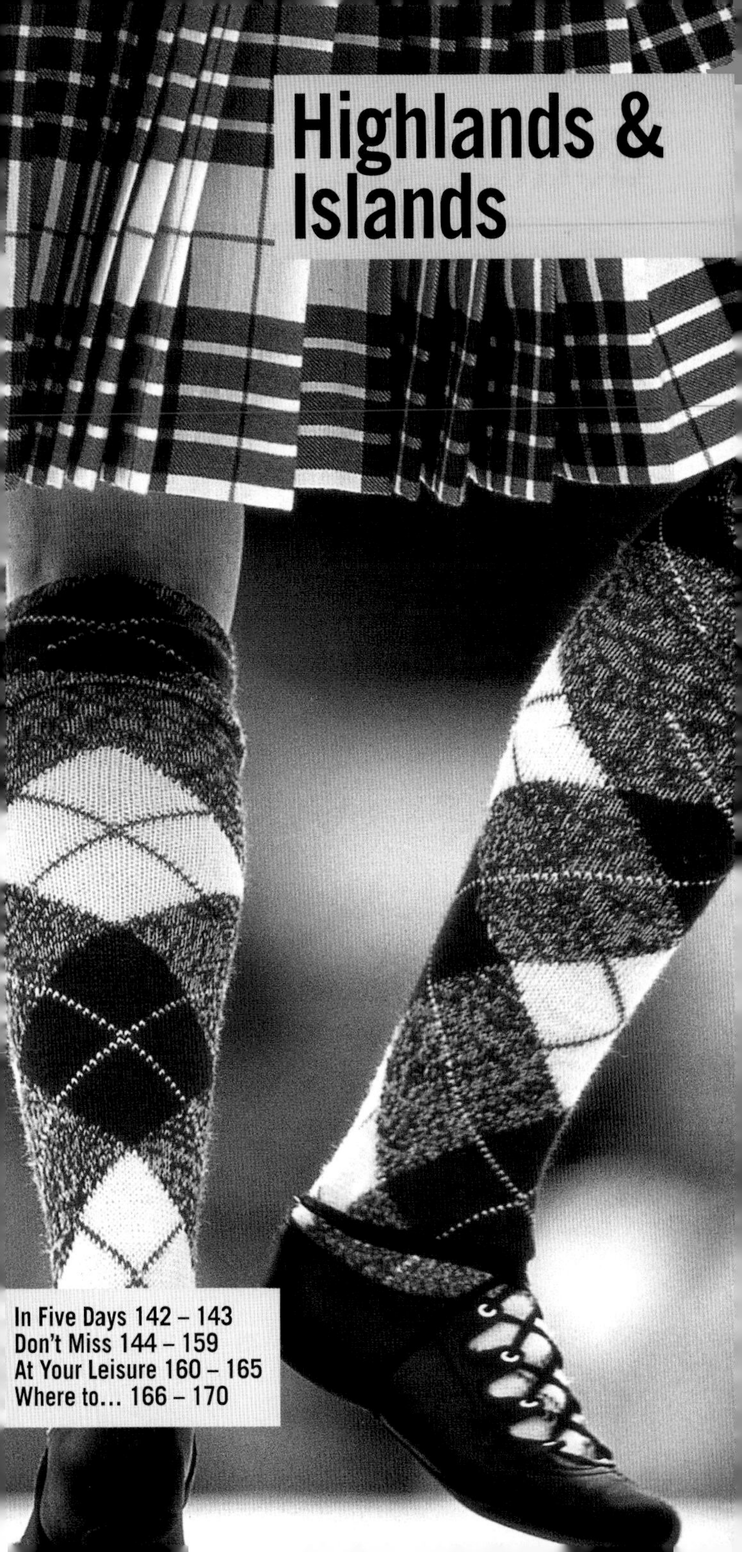

In Five Days 142 – 143
Don't Miss 144 – 159
At Your Leisure 160 – 165
Where to... 166 – 170

Getting Your Bearings

The Highlands and Islands are the Scotland of legend and postcards, of heather-clad hillsides, snow-capped mountains and sparkling lochs. On a sunny day the still waters of the lochs reflect the massive peaks and serried ranks of crags, and hills flank the glens into the distance. When the mist settles, great shoulders of rock suddenly loom before you and the black waters ripple with a chill north wind.

Here you can drive for great distances on single-track roads without meeting another soul, and at journey's end you might find a perfect beach of silver sand in a sheltered bay or a tiny hamlet of low stone cottages smelling of peat smoke. Explore the colourful harbours of the little fishing ports and then take a ferry to the islands.

The moors and cliffs of the Highlands shelter thousands of birds, including puffins, oystercatchers and curlews. Herds of deer roam freely, their russet colours blending into the bracken and peat of the moors. You'll see

The Old Man of Hoy is a spectacular sea stack on the island of Hoy, Orkney

★ Don't Miss

- 5 Glencoe ➤ 144
- 6 The Road to the Isles ➤ 146
- 7 Skye and the Western Isles ➤ 149
- 9 Loch Ness ➤ 154
- 11 The Cairngorms ➤ 156

At Your Leisure

- 1 Islay ➤ 160
- 2 Jura ➤ 160
- 3 Iona ➤ 161
- 4 Mull ➤ 161
- 8 Inverness ➤ 161
- 10 Culloden Moor ➤ 162
- 12 Aberdeen Satrosphere ➤ 162
- 13 Aberdeen Maritime Museum ➤ 162
- 14 Aberdeen Fish Market ➤ 162

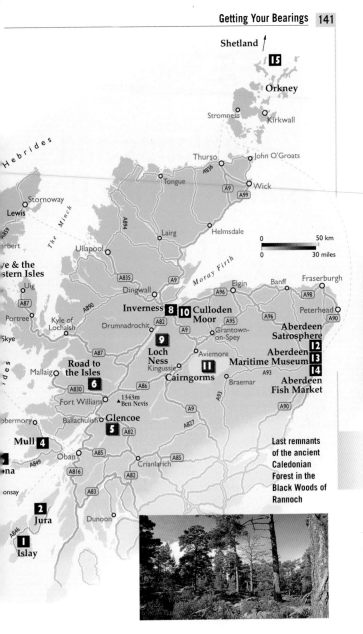

Last remnants
of the ancient
Caledonian
Forest in the
Black Woods of
Rannoch

Off the Beaten Track

15 Orkney ► 163 and
Shetland ► 165

mature stags with impressive antlers, shaggy
highland cattle with serious-looking horns and
sheep virtually everywhere.

The pace is different and sometimes unpredictable, but that gives you the chance to
appreciate the region all the more.

With so much spectacular, but at times challenging, terrain to cover, this whirlwind tour takes in a selection of the many available attractions. Make sure you check travel arrangements and ferry timetables before setting out.

Highlands and Islands in Five Days

Day 1

Morning From Crianlarich on the A82, drive right across the bleak Rannoch Moor and through Glen Coe to **Glencoe** itself (pictured right, ➤ 144). Stop here and lunch at the Glencoe Hotel, which has wonderful views over Loch Leven towards Ballachulish.

Afternoon Spend the afternoon exploring Glencoe in more detail. Starting from the visitors' centre, you should have time for the forest walk to Signal Rock or the short climb up the Devil's Staircase from Altnafeadh. Then continue on the A82 northeast to Fort William to spend the night.

Day 2

Morning Take a leisurely drive along the A830 **Road to the Isles** (➤ 146), to Mallaig, stopping at Glenfinnan for the **Monument** (➤ 146) and also to admire the white sands of Morar. Take the 30-minute ferry crossing from Mallaig (summer only) to Armadale on the **Isle of Skye** (➤ 149).

Afternoon Stop for lunch at the Hotel Eilean Iarmain at Isleornsay, about 10km to the north along the main A851 road. Continue to Portree along the A87, enjoying the unrivalled scenery.
If you have time, take a detour west along the A863 at Sligachan for views of the Cuillin Hills and the coast. Short detours off this route will take you to the **Talisker Distillery** at Carbost (➤ 151) and **Dunvegan Castle** (➤ 153). Alternatively, you can carry straight on to Portree and spend the time wandering around its picturesque harbour before spending the night in one of its hotels or guesthouses.

Day 3

Morning On a Monday, Wednesday or Friday you can take the scenic route around the Trotternish Peninsula in the north, taking in the **Old Man of Storr** (➤ 149) and the **Museum of Island Life** (➤ 150), as well as stunning coastal views to Wester Ross and the **Western Isles** (➤ 150) and then catch the 2pm ferry. But on a Tuesday, Thursday or Saturday you'll have to go direct to Uig because the ferry leaves at 9:40am. Alternatively, you could sacrifice the Golden Road on Harris and spend the time on Skye before catching the 6:20pm ferry from Uig for the 2-hour trip to Tarbert.

Have lunch either at the Uig Hotel or the Harris Hotel in Tarbert.

Afternoon If you have time, explore the delightful scenery of the Golden Road (A859) on Harris. Return by the east coast and take in the fascinating Genealogical and Exhibition Centre at Northton. Then drive north to the little port of Stornoway.

Day 4

Morning You should have time to see the **Calanais Standing Stones** (➤ 152) and the **Arnol Blackhouse** (➤ 154). Back in Stornoway, try to squeeze in the idiosyncratic Lewis Loom Centre before catching the ferry for the 3-hour journey to Ullapool. Have lunch on the boat.

Afternoon From **Ullapool** (➤ 184) drive to Inverness southeast along the A835, stopping at the Falls of Measach about 20km away. Spend the night in **Inverness** (its castle is pictured right, ➤ 161), where there is plenty to occupy you.

Day 5

Morning Take the A82 south alongside Loch Ness to Drumnadrochit. Take time to visit the **Official Loch Ness Monster Exhibition** and **Urquhart Castle** (➤ 154) before heading on to Fort Augustus where the quirky Clansmen's Centre is worth a visit. Continue on the A82 stopping just before Spean Bridge at the Commando Memorial before taking the A86 to Kingussie for lunch.

Afternoon Visit the excellent two-centre Highland Folk Museum at Kingussie (and a little further south at Newtonmore) before returning south. Alternatively, if you have time, head to the Cairngorm ski area above Aviemore and take the chairlift to the top for spectacular views in summer.

Glencoe

The novelist Charles Dickens (1812–70) imagined Glencoe as the 'burial ground of a race of giants' and it is one of the few places where non-hillwalkers or climbers can experience the sheer mass of the mountains close up. The glen is usually teeming with visitors, but its vast spaces never feel crowded. For less ambitious hikers there are short, low-level trails that will take you off-road, and the forest walk to the Signal Rock from the visitor centre or the walk around Loch Achtriochtan are not strenuous.

The mood of the glen changes with the weather and the seasons, often dramatically in one day. On a clear spring day, the snow-capped peaks, high white clouds and blue sky reflected in **Loch Achtriochtan** light up the whole glen. At dawn and dusk the low light and long shadows highlight the deep cracks and

Old roads and paths make Glencoe a walkers' paradise

Dawn breaks on Rannoch Moor, one of Scotland's last remote areas

craggy tops of the mountains, while either side is patched with light in shades of emerald and dark olive. And when it's dark and overcast, the mountains are veiled in mist and cloud.

The great bulk of **Buachaille Etive Mór** guards the entrance to the glen from the bleak expanse of Rannoch Moor. From there the road curves around below the massive peaks flanking the broad floor, to tiny Loch Achtriochtan, whose community was at the centre of the massacre of Glencoe. As the road curves away again around the woodlands at the visitor centre, look for the **Signal Rock,** where the fire was lit to signal the start of the massacre. The glen opens up at the village of Glencoe with a view up the broad waters of **Loch Leven.** On the shores near here the old chief was shot in his bed and his wife was brutally attacked.

The Massacre of Glencoe

On 13 February, 1692, government troops, led by Captain Robert Campbell of Glenlyon, who had been billeted with the MacDonald clan, rose at dawn and slaughtered their hosts. Aside from the savagery of the attack, it was the breach of the code of Highland hospitality towards all, even an enemy, that made the Campbell name a byword for treachery for centuries. Some 38 people were killed and hundreds more escaped to the hills, although many perished in the winter snows. Most of the MacDonalds escaped, including the sons of the old chief.

TAKING A BREAK

The **Clachaig Inn** is the best place for a bar lunch or evening meal. It's a little basic, but it's popular with walkers and climbers and has a great atmosphere.

Glencoe Visitor Centre
🕂 202 B5
✉ Glencoe
☎ 01855 811307
🕐 Daily 9:30–5:30, May–Aug; 10–5, Mar–Apr and Sep–Oct
🚌 Glasgow to Fort William goes through the glen
🎫 Inexpensive

GLENCOE: INSIDE INFO

Hidden gem Get away from the summer crowds by taking the B-road by Buachaille Etive Mór to Glen Etive to picnic by Loch Etive.

The Road to the Isles

Whether you're heading for the Isle of Skye or simply want to enjoy the spectacular Highland landscape, the Road to the Isles is one of the most romantic and historic journeys in Scotland. Drive or take the train from the foot of mighty Ben Nevis through dramatic loch and mountain scenery to the busy fishing port of Mallaig along the A830.

Start just outside **Fort William**, opposite the Ben Nevis Distillery, and head west on the A830. Just north of Fort William is the village of Banavie, site of the unmissable **Neptune's Staircase** on the Caledonian Canal. Thomas Telford's spectacular engineering feat of eight locks raises boats 19.5m over just 1.6km.

About 30km from Ben Nevis, the **Glenfinnan Monument** at the head of Loch Sheil marks the spot where Bonnie Prince Charlie raised his standard in 1745. Over 1,000 Highlanders gathered in this lonely and atmospheric place to greet him as his rowing boat crept from the mists of Loch Sheil. The picturesque railway station at Glenfinnan houses the **Glenfinnan Railway Museum**, with a fascinating display of memorabilia.

View the Glenfinnan Monument from the steam train as it crosses Glenfinnan Viaduct

The Iron Road to the Isles

Leave the car at home and take the train for an even better view of this spectacular scenery. You don't get such a good view of the impressive viaducts of course but the ride is exhilarating as you rumble across them, high above ground with breathtaking views of Loch Shiel or Loch Nan Uamh. In summer the Jacobite steam train runs once a day from Fort William to Mallaig and back.

Neptune's Staircase, a massive set of locks on the Caledonian Canal

As you travel west the landscape becomes more and more rugged, while the sea lochs create constantly changing perspectives of land and water. It was not until the early-19th century that a road allowing coach travel penetrated this far. The 12th-century monks at Arisaig called this high rocky countryside the Rough Bounds. At **Loch Nan Uamh,** look out for the railway viaduct and the Prince's Cairn marking the spot where Bonnie Prince Charlie left for France.

At **Arisaig** you can take a ferry to the small isles or walk along the pure white beaches. *Local Hero* and *Highlander* were filmed around here, and as you travel from Arisaig to Mallaig you may recognise the stunning scenery. Stop at **Morar** to walk along the silver sands, looking for the legendary monster of Loch Morar, or just to watch a magical sunset over the islands.

Mallaig is the end of the road and it's worth spending some time in this bustling little port. Wander through the colourful harbour, by the boats and nets, listen to the clank of chains and the screech of the seabirds and smell the fish and the engine oil. Fishing is the lifeblood of Mallaig and at **Marine World** you can discover the rich sealife that flourishes in the clear waters of the west coast. Watch an octopus sliding down the glass, spot flatfish camouflaged against shingle or wonder at strange deepwater fish with enormous ugly heads.

The Prince's Cairn marks the spot on Loch Nan Uamh where Bonnie Prince Charlie left for France

TAKING A BREAK

At Mallaig eat fresh fish at one of the tea rooms or restaurants on Main Street: the **Cornerstone Café** is particularly good.

The silver sands of Morar

Fort William Tourist Information Centre
✚ 202B5
✉ Cameron Square, Fort William
☎ 01397 703781

National Trust for Scotland Information Centre
✉ Glenfinnan, A830, 29km west of Fort William
☎ 01397 722250

Jacobite Steam Train
✉ West Coast Railway Company, Warton Road, Carnforth, Lancashire LA5 9HX
☎ 01524 732100 (info); 01463 239026 (bookings)
🕐 Services: once a day Mon–Fri, 19 Jun–22 Sep (also Sun, 30 Jul–3 Sep)

Mallaig Marine World
✉ The Harbour, Mallaig
☎ 01687 462292

THE ROAD TO THE ISLES: INSIDE INFO

Top tips The viewpoint on the hill behind the visitors' centre at **Glenfinnan** is the best place to watch steam trains cross the impressive viaduct or for taking a photograph of the monument and Loch Sheil, particularly in the early morning when the sun shines through the mist.

Hidden gem In Arisaig take the local road left, off the A830, to Rhue Peninsula for superb views towards the smaller islands of Eigg, Muck, Rum and Canna.

Skye and the Western Isles

The Hebrides, the islands off the west coast of Scotland, are at the heart of Gaelic culture. Renowned for their music, culture and legendary hospitality, this is where you can really get away from it all and relax, so take time to enjoy the islands. The high lonely peaks, the broad moorlands teeming with wildlife, the smell of peat, ancient brochs (circular stone towers) and long, narrow, winding roads are distanced from mainland pressures by the surrounding sea.

The Old Man of Storr looms over the Trotternish peninsula

Skye is the most accessible of the islands, with regular car ferries during the summer from Mallaig or the smaller car ferry from Glenelg. You can also cross at any time by the toll bridge at Kyle of Lochalsh.

In the northern part of Skye is the **Trotternish peninsula,** and it's well worth meandering around this fascinating coastline. On the eastern side the **Old Man of Storr,** a distinctive 49m sheer column of rock, appears precariously balanced below the Storr mountain. Further north, the spectacular **Kilt Rock** waterfall drops 91m to the sea, while among the pinnacles and strange rock formations of the **Quiraing** you enter a weird and wonderful landscape of legends and giants.

Things to Do

On the island of Raasay, the house where Dr Johnson and James Boswell lodged in 1773 on their epic tour of the Hebrides is now an outdoor centre offering canoeing, windsurfing, climbing, cycling and walking. You can spot otters from the hide at Kylerhea Otter Haven, south of Kyle of Lochalsh on Skye.

Check out any family connections with the Isles at the remarkable historical collection at Co Leis Thu?/Seallam, Genealogical and Exhibition Centre in Northton on Harris.

More prosaically, the **Skye Museum of Island Life**, housed in a number of thatched buildings, shows island life as it was about 100 years ago.

The most dramatic sight, visible throughout the Islands and from the mainland, is the jagged outline of **the Cuillins,** a massive range of mountains that dominates the landscape. The range includes 12 Munros, peaks over 914m (➤ 124).

The combination of Munros and weird rock formations of the Trotternish peninsula make Skye the ideal place for hill-walkers and climbers, but there are also plenty of less challenging walks. Birdwatchers may be lucky to hear the scratchy cry of the corncrake, a once common bird now extremely localised. Skye's greatest attraction is its scenery, but if it disappears into low grey clouds and fine drizzle, you can always visit the award-winning **Skye Serpentarium** near Broadford. This

32 standing stones form an intriguing cruciform pattern at Calanais

unique collection of reptiles will captivate the whole family, and you can even handle a snake. Alternatively, take a tour of the **Talisker Whisky Distillery** at Carbost and sample the distinctive peaty dram.

The Western Isles

The rugged Western Isles – **Lewis and Harris, North and South Uist, Benbecula and Barra** – stand between the harsh Atlantic Ocean and Skye and the other inner islands. The flat windswept peat bog and moorland of Lewis contrasts with the mountainous, rugged contours of adjoining Harris. To appreciate the strange beauty of Harris, take the Golden Road to

June flowers bloom on the Machair at Vatersay in the Western Isles

Leverburgh from the ferry port at Tarbert. Twisting and turning along the coast, through a moonscape of ancient rock, this single-track road is possibly the most scenic drive in the Hebrides.

On Lewis you'll find the **Standing Stones of Calanais** (or Callanish in the Anglicised spelling) once buried in a peat bog, which have stood above this bay for over 4,000 years. Although the original purpose of this complex pattern of massive stones is a mystery, the central cairn (mound) was a burial place for many years.

Further north is **Dun Carloway Broch**, built around 2,000

Thatched croft-house at the Luib Folk Museum on Skye. Below right: Dunvegan Castle, home of the Clan MacLeod

SKYE AND THE WESTERN ISLES: INSIDE INFO

Top tips There is strict Sunday observance throughout the Isles, and particularly on Lewis and Harris, so don't be surprised if attractions are closed on Sundays, even during peak seasons.
• The best way to see Skye and the Western Isles is with an 8- or 15-day **Island Rover** Ticket from Caledonian MacBrayne Ferries. Follow the **Road to the Isles** (► 146–8), explore the small Isles, then take the Skye ferry to Armadale. From Uig, cross to Tarbert on Harris or Lochmaddy on North Uist. Then take the ferry from Stornaway to Ullapool.

Hidden gem Dunvegan Castle itself may not be remarkable, but it contains a few curiosities, such as the fairy flag. This faded fragment of silk, which ensures victory in battle, was reputedly given to a chief of MacLeod by his fairy wife.

years ago. This high, round, fortified house was built with a double drystone wall to withstand the Atlantic gales.

Blackhouses were built long and low for the same reason, their thatch held in place by ropes and stone weights keeping them snug against the elements. The **Arnol Blackhouse** was last occupied in the 1960s, and the folk museum here shows a crofter's way of life that died out only recently. At the other end of the house is the byre that held the animals in stalls. You can stay in a blackhouse, albeit with modern facilities, at the youth hostel at Gearrannan Blackhouse village.

Skye and the Western Isles
🔛 206 C3
✉ Portree Tourist Information Centre, Bayfield Road, Portree, Skye
☎ 01478 612137
✉ Western Isles Tourist Board, 26 Cromwell Street, Stornoway, Lewis
☎ 01851 703088

Dunvegan Castle
🔛 206 B3
✉ A850 north of Dunvegan, Skye
☎ 01470 521206
🕐 Daily 10–5:30, mid-Mar–Oct; 11–4, Nov–mid-Mar 🍴 (£££)
💷 Moderate

Skye Serpentarium
🔛 204 A1
✉ The Old Mill, Harrapool, Broadford
☎ 01471 822209
🕐 Mon–Sat 10–5, Easter–Oct; Sun Jul–Aug and Bank holidays 🚌 Bus from Kyle, Kyleakin and Armadale 💷 Inexpensive

Skye Museum of Island Life
🔛 206 B4
✉ A855 north of Uig ☎ 01420 552206
🕐 Mon–Sat 9:30–5:30, Apr–Oct
🚌 Bus from Portree to Kilmuir
💷 Inexpensive

Calanais (Callanish) Standing Stones and Visitor Centre
🔛 206 B5
✉ A858 at Calanais, Lewis ☎ 01851 621422
🕐 Open access to stones; visitor centre: Mon–Sat 10–7, summer; Mon–Sat 10–4, winter
🍴 (£) 🚌 Bus from Stornoway

Dun Carloway Broch and Doune Broch Visitor Centre
🔛 206 B5
✉ A858 south of Carloway, Lewis
☎ 0131 6688800; 01851 643338
🕐 Open access to broch; visitor centre: Mon–Sat 10–5, 15 May–16 Sep
🚌 Bus from Stornoway

Arnol Blackhouse
🔛 206 B5
✉ 42 Arnol, Barvas, Lewis ☎ 01851 710395
🕐 Mon–Sat 9:30–6:30, Apr–Sep; Mon–Thu and Sat 9:30–4:30, Oct–Mar
🚌 Bus from Stornoway
💷 Inexpensive

Lewis Loom Centre
🔛 206 C5
✉ 3 Bayhead Street, Stornoway, Lewis
☎ 01851 703117
🕐 Daily 9–6
💷 Inexpensive

Loch Ness

The beauty of the steep tree-lined banks of Loch Ness makes a striking backdrop to the moody waters below. The best way to see the loch is aboard the Loch Ness Cruiser, which runs from the pier at Fort Augustus, next to the Clansman Centre.

In its ice-cold depths, some 213m below the surface, scientists recently discovered a population of Arctic charr, fish undisturbed since the last Ice Age. And only the most hardened cynic could look out over these mysterious waters without scanning the surface for a glimpse of Nessie, the legendary monster. In such a vast body of water it's easy to understand how some large beast could possibly haunt the depths, eluding the sonar probes of the scientists.

A Monster Hit

Nessie's first appeared when the Irish missionary and abbot St Columba (c521–97) allegedly drove away a sea monster in AD565. But it was not until the construction of the A82 road in the 1930s that sightings increased, as did the appearance of indistinct and somewhat dubious photographs. More recently, highly sophisticated scientific equipment has failed to find any conclusive proof of the monster. However, the evidence amassed about the teeming life below the surface of these still, dark waters is presented in a fascinating audio-visual display at

Vital Statistics

Loch Ness is the largest body of fresh water in Britain

Length: around 37km

Width: 3.2km

Depth: 230–250m

The now-ruined Urquhart Castle was once the largest in Scotland

the Official Loch Ness Monster Exhibition Centre in Drumnadrochit.

TAKING A BREAK

At Brackla, just beyond Abriachan off the A82 between Inverness and Drumnadrochit, is **The Clansman** (tel: 01456 450326), which has a superb panorama bar overlooking Loch Ness and a small marina connected to the hotel by a subway.

➕ 204 C1   ✉ Between Inverness and Fort Augustus

LOCH NESS: INSIDE INFO

Top tips The best view of the loch is from **Urquhart Castle** near Drumnadrochit.

Hidden gems About 3km south of Urquhart Castle, on the loch side of the road, stands the **Cobb Memorial**, a cairn commemorating John Cobb, who died on 29 September, 1952 while breaking the world water speed record in his speed-boat *Crusader*.
• Follow the well-marked forest paths from the pretty village of Invermoriston to where the **River Moriston** tumbles over waterfalls towards Loch Ness. A partly ruined Telford bridge, spanning the falls and the salmon pools below, can still be crossed on foot.

One to miss The Original Loch Ness Monster Exhibition is little more than a gift shop. If you want information, go to the Official Loch Ness Monster Exhibition at Drumnadrochit (tel: 01456 450573).

The Cairngorms

The Cairngorm Mountains take their name from Cairn Gorm, a peak of 1245m. An incredibly varied landscape, the area is scheduled to become Scotland's second national park in 2001. Here you'll find alpine tundra, heather and moorland and remnants of ancient Caledonian pine forests.

A Centre of Activity

Whether you're based in one of the sleepy villages or in the brash resort of Aviemore, you'll find plenty to do, from fly fishing on a remote inland loch, training for the rigours of mountaineering at Glenmore Lodge or enjoying a leisurely drive through the historic Spey Valley.

The Cairngorm plateau has four of the highest peaks in Scotland and is one of the best areas in Britain for rock and ice climbing. In summer the area attracts watersports enthusiasts with sailing, windsurfing and canoeing at the **Loch Morlich Water Sport Centre** about 12km from Aviemore. There's more of the same at the watersports centre on **Loch Insh,** which also has a dry-ski slope and mountain bikes to hire.

Aviemore, Scotland's premier ski resort, is home to a number of rare wildlife species, including the Scottish wild cat, red squirrels, pine martens and the threatened capercaillie.

Aviemore was purpose built in the 1960s to cater for the growing number of skiers attracted to the slopes of Cairn Gorm, and is currently undergoing a revamp, with much of its concrete development being demolished. The town has all the facilities you need, including a reasonable nightlife, restaurants, pubs, and outfitters for walkers, climbers, cyclists and anglers,

Loch Morlich and the Cairngorms, which contain four of the highest mountains in Britain

as well as skiers.

At the centre of the Cairngorms, **Rothiemurchus Estate** has belonged to the Grant family since the early-16th century and is one of the best recreational facilities in the Highlands. Here you can try off-road driving or clay-pigeon shooting, or go walking, birdwatching, mountain biking or fishing. You could easily spend days on the estate, but make sure you see the largest section of almost completely natural Caledonian pine forest in Scotland, stretching for over 32km. Pine forests once covered most of the country, but centuries of clearing for fuel, timber and agriculture have left them virtually extinct.

Cairngorm, Scotland's premier skiing area

At **Loch an Eilein** are the remains of a 15th-century castle, and at the visitor centre you can learn all about 200 years of the great estate of Rothiemurchus. Elizabeth Grant of

Rothiemurchus has left a fascinating account of life here 200 years ago in her book *Memoirs of a Highland Lady* which you can buy and read after your trip is over.

Quiet walkers may find a capercaillie in the under-growth

Quieter Pastimes

For more sedate tastes, further south, in the beautiful Spey Valley, is the little town of Kingussie which, together with nearby Newtonmore, is home to the **Highland Folk Museum.** The museum covers all aspects of Highland life such as farming in reconstructed buildings that include a smokehouse, mill and a blackhouse from the Hebridean islands. Near by, the impressive ruin of **Ruthven Barracks,** built to quell Highland unrest after the Jacobite rebellion of 1715, stands proud and roofless against the sky. It was captured by Bonnie Prince Charlie's army in 1746, who blew it up when news reached them of defeat at Culloden. From Ruthven you can walk a stretch of **General Wade's military road** (▶ 183), which crosses a perfectly preserved Wade Bridge near Dalwhinnie.

TAKING A BREAK

You'll find superb restaurants and tea rooms throughout the area, but try **Littlejohn's** restaurant on Grampian Road in

The impressive ruins of Ruthven Barracks are a reminder of a turbulent period of Scotland's history

Aviemore if you're looking for a pleasant, child-friendly place. In addition to main meals, it offers a good choice of coffee.

There can be few sights more rewarding than the ospreys at Loch Garten

Aviemore Tourist Information Centre
➕ 204 C1
✉ Grampian Road
☎ 01479 810363
🕐 Mon–Sat 9–6 (9–7 in summer), Sun 10–5; closed Sun, Dec–Jan
🍴 Plenty of eating places, cafés and restaurants (£–££)
🚌 From Inverness, Glasgow and Edinburgh stop on Grampian Road, Aviemore

THE CAIRNGORMS: INSIDE INFO

Top tips In summer take the **chairlift** to the Cairngorm plateau and then walk the short distance to the summit. On a clear day you can see past Loch Morlich to Aviemore and beyond.
• To get away from the bustle of Aviemore base your trip at one of the quieter villages in the area: nearby Coylumbridge is in the heart of Rothiemurchus Estate and the fine Georgian town and ski resort of Grantown-on-Spey is particularly popular with anglers looking for trout and salmon.

Hidden gem The **osprey**, a fish-eating hawk, was not seen in Britain for 50 years but in 1954 a pair built a nest near Loch Garten and returned each year. Other nesting pairs have now become established in the Highlands. The Loch Garten site is part of the Abernethy Forest reserve belonging to the Royal Society for the Protection of Birds (RSPB) and during the nesting period (April to August), visitors can view the birds from a hide equipped with a closed-circuit television link to their nest.

In More Depth The Cairngorms region is ideal walking country for people of all abilities. There are plenty of low-level walks and nature trails, especially on the Rothiemurchus Estate and around Loch Morlich. For something a little more adventurous, the Lairig Ghru is the finest mountain pass in Britain, carved by glaciers. Running 32km from near Coylumbridge to the Linn of Dee near Braemar, it links Speyside with Deeside. But this route is quite challenging and only suitable for fit and experienced walkers who are properly equipped, as even in summer a change in the weather can bring the risk of exposure. For a shorter option there's a six-hour hike up to the pass from Coylumbridge and back.

At Your Leisure

1 Islay

This is serious malt whisky country, as any lover of a dram will tell you. The water, the peat and generations of skill and knowledge produce the distinctive smoky flavours of Lagavulin, Laphroaig and Bowmore whiskies. As well as a distillery visit at Bowmore, look out for the 18th-century round church built without corners to deny the Devil an opportunity to lurk. Birdwatching is another attraction and the RSPB site at Gruinart (tel: 01469 850505) has guided walks. There is also a great deal of historical interest on the island.

Access to Islay is by air from Glasgow, twice daily Monday to Friday and once on Saturday. CalMac Ferries operate a car ferry from Kennacraig on the Kintyre Peninsula to Port Ellen.

➕ 202 A1 ✉ Bowmore Tourist Information Office ☎ 01496 810254 🕐 Mon–Sat 9:30–5, summer (also 5:30 in Jul–Aug), Sun 2–5; Mon–Fri noon–4, winter

Iona Abbey was restored in the early-20th century and is now a spiritual retreat

2 Jura

If you want to get away from it all go to Jura – there's only one road, most of the interior is inaccessible by car and the blinding white, sandy beaches to the west can only be reached on foot. You can climb the Paps of Jura, or walk for days without meeting another soul. Because of depopulation, deer far outnumber people. From Kinuachdrach at the end of a decrepit track, a 3.2km hike takes you to the northern tip where you might get an unusual sight of the infamous Corrievreckan Whirlpool, classified as unnavigable by the Royal Navy.

Don't forget to visit the Isle of Jura Distillery, while Stephen and Bev's island store is the nearest thing to an information and advice centre.

➕ 202 A3 ✉ Jura Stores, access by car ferry from Islay ☎ 01496 820231; e-mail: jura@stores.demon.co.uk; www.stores.demon.co.uk/index.html

3 Iona

Just a five-minute trip by passenger ferry from Fionnphort on Mull, Iona has been a place of pilgrimage since the days of St Columba. It's still a religious retreat and a sense of peace surrounds the 12th-century abbey. Iona was supposedly the burial place of the kings of Scotland, including Duncan and Macbeth, but there's no evidence to support this. A more recent and a poignant memorial is the simple headstone of John Smith (1938–94), former leader of the Labour Party, carved on a mighty boulder at St Oran's Chapel.

If you get the chance, take the boat trip to Staffa, with its massive basalt columns and the incredible Fingal's Cave, which inspired Mendelssohn's Hebridean Overture.

➕ 206 B1 ✉ Iona, ferry from Fionnphort, Mull ⑪ The Coffee House, west of the Abbey (£)

4 Mull

If Mull is your first introduction to the Hebrides, take a slow drive around the island's narrow winding roads to appreciate the wonderful scenery as you glimpse the sea and the islands or small lochs glistening in the glens between the hills. From the brightly coloured houses that line Tobermory harbour to Toronsay Castle, with its extensive gardens and Venetian statues and the rugged cliffs at Loch na Keal, allow yourself a couple of days to do it justice.

➕ 206 C1 ✉ Craignure Tourist Office, by the pier ☎ 01680 812377 🕐 Daily from very early to late, depending on CalMac''s ferry timetable 🚌 Infrequent buses to Fionnphort and Tobermory 🚢 Oban and then ferry to Craignure

8 Inverness

Situated on the River Ness at the head of the Great Glen, Inverness is a great base for exploring the Highlands. It is the largest town in the HIghlands and predominantly dates back to the 19th century – most of the older buildings were regularly destroyed during times of turbulence. Even the castle was built only between 1834 and 1847, although its attractive setting is far older. Today, it is the Sheriff Court.

The wreck of a gold-laden Spanish frigate reputedly lies beneath Tobermory harbour

Another enjoyable place to visit is the Kiltmaker Centre where you can kit yourself out in the factory shop.

☩ 204 C2 ✉ Inverness Tourist Information Centre, Castle Wynd ☎ 01463 234353 🕐 Mon–Sat 9–5, Sun 10–4; longer in summer, call to check 🚉 Inverness

🔟 Culloden Moor

Site of the last battle fought on British soil, in 1746, this was where the Jacobite cause had finally foundered. The battlefield has been restored to its condition at that fateful time. Flags mark the lines of Government and

The memorial cairn at Culloden

Jacobite forces and each clan and regiment is faithfully located. It's easy to see why the battle charge of the Highlanders, in this boggy ground against heavy artillery, was doomed to failure. Near the cairn lie the mass graves of the Highlanders and a melancholy air of desolation still clings to this bleak and barren moor.

☩ 204 C2 ✉ NTS Visitors' Centre, Culloden Moor ☎ 01463 790607 🕐 Daily 9–6, Apr–Oct; 10–4, Feb–Mar and Nov–Dec 🍴 Restaurant in visitors' centre (££) 🚌 bus from Inverness 🚉 Inverness 💷 Inexpensive

🔢 Aberdeen Satrosphere

If you're visiting with children this is the place to take them. Lots of hands-on experiences make this a fun

place for the whole family that's also very educational. You can create a giant soap bubble, play with computers and telecommunications equipment, have a look inside anthills and beehives, try TV newsreading and balance balls on streams of air. Allow at least half a day for a visit.

☩ 205 F1 ✉ 19 Justice Mill Lane ☎ 01224 213232 🕐 Mon–Sat 10–4, Sun 1:30–5 🍴 Café on site (£) 🚉 Aberdeen 💷 Inexpensive

🔢 Aberdeen Maritime Museum

Based in the oldest building in the city – 16th-century Provost Ross's House, plus a modern extension – the museum covers Aberdeen's entire maritime past, from the early days of whaling and herring fishing to the 20th-century oil industry. A huge suspended model of an oil rig forms a dramatic centrepiece.

☩ 205 F1 ✉ Shiprow ☎ 01224 337700 🕐 Mon–Sat 10–5, Sun noon–3 🍴 Café (£) 🚉 Aberdeen 💷 Free

🔢 Aberdeen Fish Market

Fish has been the mainstay of Aberdeen for hundreds of years and if you get up early and head for the harbour you'll find the fish market in full swing. Auctioneers keep up a fast, incomprehensible spiel, while buyers make mysterious gestures. It's a complete sound, sight and smell show but it's all over by 8am, when you'll be longing for a fish breakfast.

☩ 205 F1 ✉ The Harbour 🚉 Aberdeen 💷 Free

Off the Beaten Track

🔟 Orkney

Scotland's latest World Heritage Site, designated in 1999, covers the neolithic remains on Orkney, and particularly Skara Brae, Maes Howe, the Stones of Stenness and the Ring of Brodgar.

Orkney Tourist Board
➕ 205 E5 ✉ 6 Broad Street, Kirkwall
☎ 01856 872856; fax: 01856 875056;
e-mail: orkneytb@csi.com;
www.orkney.com ⏱ Mon–Sat 9:30–5,
Oct–Mar; daily 9–6, Apr; 8:30–8,
May–Sep 🍴 Plenty of cafés, restaurants and tea rooms in Kirkwall (£–££)

Cutting edge domestic furniture from the Stone Age, on display in a living room at Skara Brae

Skara Brae

In a country littered with neolithic remains, standing stones, chambered tombs and prehistoric relics, Skara Brae is an overwhelming archaeological site. This small village takes you to the heart of a community at the dawn of history, showing how the people lived, ate and slept.

The excellent interpretation centre explains how Skara Brae was revealed to the world in 1850 when a great storm uncovered it, how the landscape and climate have changed over the millennia and how the evidence has helped to re-create an ancient way of life. In the reconstructed house outside you can creep through the low narrow passages, walk round the central hearth and imagine the smoke drifting up into the restored rafters tied together with twine. The box beds are complete with heather mattresses and warm fleece, the stone dresser is adorned with ornaments and shells, while nearby a lobster lies as if ready to eat.

The walk to the village itself is a timeline to the past. Start from a depiction of Neil Armstrong on the moon, past the invention of the telephone and the American Declaration of Independence. Go back past the fall of Rome and the birth of Christ, then further back past the building of the Parthenon in Athens and the construction of the Pyramids in Egypt to Skara Brae at the end of the line, 5,000 years ago. Yet in this little cluster of roofless dwellings, built in mounds of midden (refuse) for stability and warmth, the past somehow seems very near.

➕ 205 D5 ✉ Stenness ☎ 01856 841815
⏱ Daily 9:30–6:30, Apr–Sep; Mon–Sat 9:30–4:30, Sun 2–4:30, Oct–Mar
🍴 Café (£) 💳 Inexpensive

Maes Howe

When the Neolithic chambered tomb at Maes Howe was built around 5,000 years ago it was aligned with such precision that the midwinter sunset, streaming along the narrow entrance tunnel, lit the back wall of the chamber. This prehistoric workmanship is among the best in Western Europe. The mound was excavated in 1861, revealing a central chamber with three small chambers in the walls but no prehistoric remains.

The tomb had suffered the depredations of the Vikings centuries before. It's not clear whether they took anything, but they left masses of ribald Runic graffiti which wouldn't be out of place on lavatory walls today.

✚ 205 D5 ✉ Stenness ☏ 01856 761606 🕘 Daily 9:30–6:30, Apr–Sep; Sat–Wed 9:30–4:30, Thu morning, Sun 2–4:30, Oct–Mar 🍽 Café (£) 💧 Inexpensive

Other Orcadian Highlights

Orkney has more than its fair share of other attractions: for example, **St Magnus Cathedral** in Broad Street, Kirkwall (tel: 01856 874894) was founded by Jarl Rognvlad in 1137 in honour of his uncle, St Magnus. It

The people of Orkney tracked down the original builders to restore the Italian Chapel when it began to deteriorate

took over 300 years to complete, and has architectural details ranging from Norman to early Gothic.

At the opposite end of the scale the delightful tiny **Italian Chapel** at Lamb Holm is an inspiring example of faith and dedication. World War II Italian prisoners of war, with nowhere to worship and little more than concrete, wire and paint, constructed this unique sanctuary from two Nissen huts. The interior, by artist Domenico Chiocchetti, is a masterpiece of *trompe l'œil* stonework and windows, with a magnificent fresco altarpiece behind a wrought-iron screen.

Diving for Wrecks

The natural harbour of Scapa Flow, surrounded by Hoy, South Ronaldsay and the mainland, has been used since the time of the Vikings. But it was the scuttling of the German fleet here on 21 May, 1919 that made it the world's premier wreck-diving location. Although most of the fleet was salvaged there are still seven wrecks here, some on their sides and highly accessible and others only 9m deep.

➕ 205 D5 ✉ Scapa Scuba , 13 Ness Road, Stromness ☎ 01856 851218

ⓑ Shetland

Scotland's most northerly outpost is easily accessible by air from Glasgow or Edinburgh. In fine weather Shetland is indescribably beautiful, but when the weather closes in it disappears in grey. Travel the length of the islands to the north to appreciate the bright greens, the sandy beaches and the sparkling blue sea all around. Then send a postcard from the most northerly post office in the UK on the island of Unst.

The narrow flagstoned main street of Lerwick, Shetland's largest town, has lots of narrow wynds and passages branching to the busy and colourful harbour or up through the houses huddled on the hill.

Shetland's annual fire festival, Up Helly Aa, is held in January regardless of the weather. Over 1,000 men carrying blazing torches drag a Viking longship through the darkened town. Finally, the craft is burned and everyone parties all night in halls throughout Lerwick. The next day is a public

The Up Helly Aa procession snakes through the streets of Lerwick like a river of fire

holiday and nobody stirs. Get a flavour of the festival at the Up Helly Aa Exhibition off St Sunniva Street, or glimpse Shetland's Scandinavian past at the fascinating Viking settlement of Jarlshof to the south of Lerwick close to the airport.

Fiddle Music

The distinctive Shetland fiddle style has evolved over the years through the playing of Aly Bain and others. Remnants of an older style can still be heard and you may come across some old men playing in the strangely discordant style of Papa Stour. The Lounge Bar in Lerwick is a good place to hear local traditional musicians.

Mousa Broch

On the tiny island of Mousa, reached by boat from Leebitton in Sandwick, is the best-preserved prehistoric broch in Britain, built around 2,000 years ago. You can still climb the dark winding stairs in the stone walls to the top, where only the roof is missing.

➕ 205 A4 ✉ Shetland Islands Tourism, Market Cross, Lerwick
☎ 01595 693434; fax: 01595 695807;
e-mail: info@sit.ossain.net;
www.shetland-tourism.co.uk
🕐 Mon–Fri 8–6, Sat 8–4, Apr–Sep;
Mon–Fri 9–5, Oct–Mar

Where to...
Eat and Drink

Prices

The £ amounts indicate what you can expect to pay for a three-course meal for one person, including coffee and service.

£ = under £15 **££** = £15–25 **£££** = over £25

RESTAURANTS

Altnaharrie Inn £££

You come to Altnaharrie for the food, but you have to stay as well, as it's only reached by boat. The wild setting, the simple croft with open fires, white walls, rugs, candles and flowers, and the tasteful bedrooms form an exquisite setting. In the intimate dining-room, Gunn Eriksen's delicate, modern cooking is considered the best in Scotland.

🚹 204 B3 ☒ Ullapool ☎ 01854 633230 ⊚ Dinner daily at 8; closed early Nov–Easter

Bonaventure ££

Located about 32km west of Stornaway, Richard Leparoux's tiny restaurant must be the most westerly in the UK, and it's often fully booked for dinner. Here, Scottish food has a French accent, built around the finest local ingredients. The setting is unusual: a former RAF base that's been jazzed up with a nautical theme. There are also three rooms for bed and breakfast.

🚹 206 B5 ☒ Aird Uig, Timsgarry, Isle of Lewis ☎ 01851 672474 ⊚ Lunch and dinner Tue–Sat; closed mid-Jan to Feb and Nov

The Creel ££–£££

The appeal of Joyce and Alan Craigie's remote island restaurant lies in the sheer quality of local ingredients. Orkney beef, North Ronaldsay lamb and a wealth of seafood are all used to good effect in a repertoire that can call on the Mediterranean and beyond for inspiration. Scotland, however, cannot be beaten for clootie dumplings, beremeal bannocks and soda bread – all are irresistible. There are also three *en-suite* bedrooms.

🚹 205 E4 ☒ Front Road, St Margaret's Hope, South Ronaldsay, Orkney ☎ 01856 831311 ⊚ Daily 7pm–9:30; closed Jan–Feb and 2 weeks in Oct

Harlosh House £££

A former tackman's house dating from the mid-18th century, this small, intimate restaurant-with-rooms still retains some original features, including lovely timber beams, and offers great views over Loch Bracadale. Peter Elford opens for dinner only, and he puts great emphasis on local seafood, served as part of a four-course set menu. Dessert could include a selection of Scottish cheeses. The six cottage-style bedrooms are charming.

🚹 206 B3 ☒ Harlosh, Isle of Skye ☎ 01470 521367 ⊚ Daily 7pm–8:30; closed Oct–Easter

Killiecrankie Hotel £–££

Colin and Carole Anderson maintain a village inn atmosphere at their inviting hotel. Excellent bar lunches are served in the sun lounge, but head for the elegant restaurant for more serious evening meals. The menu changes daily and the kitchen makes use of local produce in its innovative Scottish cooking. The wine list has something for all tastes. The hotel's ten cosy bedrooms are bright and airy.

🚹 203 D5 ☒ Killiecrankie, near Pitlochry, ☎ 01796 473220; fax: 01796 472451 ⊚ Daily 7pm–8:30; closed Jan–Feb and 10 days before Christmas

The Loft £-££

The corner of a caravan park behind the Tilt Hotel is an odd location for this small but sophisticated country restaurant. The former hayloft is characterised by beams, stone walls, oak floors and a warm Provençal décor, plus a splendid conservatory with access to the roof terrace, where lighter meals are served. The cooking is modern with a slight French bias, dinner being more adventurous than the simple lunch.

🚹 **203 D5** ⌂ **River Tilt Park, Blair Atholl** ☎ **01796 481377** 🍽 **Lunch and dinner daily; closed Mon in Jan-Apr**

Old Station Restaurant ££

At around 16km from Fort William, Richard and Helen Bunney's fine old Victorian station is well worth a detour. Fully restored to create an attractive restaurant, complete with appropriate railway memorabilia, the Old Station offers outstanding modern Scottish cooking with the emphasis on west-coast seafood and

a good vegetarian selection. It's still a working station so you can watch the trains arrive and depart.

🚹 **202 B5** ⌂ **Station Road, Spean Bridge** ☎ **01397 712535** 🍽 **Dinner daily 6-9; closed Mon in Oct-April**

La Riviera £-££

Set on the north bank of the River Ness, the smart Glenmoriston Town House hotel is noted locally for the classic Italian cooking served in its comfortably elegant La Riviera restaurant. Specialities are worth checking out, but the fixed-price menus are excellent value. Wines display an Italian bias, but lovers of single-malt whisky should take note: the Moriston bar stocks around 100 of them.

🚹 **204 C2** ⌂ **20 Ness Bank, Inverness** ☎ **01463 223777** 🍽 **Lunch and dinner daily**

Three Chimneys Restaurant ££-£££

This wonderful stone crofter's cottage stands in rugged countryside, enjoying views of the sea and distant mountains. A steadily growing following enjoys the stunningly fresh seafood and honest approach evident in the cooking. The tried-and-tested menu requires no embellishments as the quality of local and regional ingredients is a keynote. The six luxurious en-suite bedrooms are recommended, and the breakfast room looks straight on to the sea.

🚹 **206 B3** ⌂ **Colbost, Dunvegan, Isle of Skye** ☎ **01470 511258** 🍽 **Lunch and dinner daily; closed Sun lunch in mid-Jan to mid-Feb**

The Cross £££

Visitors to the Hadleys' converted tweed mill focus on the merits of the kitchen, but this is also a charming small hotel with nine bedrooms. Ruth Hadley's five-course dinners are high quality with a modern edge that notes the seasons. The emphasis is always on local produce, whether seafood, meat or vegetables. A passion for fine wine distinguishes the wine list and Tony Hadley will always give advice.

🚹 **204 C1** ⌂ **Tweed Mill Brae, Ardbroilach Road, Kingussie** ☎ **01540 661166** 🍽 **Wed-Mon 7pm-8:30; closed Dec-Mar**

Old Pines Restaurant with Rooms ££

The Barbers' superb Scandinavian-style house is right in the middle of some of Scotland's most dramatic and desolate scenery, yet visitors travel from far and wide to sample the excellent Scottish regional cooking, sharing tables and experiences. Light meals are served all day. The set five-course dinner menu changes daily, offering honest, straightforward cooking and using home-grown produce. The eight en-suite rooms are each named after a flower and furnished accordingly.

🚹 **202 B5** ⌂ **Spean Bridge, near Fort William** ☎ **01397 712324; fax: 01397 71243** 🍽 **Dinner daily from 8pm; closed dinner Sun in May-Sept except for residents. Closed Dec-Mar**

Where to... Stay

Prices

Price categories are per person, including English breakfast.

£ = under £30 per night   ££ = £30–60 per night   £££ = over £60 per night

Ardvourlie Castle ££

Ardvourlie is more a Victorian hunting lodge than a castle, though it looks impressive when viewed across the waters of Loch Seaforth. Derek Martin is to be applauded for his excellent period restoration that gives unusual elegance and charm to the place. The hotel's peaceful setting, with views to the mountains is enhanced by open fires, a pleasant library and four very comfortable bedrooms with huge bathrooms; all complemented by superb dinners served by gaslight.

✚ 206 B4 ☒ Ardvourlie, Isle of Harris ☎ 01859 502307; fax: 01859 502348

Baile-na-Cille £–££

This remote but soothingly peaceful, easy-going beachside hotel – set on a grassy bank in front of a swath of white sand – is noted for its warm welcome towards families. The air of relaxation and informality is something children appreciate as much as the wide, safe beach outside. All 12 of the hotel's en-suite rooms are comfortable, and Joanna Gollin's simple and wholesome cooking seems to reflect the philosophy of the hotel and its setting.

✚ 206 B5 ☒ Timsgarry, Isle of Lewis ☎ 01851 672242; fax: 01851 672241
E-mail: randigollin@compuserve.com

Ballachullish House ££

Located about 5km north of Glencoe, the Ballachullish is one of Scotland's oldest hotels and is reputed to be one of the most haunted houses in the country. Set above Loch Linnhe, there are splendid views from all the public rooms. The comfortable atmosphere is created by the combination of antiques, an historic feel and stylish bedrooms – the best ones making great use of the light, space and scenery. For evening entertainment, there is a billiards room, games and two bars.

✚ 202 B5 ☒ Ballachullish, Highland ☎ 01855 811266; fax: 01855 811498
E-mail: mclaughlins@btconnect.com

Ben Loyal Hotel ££

There are lovely views up to Ben Loyal and out over the Kyle of Tongue (castle) from this very well-run, centrally located hotel. The pine-furnished bedrooms are pretty, with those in the annexe being less expensive. There's traditional live music in the lounge bar in summer, and Elaine and Paul Lewis have built the restaurant into one of the best places to eat along the whole north coast.

✚ 204 C4 ☒ Tongue, Highland ☎ 01847 611216; fax: 01847 611212
E-mail: thebenloyalhotel@btinternet.com

Busta House ££

Set in pleasant grounds overlooking Busta Voe, this historic laird's home dates from the 16th century. High standards are evident throughout, but especially in the 20 country-house style bedrooms that maximise all available space. Day rooms include several lounges, a bar well stocked with malts (and popular for taking light meals), as well as an attractive dining-room offering two fixed-price menus, one of which offers vegetarian fare.

✚ 204 A4 ☒ Brae, Shetland ☎ 01806 522506; fax: 01806 522588
E-mail: busta@mes.co.uk

Culloden House Hotel £££

It was from this historic Georgian mansion that Bonnie Prince Charlie left for the Battle of Culloden in 1746. Today, marble fireplaces, chandeliers and plasterwork are testament to the period, while the restaurant, designed by Robert Adam, features a 5.5m-high ceiling. Bedrooms range from opulent period suites and master rooms to smart contemporary rooms, while six non-smoking suites are in a separate mansion house in the extensive grounds. The hotel exudes an air of refinement and comfort.

➕ 204 C2 ☒ Culloden, Inverness
☎ 01463 790461; fax:01463 792181
E-mail: user@cullodenhouse.co.uk

Dalmunzie House ££

Surrounded by a 2,600ha mountain estate, this is a splendid turreted baronial house that offers plenty to keep visitors busy. There's a nine-hole golf course, burn fishing and hard-court tennis, as well as skiing in winter. Individually furnished bedrooms are generally large with superb views, and there are seven self-catering cottages in the grounds. Traditional Scottish meals are served in the dining-room.

➕ 203 D5 ☒ Blairgowrie, Spital of Glenshee ☎ 01250 885224; fax: 01250 885225
E-mail: dalmunzie@aol.com

Druimard Country House Hotel £££

There's a comforting homeliness to Haydn and Wendy Hubbard's Victorian country house. It's set in a sleepy hamlet on the northwest of Mull, has outstanding views over the glen and the River Bellart and offers six pretty bedrooms that vary in size but are full of thoughtful touches. All this forms a backdrop to some of the best cooking on the island, served in the smart but unstuffy restaurant which offers five-course set dinner menus.

➕ 202 A5 ☒ Dervaig, Isle of Mull
☎ 01688 400345/400291; fax: 01688 400345

Inverlochy Castle £££

Inverlochy is one of the most impressive destination hotels in the world – the Great Hall sets the tone of Victorian grandeur and it remains a castle built for comfort rather than defence. Antiques are everywhere, in the public rooms and in the luxurious bedrooms, each complete with sofas, armchairs, fresh flowers and enormous bathrooms. Views over the gardens and loch are stunning. Three elegant dining rooms, each decorated with elaborate furniture presented as gifts from the King of Norway, are the setting for inventive, ambitious cooking.

➕ 202 B5 ☒ Torlundy, Fort William
☎ 01397 702177; fax: 01397 702953
E-mail: info@inverlochy.co.uk

Kinloch Lodge £££

Kinloch Lodge dates from 1540 and features splendid views over Loch Na Dalit. This comfortable country house hotel, Lord and Lady MacDonald's secluded home retains the atmosphere of a private house, with open fires, drawing rooms filled with antiques and an elegant dining-room adorned with family portraits and silver. Dinner showcases cooking that reveals a refreshing simplicity and features the best of island produce.

➕ 204 A1 ☒ Isle of Ornsay, Isle of Skye ☎ 01471 833214; fax: 01471 833277 E-mail: kinloch@dial.pipex.com

Merkister Hotel £–££

Immensely popular and famous as a fishing hotel – the brown-trout fishing is among the best in the world, and boats can be arranged – the Merkister stands in its own grounds in a picturesque spot overlooking Merkister Bay on Loch Harray. The centre of affairs is the bar, where the largest trout caught in the UK can be seen. Modest bedrooms are all en suite and comfortable. Birdwatchers appreciate the hide in the grounds.

➕ 205 D5 ☒ Loch of Harray, Harray, Orkney ☎ 01856 771366;
fax: 01856 771515
E-mail: merkisterhotel@hotmail.com

Where to...
Shop

TARTANS AND TWEEDS

Tweeds and knitwear are the main specialities of this region, and you will not be able to buy Harris tweed cheaper than on Harris itself.

The **Lewis Loom Centre** in Stornoway, Isle of Lewis, will sell you Harris tweed by the metre, or you can try some of Ronnie MacKenzie's ready-made range. He also produces high-quality knitwear. Elsewhere on Harris signs along the Golden Road advertise locally produced tweed. The **Mackays** at No 6 Luskentyre make a fine selection of tartan tweeds and welcome visitors.

On Orkney, the excellent **Judith Glue's** near St Magnus Cathedral in Kirkwall specialises in Orcadian knitwear with runic designs. It also sells jewellery, pottery, stoneware and local preserves.

CRAFTS

Highland Stoneware in Ullapool (tel: 01854 612980) has a huge range of hand-painted stoneware and pottery, and **Caithness Glass** is a good source of crystal glasses and ornaments. There are outlets throughout the Highlands, but try the one at the Waterfront Centre, by the railway pier in Oban.

FOOD

Local preserves and condiments let you to take a taste of Scotland home with you. The **House of Bruar**, by the main A9 north of Pitlochry, has a good range, plus a variety of Scottish cheeses. **Brodie Country Fare**, on the main road from Nairn to Forres, has a similar range that includes chutneys and other mouthwatering deli delights.

Where to...
Be Entertained

CONCERTS AND CEILIDHS

During the summer the Highlands are jumping. The very best events are the local ceilidhs in small village halls, but you'll need to search for them. Ask at tourist information offices or look out for posters in shops, on telegraph poles and bus shelters in the area.

The **Ceilidh Place** (tel: 01854 612135) in Ullapool is absolutely the best place in the Highlands for live traditional music and dancing, every evening during the summer. In Aberdeen the **Lemon Tree** arts centre, café and restaurant (tel: 01224 642230), while in Inverness the excellent **Balnain House**, on Huntly Street by the riverside, holds regular ceilidhs and concerts.

THEATRE

With only 43 seats, **Mull Little Theatre** (tel: 01688 400245) at Dervaig is the smallest in Scotland but also one of the best. This converted coach house is home to a professional theatre company. The 500-seater **Festival Theatre** at Pitlochry (tel: 01796 484626; closed winter) is another gem producing modern plays and the classics as well as offering an array of art exhibitions, music, films, readings and appearances by famous authors. The **Eden Court**, Inverness (tel: 01463 234234) is among the top provincial theatres in Britain, staging not only classical drama, dance, pop music and opera but also holding ceilidhs and piping events in the summer.

Walks
and Tours

1 Whisky & Castle Trail 172 – 175
2 Border Tour 176 – 177
3 Glasgow Walk 178 – 180
4 Great Glen Tour 181 – 183
5 Ullapool & Loch Broom Walk
   184 – 186

THE WHISKY AND CASTLE TRAIL

Tour

Scotland is famous for its ancient castles and for its whisky, and this tour of Speyside covers both. Scotland's Malt Whisky Trail and Scotland's Castle Trail have been specially devised and signposted by the Aberdeen and Grampian Highlands Tourist Board. Free maps for both trails and also for the Victorian Heritage, Stone Circles and Coastal Trails are available from local tourist information offices or on the internet.

The two trails are too extensive to cover in full here, so this tour combines some of the highlights of both. Note that Scotland has severe drink-driving laws, so don't drink if you're the driver. Instead of accepting the complimentary wee dram at the end of the distillery tour, ask for a miniature to enjoy later.

DISTANCE 134km **TIME** 4–6 hours depending on stops
START/END POINT Huntly, on the A96 about 60km northwest of Aberdeen ✚ 205 E2

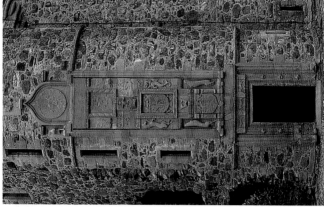

1–2

Huntly stands at the confluence of the rivers Bogie and Deveron and offers some fine fishing. Set in parkland beside the River Deveron is the roofless **Huntly Castle**, with a magnificent south front, massively inscribed across the beautiful oriel windows. Its splendid ornate heraldic doorway has carved coats of arms stretching up the tower, but the religious figures are sadly defaced. You can still see the motte and bailey of the original 12th-century wooden keep and the shape and position of the medieval tower house which replaced it. The extensive ruins of the 17th-century palace vividly evoke the life of the building. Narrow stairs lead from the steward's room to the lord's chamber above. The 16th-century graffiti in the basement corridor recall the former inhabitants, and looking down into the dungeon pit will cause a shiver.

The stone carvings on Huntly Castle give a clue to previous occupants

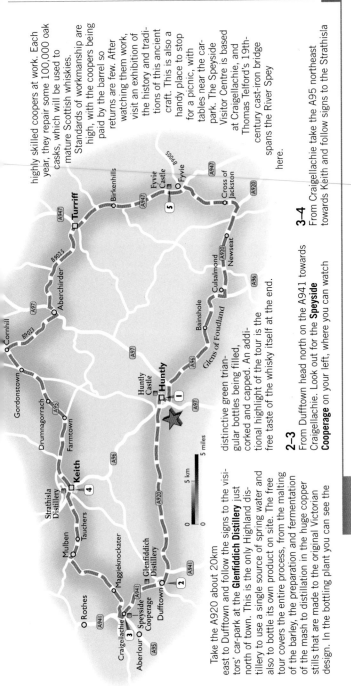

highly skilled coopers at work. Each year, they repair some 100,000 oak casks, which will be used to mature Scottish whiskies.

Standards of workmanship are high, with the coopers being paid by the barrel so returns are few. After watching them work, visit an exhibition of the history and traditions of this ancient craft. This is also a handy place to stop for a picnic, with tables near the carpark. The Speyside Visitor Centre is based at Craigellachie, and Thomas Telford's 19th-century cast-iron bridge spans the River Spey here.

Take the A920 about 20km east to Dufftown and follow the signs to the visitors' car-park. This is north of town. This is the only Highland distillery to use a single source of spring water and also to bottle its own product on site. The free tour covers the entire process, from the malting of the barley, the preparation and fermentation of the mash to distillation in the huge copper stills that are made to the original Victorian design. In the bottling plant you can see the distinctive green triangular bottles being filled, corked and capped. An additional highlight of the tour is the free taste of the whisky itself at the end.

2–3
From Dufftown head north on the A941 towards Craigellachie. Look out for the **Speyside Cooperage** on your left, where you can watch

3–4
From Craigellachie take the A95 northeast towards Keith and follow signs to the Strathisla

4–5

Continue northeast on the A95 for about 20km until you reach the hamlet of Cornhill, where you turn right on to the B9023. In another 8km turn left on to the A97, then right on to the B9025 for 10km to Turriff. At Turriff turn right on to the A947 towards Fyvie 13.5km away. On your left just before you reach the town is **Fyvie Castle**, originally dating from the 13th century and one of the finest examples of Scottish Baronial architecture in existence. Endlessly extended and improved over the centuries, it's said that five of its owners added a tower bearing their name. The great 16th-century spiral staircase is the best example in Scotland. Rising up the Gordon Tower to the dining-room, its 3m-wide steps supposedly enabling horses to be ridden up them for a bet. There's a collection of portraits, fine armour and 16th-century tapestries, plus an ice house, a racquets court and a tenpin bowling alley.

5–6

From Fyvie, continue for a further 0.8km on the A947 and turn right on to the local road. Drive for 6.75km via the hamlet of Cross of Jackston to the junction with the A920 and turn right. After another 11km turn right on to the A96 and continue for 14.5km back to Huntly.

Distillery, just 200m from the railway station. Enjoy an unhurried self-guided tour round the oldest working distillery in the Highlands, opened in 1786, which produces the legendary Chivas Regal. You can learn about the art of whisky blending and take lessons in whisky nosing before enjoying a dram or, if you prefer, some shortbread and coffee.

Taking a Break

While in Craigellachie, try the Highlander Inn, 10 Victoria Street, for enjoyable home-cooked dishes of local produce in a riverside setting.

Through memorable audio-visuals and tours, the Glenfiddich Distillery Visitor Centre explains all the stages of whisky-making from malting to bottling

Aberdeen and Grampian Highlands Tourist Board

27 Allbyn Place, Aberdeen

01224 632727; fax: 01224 620415; e-mail: info@agtb.org; www.agtb.org; www.maltwhisky-trail.com

Places to visit
Huntly Castle

/fax 01466 793191

Glenfiddich Distillery, Dufftown

A941. 1.6km north of Dufftown

01340 820373; fax: 01340 820805 (advance booking necessary)

Speyside Cooperage Visitor Centre

Dufftown Road, Craigellachie, Aberlour

01340 871108; fax: 01340 881437

Strathisla Distillery

Seafield Avenue, Keith

01542 783044; fax: 0142 783039

Fyvie Castle

Near Turriff 01651 891266; fax: 01651 891107; e-mail: ybell@nts.org.uk

Fyvie Castle: The original 13th-century fortress evolved to become the elegant stately home it is today

2 SIR WALTER SCOTT'S BORDER

Tour

The pioneer of the historical novel in Britain, this Edinburgh lawyer's work featured the Scotland of romance and myth (▶ 8). Scott also established tartan as the Scottish national dress and rediscovered the Scottish crown jewels. This tour explores some of the places associated with Scott, and also takes in the evocative and historic Border Abbeys (▶ 110).

DISTANCE 129km **TIME** Half a day
START/END POINT Abbotsford ✛ 203 E3

1–2

Start at Scott's home beside the River Tweed in **Abbotsford**. Originally a farmhouse, he turned it into the Baronial mansion of today, where his descendants still live. Most of his furniture, historical relics, weapons and armour are on display and the highlight is the great library of 9,000 books. After visiting the house, walk through the gardens and alongside his beloved river.

Take the B6360 out of Abbotsford and after 3.2km turn left on to the A7 to Selkirk. In the Market Square you can visit

Scott's **courtroom** (tel: 01750 20096) where he sat in judgement as the county sheriff. An exhibition tells of his life and writings.

2–3

Return to the A7, turn left and continue via Galashiels to the village of Stow. Turn right on to the B6362 and drive via Lauder to the junction with the A697 and turn right. After 4km turn right again on to the A6089, signposted to Gordon. At the crossroads in Gordon, turn right on to the A6105 and after about

Smailholm Tower shrouded in mist and history

7km turn left on to the B6397 and follow it for 6km to Smailholm. From here follow the signs south on the local road to 16th-century **Smailholm Tower** (tel: 01573 460365), atop a crag beyond Sandyknowe farm, home of Scott's grandfather, and where young Walter convalesced after contracting polio. It was here that he first heard the old tales, ballads and legends that gave him a lifelong love of Scottish history and a taste for adventure. One of his earliest works, inspired by his visit to Smailholm Tower, was a collection of ancient songs and ballads, published as the *Minstrelsy of the Scottish Borders*. A display of tapestries and costumed figures within the tower illustrates that work.

Stow

Lauder

Thirlestane

Bassendean

Gordon

A7

A68

A697

A697

A6089

A6105

B6362

B6361

B6361

Taking a break

Either stop for a picnic on the well-kept lawns of Dryburgh Abbey or try **Burt's Hotel**, Market Square, Melrose (tel: 01896 822285), a popular former coaching inn with a good selection of malt whiskies.

3–4

Return to the B6397 and continue to the junction with the A6089 and turn right for Kelso. Stroll round the wide market square surrounded by fine Georgian buildings then briefly look at the ruins of **Kelso Abbey** (▶ 110). Leave Kelso on the A698 and after 14.5km turn left on to the A68, signposted for **Jedburgh**. Jedburgh is a quaint town of twisting wynds and closes and **Jedburgh Abbey** is superb (▶ 110). Mary, Queen of Scot's House (so called only because she once stayed there) is a fine 16th-century dwelling and contains a copy of her death mask and a rare portrait of the Earl of Bothwell, Mary's chief adviser and third husband.

4–5

Return on the A68 north from Jedburgh and at St Boswells turn right on the B6404. After 2.4km turn left on to the B6356 and shortly afterwards turn left and follow the signs for 12th-century **Dryburgh Abbey** (▶ 110). Dryburgh has the most attractive setting of the Border Abbeys in a valley by the River Tweed with a striking backdrop formed by the Eildon Hills.

5–6

From Dryburgh continue along the B6356 and after about 1.6km you'll come to **Scott's View**, his favourite vista. Take the next local road on the left, keep left at the next junction and fork left. Take the B6360, then immediately join the A68. At the roundabout take the A6091, following the signs for **Melrose** to visit the richest of the abbeys and the burial place of Robert the Bruce's heart (▶ 110).

6–7

Leave Melrose on the B6374, turn left on to the B6360 and right on to the A6091. Finally, turn left on to the A7 and left again, taking the local road and following the signs back to Abbotsford.

George Square is a favourite spot for office workers to eat lunch, but it hosts outdoor festivals as well

THE STREETS OF GLASGOW
3
Walk

If the rest of the world needed awakening to the merits of Glasgow, it came in 1990, the year it was designated 'European City of Culture'.

DISTANCE 10km **TIME** 4 hours
START/END POINT George Square, opposite Queen Street Station (▶ 75) ✚ 201 D3

Further distinction has come from the Arts Council, which honoured it as '1999 UK City of Architecture and Design'.

1–2

You can park in the multistorey car-park behind Queen Street Station. From the south side of the station cross into vibrant George Square. The square is dominated by the Victorian **City Chambers,** built in Italian Renaissance style (▶ 75). Turn left, then left again up Hanover Street and turn right on to Cathedral Street, which gets very busy. At the end of the road cross over into a little square encircling 12th-century **Glasgow Cathedral** (▶ 86), founded by St Mungo, the city's patron saint.

Overlooking it are the elaborate Doric columns and neo-classical temples of the cemetery known as

the Necropolis, modelled on the Père Lachaise cemetery in Paris. Opposite the cathedral, in the High Street, is the gloomy-looking 15th-century **Provand's Lordship,** Glasgow's oldest house (▶ 86)

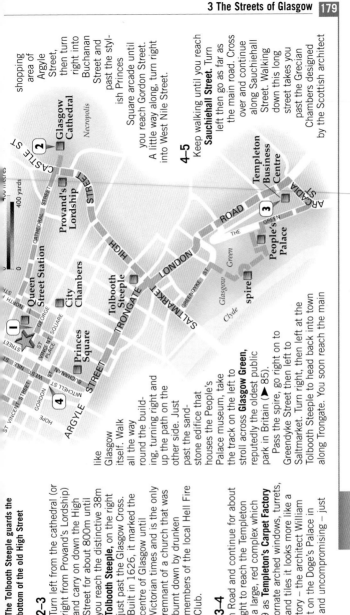

The Tolbooth Steeple guards the bottom of the old High Street

shopping area of Argyle Street, then turn right into Buchanan Street and past the stylish Princes Square arcade until you reach Gordon Street. A little way along, turn right into West Nile Street.

4–5

Keep walking until you reach **Sauchiehall Street.** Turn left then go as far as the main road. Cross over and continue along Sauchiehall Street. Walking down this long street takes you past the Grecian Chambers designed by the Scottish architect

2–3

Turn left from the cathedral (or right from Provand's Lordship) and carry on down the High Street for about 800m until you reach the distinctive 38m **Tolbooth Steeple,** on the right just past the Glasgow Cross. Built in 1626, it marked the centre of Glasgow until Victorian times and is the only remnant of a church that was burnt down by drunken members of the local Hell Fire Club.

like Glasgow itself. Walk all the way round the building, turning right and up the path on the other side. Just past the sandstone edifice that houses the People's Palace museum, take the track on the left to stroll across **Glasgow Green,** reputedly the oldest public park in Britain (▶ 85).

Pass the spire, go right on to Greendyke Street then left to Saltmarket. Turn right, then left at the Tolbooth Steeple to head back into town along Trongate. You soon reach the main

3–4

Cross into London Road and continue for about 1km, then turn right to reach the Templeton Business Centre, a large, red complex which was built in 1889 as **Templeton's Carpet Factory** (▶ 85). With its ornate arched windows, turrets, delicate mosaics and tiles it looks more like a palace than a factory – the architect William Leiper modelled it on the Doge's Palace in Venice. It is bold and uncompromising – just walk up the rather scruffy-looking Renfrew Street. But soon you come to the **Glasgow School of Art** (▶ 87), Charles Rennie Mackintosh's most famous, and some would argue most important, work. Simple and elegant, this is art deco at its most striking.

Go into Dalhousie Street, turn right, then left into Sauchiehall Street. Turn right along Hope Street, then left along St Vincent Street. Follow the road back into George Square to complete your circuit of Glasgow's architectural treasures.

The Mackintosh Room at Glasgow School of Art

Taking a break

Pop into Mackintosh's famous **Willow Tea Room** (▶ 90), at 217 Sauchiehall Street, for a grand selection of tea and cakes.

Alexander 'Greek' Thomson, past Charles Rennie Mackintosh's **Willow Tea Room** (▶ 90) and out into the West End. The city's wealthier residents began to move here in the 19th century, when industrialisation brought rapid growth to Glasgow. The streets become quieter around

here and there are elegant terraces, notably the broad white sweep of Royal Crescent.

5–6

Cross over, then turn right up Kelvin Way past bowling greens and tennis courts.

Just before you reach the large, red sandstone **Kelvingrove Museum** and **Art Gallery** (▶ 81–3), the route takes you over the River Kelvin and gives good views of the Gothic-style Glasgow University buildings. Go over the bridge, turning right at the roundabout into Gibson Street. Follow this road then, at a mini-roundabout, turn right and uphill into Park Avenue, just by Glasgow Caledonian University buildings. Turn left at the top into Park Drive, then right up Cliff Road.

6–7

Turn left and keep walking round to the three towers of Trinity College. Go left into Lynedoch Street and right at the end into Woodlands Road. At traffic lights turn right and walk over the footbridge. The peace of the West End is left on the other side of the motorway as you

Glasgow University is the oldest of the city's three universities

4 THE GREAT GLEN

Tour

DISTANCE 134km along steep and narrow roads in places **TIME** Half a day
START POINT Fort William ☐ 202 B5
END POINT Inverness ☐ 204 C2

The Great Glen was formed over 300 million years ago, and for centuries it has linked the east and west coasts between Inverness and Fort William. Along its rugged 100km is the Caledonian Canal, Thomas Telford's 19th-century engineering masterpiece which linked the four lochs of the glen – Ness, Lochy, Oich and Linnhe – with a series of channels, enabling ships sailing from east to west to avoid the treacherous seas to the north. Its 29 locks raised large sea-going vessels to a height of 32m above sea level at Loch Oich and back to the sea again.

This leisurely drive along the canal's 35-km length has options for the final stretch along Loch Ness from Fort Augustus to Inverness. Alternatively, you could make the journey by boat, or try the Great Glen Walk along towpaths and forest trails, with optional hill climbs to the most impressive views. There's even the two-wheeled option of the Great Glen Cycle Route.

1–2

In Fort William spend some time at the West Highland Museum, which has some excellent Jacobite relics. The Great Glen was Bonnie Prince Charlie's escape route into the Highlands after Culloden. If you have time take a look at **Neptune's Staircase**, the great flight of locks on the Caledonian Canal at Banavie, just west of Fort William on the A830 (▶ 146).

Leave Fort William on the A82 and drive 16km northeast to Spean Bridge. Continue on the A82 for around 1.5km to the junction with the B8004 and stop at the Commando Memorial – massive bronze soldiers commemorating the commandos who trained here and who died in World War II. If you continue on the B8004 and turn right on to the B8005 you'll find **Achnacarry House**, the heart of the Commando Basic Training Centre during the war. It's now home to Cameron of Lochiel,

The Commando Memorial, a poignant reminder of the men who fought and died in WWII

whose ancestor fought for the Jacobite cause, and opposite is the Clan Cameron Museum.

2–3

Return to the A82 and continue northeast via Laggan to Invergarry. Turn left on to the A87 and after 16km turn right on to the A887. In a further 22.5km turn right at Invermoriston.

Hidden gems

Just before the end of the B8005 at Loch Arkaig, stop at the little humpbacked bridge for a view of the **Cia-aig waterfall** with the Witch's Cauldron pool at its foot. The legend is that when some of Cameron's cattle became sick, an old crone living near the Loch was blamed. The men sent to apprehend her found nothing at her house but a wild-looking cat that they put in a sack, weighted and threw in the water. Of course the cat immediately changed into the old woman, who drowned and the curse on the cattle was lifted.

● If you clamber up through the trees here you may find the cave that Bonnie Prince Charlie hid in for two weeks after he escaped from Culloden.

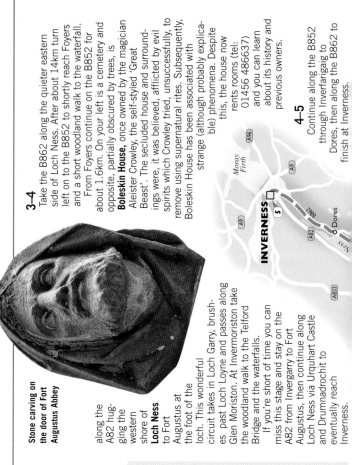

Stone carving on the door of Fort Augustus Abbey

along the A82 hugging the western shore of **Loch Ness** to Fort Augustus at the foot of the loch. This wonderful circuit takes in Loch Garry, brushes past Loch Loyne and passes along Glen Moriston. At Invermoriston take the woodland walk to the Telford Bridge and the waterfalls.

If you're short of time you can miss this stage and stay on the A82 from Invergarry to Fort Augustus, then continue along Loch Ness via Urquhart Castle and Drumnadrochit to eventually reach Inverness.

3–4

Take the B862 along the quieter eastern side of Loch Ness. After about 14km turn left on to the B852 to shortly reach Foyers and a short woodland walk to the waterfall. From Foyers continue on the B852 for about 1.6km. On your left is a cemetery and opposite, partially obscured by trees, is **Boleskin House**, once owned by the magician Aleister Crowley, the self-styled 'Great Beast'. The secluded house and surroundings were, it was believed, afflicted by evil spirits which Crowley tried, unsuccessfully, to remove using supernatural rites. Subsequently, Boleskin House has been associated with strange (although probably explicable) phenomena. Despite this, the house now rents rooms (tel: 01456 486637) and you can learn about its history and previous owners.

4–5

Continue along the B852 through Inverfarigaig to Dores, then along the B862 to finish at Inverness.

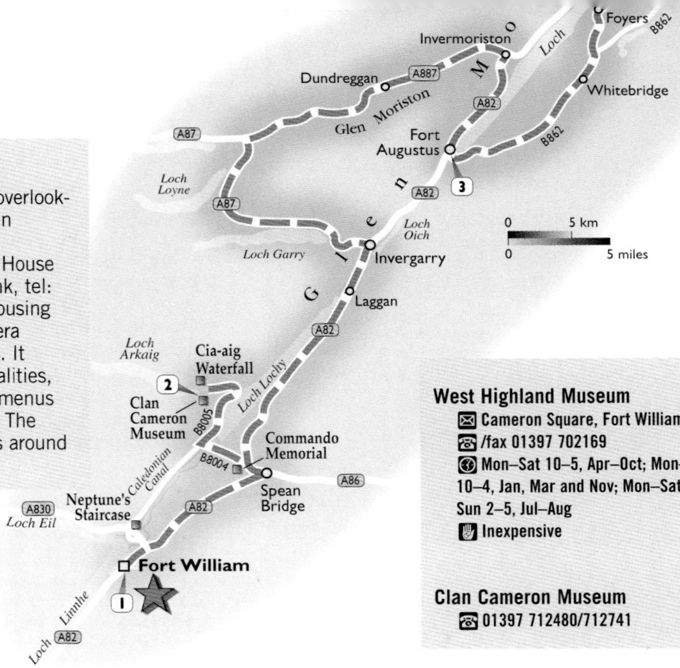

Wade Roads

The B862 follows the line of General George Wade's old military road of 1742. The English soldier Wade was posted to the Highlands to build roads and bridges to help control the Jacobite clans after the 1715 rebellion. For some serious walking the most famous stretch of Wade Road runs from Fort Augustus over the Corrieyairack Pass, in its time the highest road in Britain, and at 19km it's the longest surviving stretch of his original road. It was actually a drovers' route long before Wade's arrival.

🕐 Daily 1:30–5, Easter–mid-Oct; 11–5, Jul–Aug

💷 Inexpensive

Achnacarry House

Not generally open to the public, but Cameron of Lochiel welcomes members of his clan to the house if notified in advance through the museum.

West Highland Museum

✉ Cameron Square, Fort William
☎/fax 01397 702169
🕐 Mon–Sat 10–5, Apr–Oct; Mon–Sat 10–4, Jan, Mar and Nov; Mon–Sat 10–5, Sun 2–5, Jul–Aug
💷 Inexpensive

Clan Cameron Museum

☎ 01397 712480/712741

Taking a break

On the north bank overlooking the River Ness in Inverness is the Glenmoriston Town House Hotel (20 Ness Bank, tel: 01463 223777) housing the elegant La Riviera restaurant (▶ 167). It serves Italian specialities, but the fixed-price menus are excellent value. The Moriston Bar stocks around 100 malts.

5 ULLAPOOL, LOCH BROOM AND THE DROVE ROADS

Walk

DISTANCE 13km, gradual ascent over surfaced paths, and hillside **TIME** 3–4 hours
START/END POINT Safeway supermarket car-park, Ullapool ✚ 204 B3

A herd of cattle being driven through a mountain pass is a familiar scene in countless Hollywood westerns. But instead of blue sky and buckskinned cowboys on horseback, picture grey drizzle and cowboys on foot, wrapped in lengths of woollen plaid cloth. This was the wild west of Scotland, and the cowhands were Highlanders on a drove road herding their cattle to the markets of the South. This walk follows the tracks of drovers bringing cattle from the Islands.

1–2

From the car-park next to the Safeway supermarket, exit to Latheron Lane and turn left into Quay Street. At the Riverside Hotel, where the

This walk offers the most breathtaking views over Loch Broom and Ullapool

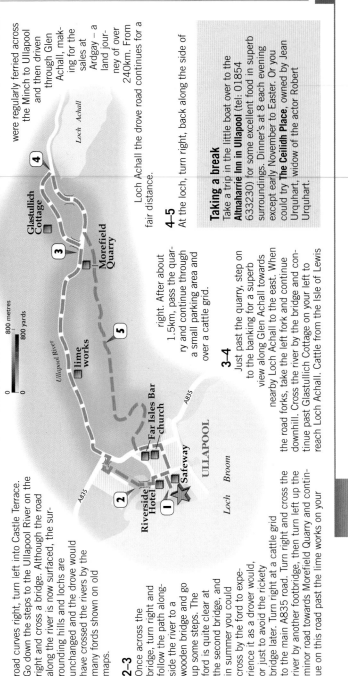

road curves right, turn left into Castle Terrace. Go down the steps to the Ullapool River on the right and cross a bridge. Although the road along the river is now surfaced, the surrounding hills and lochs are unchanged and the drove would have crossed the rivers by the many fords shown on old maps.

2–3

Once across the bridge, turn right and follow the path alongside the river to a wooden bridge and go up some steps. The ford is quite clear at the second bridge, and in summer you could cross by the ford to experience it as a drover would, or just to avoid the rickety bridge later. Turn right at a cattle grid to the main A835 road. Turn right and cross the river by another footbridge, then turn left up the minor road towards Morefield Quarry and continue on this road past the lime works on your right. After about 1.5km, pass the quarry and continue through a small parking area and over a cattle grid.

3–4

Just past the quarry, step on to the banking for a superb view along Glen Achall towards nearby Loch Achall to the east. When the road forks, take the left fork and continue downhill. Cross the river by the bridge and continue past Glastullich Cottage on your left to reach Loch Achall. Cattle from the Isle of Lewis were regularly ferried across the Minch to Ullapool and then driven through Glen Achall, making for the sales at Ardgay – a land journey of over 240km. From Loch Achall the drove road continues for a fair distance.

4–5

At the loch, turn right, back along the side of

Taking a break

Take a trip in the little boat over to the **Altnaharrie Inn in Ullapool** (tel: 01854 633230) for some excellent food in superb surroundings. Dinner's at 8 each evening except early November to Easter. Or you could try **The Ceilidh Place**, owned by Jean Urquhart, widow of the actor Robert Urquhart.

You can visit the mostly uninhabited Summer Isles on Loch Broom by boat during the summer

the loch, to a rickety wooden bridge. It's signed 'Dangerous Bridge', but you can cross with a lot of care. When you reach the cattle grid a little further along, veer left up the side of a line of trees. The path is not obvious at this point, but in about 90m you'll see a deer fence with a kissing gate. Go through the gate and follow the well-defined path along the side of the hill, and through another kissing gate and deer fence. When the path forks, choose the left-hand route up the side of the hill.

Ancient Tracks
Droving in Scotland goes back at least to the 14th century. Meat did not form a substantial part of the Scottish diet, and with no means of sustaining cattle through the harsh winter, they had to be driven south and sold. The drove roads followed the line of least resistance through straths (broad river valleys) and glens. While some of these ancient tracks are now buried under the tarmac of modern highways, many remain as rights of way.

5–6
Follow the rough, winding path down the side of the hill, through a kissing gate and out to the main road (A835). Turn left and follow the road,

passing the Far Isles Bar and Restaurant on the right-hand side, to the church in Ullapool. Turn right here and follow the signs back to the supermarket car-park.

Unromantic Trysts
Moving 16km a day, drovers would sleep beside their animals and rise at dawn for another weary day on the road to the great cattle trysts (fairs) at Ardgay, Muir of Ord, Crieff and Falkirk. The trysts were colourful affairs, with musicians, beggars, pickpockets and pedlars mingling with the drovers and buyers. Drinking dens in makeshift tents enhanced the atmosphere, while huge bubbling cauldrons of broth provided a warming change from weeks of oatmeal. The whole event had the atmosphere of a fair or carnival.

GETTING ADVANCE INFORMATION

Websites
- Scottish Tourist Board:
www.holiday.scotland.net
- British Tourist
Authority:
www.visitbritain.com

In Scotland
Scottish Tourist Board
Edinburgh
☎ 0131 332243

In Ireland
British Tourist Authority
Dublin
☎ 971 725396

BEFORE YOU GO

WHAT YOU NEED

- ● Required
- ○ Suggested
- ▲ Not required
- △ Not applicable

	UK	Germany	USA	Canada	Australia	Ireland	Netherlands	Spain
Passport/National Identity Card	▲	●	●	●	●	▲	▲	●
Visa	▲	▲	▲	▲	▲	▲	▲	▲
Onward or Return Ticket	▲	○	○	○	○	▲	○	○
Health Inoculations (tetanus and polio)	▲	▲	▲	▲	▲	▲	▲	▲
Health Documentation	▲	●	●	●	●	●	●	●
Travel Insurance	○	○	○	○	○	○	○	○
Driving Licence (national)	●	●	●	●	●	●	●	●
Car Insurance Certificate	●	●	△	△	△	●	●	●
Car Registration Document	●	●	△	△	△	●	●	●

WHEN TO GO

Edinburgh

High season | Low season

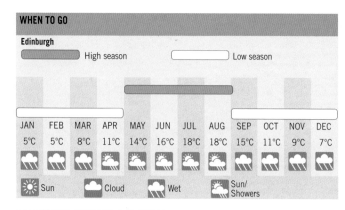

JAN	FEB	MAR	APR	MAY	JUN	JUL	AUG	SEP	OCT	NOV	DEC
5°C	5°C	8°C	11°C	14°C	16°C	18°C	18°C	15°C	11°C	9°C	7°C

☀ Sun ☁ Cloud 🌧 Wet ⛅ Sun/Showers

Temperatures are the **average daily maximum** for each month. The best times of the year for decent weather are in the spring and early summer (April and June) when the countryside looks its best. In high summer (July and August) the weather is changeable and can be cloudy and wet. Generally autumn (September and October) is more settled and there's a better chance of good weather, but nothing is guaranteed. The winter months, from November to March, can be dark, wet and dreich (dreary), but clear sunny days are great, even when cold. Winter can also bring severe conditions to the Highlands and high ground. But no one comes to Scotland for the weather, so consider it a bonus if it's fine, but be prepared for rain. The cities are great to visit any time regardless of the weather.

In the US
British Tourist Authority
New York
☎ 212/986-2266

In Canada
British Tourist Authority
Toronto
☎ 905 405-1720

In Australia
British Tourist Authority
Sydney
☎ (2) 9377 4400

GETTING THERE

By air Glasgow and Edinburgh airports are connected with London by dozens of daily flights. From Heathrow, the main airlines to both airports are British Airways (0845 77 333 77) and British Midland (0870 60 70 555); from Gatwick, BA; from London City, ScotAirways (0870 606 0707); and from Luton, easyJet (0870 600 0000). Edinburgh is also served from Stansted by Go (0845 60 54321) and from London City by British European (08705 676 676). There are flights to Glasgow and Edinburgh from most other cities in the UK and Ireland. To Aberdeen and Inverness, BA flies from Gatwick; BA also flies to Aberdeen from Heathrow, Birmingham, Manchester and Newcastle. Prestwick is served from Stansted by Ryanair (08701 569 569).

The cheapest links from continental Europe are on Ryanair from Beauvais (north of Paris) and Hahn (west of Frankfurt) to Prestwick. There are non-stop flights from leading European cities to Edinburgh and Glasgow. From the US, the only direct link is from New York (Newark) to Glasgow on Continental Airlines; there is a variety of scheduled and charter flights from Canada to Glasgow. Australia and New Zealand flights involve a connection at London.

By rail The main links from England to Scotland are on Virgin Trains (08457 222333) and GNER (08457 225225), both of which serve Edinburgh and Glasgow with extensions to Dundee and Aberdeen; GNER also runs trains through to Inverness. Overnight trains from London are run by Scotrail (08457 550033) to Edinburgh, Glasgow, Aberdeen, Inverness and Fort William.

TIME

In common with the rest of Britain, Scotland follows Greenwich Mean Time (GMT) in winter, but British Summer Time (BST), or daylight saving time (GMT plus one hour) operates from late March until late October.

CURRENCY AND FOREIGN EXCHANGE

Currency The basic unit of currency in the UK is the **pound sterling** (£), divided into 100 pence (p). **Banknotes** come in denominations of £5, £10, £20 and £50. Scotland, unlike the rest of the UK, also has £1 notes. Notes are produced by Scottish banks and therefore feature different designs to those originating in England. Note that although Scottish banknotes are legal tender elsewhere in Britain, some places may be reluctant to accept them. You can, of course, change them at any bank. There are **coins** for 1p and 2p (copper), 5p, 10p, 20p and 50p (silver), £1 (gold-coloured) and £2 (silver and gold-coloured).

Sterling and US dollar **travellers' cheques** are the safest and most convenient way to carry money. All major credit cards are recognised.

Exchange All banks offer exchange facilities, and bureaux de change are common in Glasgow and Edinburgh, at airports and larger rail stations. They often operate longer hours than banks but offer poorer rates of exchange. Most banks have cashpoints for cash withdrawals, and you'll also find them at airports, railway stations and in larger supermarkets and filling stations.

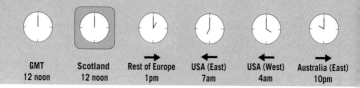

GMT 12 noon	Scotland 12 noon	→ Rest of Europe 1pm	← USA (East) 7am	← USA (West) 4am	→ Australia (East) 10pm

WHEN YOU ARE THERE

CLOTHING SIZES

UK	Rest of Europe	USA	
36	46	36	
38	48	38	
40	50	40	Suits
42	52	42	
44	54	44	
46	56	46	
7	41	8	
7.5	42	8.5	
8.5	43	9.5	Shoes
9.5	44	10.5	
10.5	45	11.5	
11	46	12	
14.5	37	14.5	
15	38	15	
15.5	39/40	15.5	Shirts
16	41	16	
16.5	42	16.5	
17	43	17	
8	34	6	
10	36	8	
12	38	10	Dresses
14	40	12	
16	42	14	
18	44	16	
4.5	38	6	
5	38	6.5	
5.5	39	7	Shoes
6	39	7.5	
6.5	40	8	
7	41	8.5	

NATIONAL HOLIDAYS

1 Jan	New Year's Day
2 Jan	New Year's Holiday
Mar/Apr	Good Friday, Easter Monday
First Mon May	May Day
Last Mon May	Bank Holiday
Last Mon Aug	Bank Holiday
25 Dec	Christmas Day
26 Dec	Boxing Day

When a national holidays falls on a weekend, the following Monday is observed as the holiday. The 2 Jan holiday is movable depending on when the New Year's Day holiday is taken.

In common with the rest of Britain, many large shops remain open in Scotland, particularly if the holiday falls in the summer. Likewise, tourist attractions are most popular over bank holiday weekends.

OPENING HOURS

○ Shops ● Post Offices
● Offices ● Museums/Monuments
● Banks ● Pharmacies

8am 9am 10am noon 1pm 2pm 4pm 5pm 7pm

□ Day   ■ Midday   □ Evening

These are general times. Shops remain open at lunchtime and on Sundays in larger towns, cities and holiday resorts. Supermarkets open seven days a week and closing times may be between 7pm and 10pm, but some now offer 24-hour opening. In rural areas shops may close for an hour at lunchtime, for one afternoon each week and all day Sunday. There is strict Sunday observance in the Highlands and Islands, and you may find that attractions are closed on Sundays in the summer.

PERSONAL SAFETY

Theft from cars is common in Scottish cities, as are bag-snatching and pick-pocketing. Report any crime to the police, and ask for a written report for an insurance claim. Otherwise, take reasonable precautions:

- Never leave anything of value in your car.
- Keep passports, tickets and valuables in the hotel safe.
- Don't carry money, credit cards or valuables in a bumbag – this marks you out as a tourist and is a magnet for pickpockets.
- Don't walk alone in dimly lit areas at night.

Police assistance:
☎ **999** from any phone

TELEPHONES

can only be used with prepaid phone cards, available from newsagents, post offices and supermarkets. Some phones also take credit cards. In rural areas you'll come across the occasional old red telephone box, but they are now few and far between. Mobile phones have also affected availability.

Public telephones are found on streets and in bars, hotels and restaurants. Some accept only 10p, 20p, 50p, £1 and £2 coins, while others

International Dialling Codes
Dial 00 followed by

USA:	1
Ireland:	353
Australia:	61
Germany:	49
Netherlands:	31
Spain:	34

POST

Towns and many large villages have at least one post office. Opening hours are Mon–Fri 9–5:30, Sat 9–12:30, closed Sun; small branches close for lunch. You can also buy stamps in supermarkets, filling stations, newsagents and shops selling postcards.

ELECTRICITY

In common with the rest of the UK, the power supply is 240 volts (50Hz) AC.

Sockets take square three-pin plugs for 3, 5 and 13 amp fused appliances. All visitors from other countries will need an adaptor, which are widely available.

TIPS/GRATUITIES

As a general guide:
Yes ✓   No ✗

Restaurants (if service not included)	✓	10%
Cafés / Bar meals	✓	10%
Tour guides	✓	£1
Hairdressers	✓	£1–2
Taxis	✓	10%
Chambermaids	✓	£2 a day
Porters	✓	£1 per bag

CONSULATES and HIGH COMMISSIONS

 USA
☎ 0131 556 8315

 Spain
☎ 0131 220 1843

 Germany
☎ 0131 337 2323

 Netherlands
☎ 0131 2203226

 New Zealand
☎ 0131 225 795

HEALTH

 Insurance European Union nationals (EU) and certain other countries are entitled to free emergency medical treatment in the UK with the relevant documentation; private medical insurance is still advised and is essential for all other visitors.

 Dental Services Dental treatment is very limited under the National Health Service (NHS) scheme and even EU nationals will probably have to pay. However, your private medical insurance should cover dental treatment. There are dentists in most small towns.

 Weather Even in a country with a reputation for so much rain it's still possible to get sunburn and sunstroke, particularly during the summer months. Avoid prolonged exposure to the sun, and use sunblock or cover up.

 Drugs Prescription and non-prescription drugs and treatments are available from pharmacies. Over-the-counter items are also widely available in supermarkets, filling stations and other shops such as newsagents. Pharmacies tend to keep shop hours but operate a rota system to ensure there is usually late opening somewhere nearby.

 Safe Water Tap water is safe to drink, particularly in rural areas and the Highlands. Mineral water is cheap and readily available.

CONCESSIONS

Students Holders of an International Student Identity Card (ISIC) are often entitled to a discount at museums and galleries. Some places also accept a matriculation or NUS card (university/college ID), if it has a photo. The Young Person's Railcard, available from railway stations to those under 26, gives a 34 per cent discount on many rail fares in Britain, and the National Express Discount Card allows 30 per cent off coach fares.
Senior Citizens get some reductions on services and at museums and galleries on proof of age. The Senior's railcard provides a discount similar to that for young people, and the National Express card is also available for coach travel.

TRAVELLING WITH A DISABILITY

Increasing numbers of accommodation and other public buildings are being adapted or purpose-built to cater for travellers with disabilities, but much remains to be done, so make sure you establish what facilities are available when booking accommodation.

CHILDREN

Well-behaved children are generally made welcome everywhere. Pubs and bars operate individual admission policies and may admit children during the day and early evening. Concessions on transport and entrance fees are generally available.

TOILETS

Public toilets are mainly clean and safe, especially in shopping malls, large supermarkets, department stores, chain bookshops etc. Some are coin entry, particularly in railway stations (usually 10p or 20p) or have an attendant, while others are free.

LOST PROPERTY

You should report the loss of property to the nearest police station and get a signed and dated copy of the paperwork for insurance claims. Items lost on public transport should be reported to the operator.

Abbotsford 176
Aberdeen 162
Aberdeen Fish
    Market 162
Aberdeen Maritime
    Museum 162
Aberdeen
    Satrosphere 162
Aberfoyle 128
accommodation
    36–7
    see also
    individual areas
Achnacarry House
    181–2, 183
admission charges 33
airports and air
    travel 32, 35, 189
Alloway 104, 105,
    106
Alyth 131
Angus Glens 131
Anstruther 132
Arisaig 147
Arnol Blackhouse
    153
Arran 109
Arrochar 122
Arthur's Seat 60
Aviemore 157

Balmaha 124
Balquhidder 120,
    129
Banavie 146
banks 189, 190
Bannockburn 126–7
Barra 151
Barrack Street
    Museum 131
The Barras 85–6
Barrie, J M 8
bed and breakfast
    36, 37
Bell's Cherrybank
    Garden 130
Ben Lomond 122
Benbecula 151
Biggar 108–9
    Biggar Gasworks
        Museum 109
    Biggar Puppet
        Theatre 109
    Gladstone Court
        98, 108–9
    Greenhill
        Covenanters
        Museum 109
    Moat Park
        Heritage Centre
        108, 109
Birnam Wood 130
Black Watch
    Museum 130
Black Woods of
    Rannoch 141

Boleskine House 182
Bonnie Prince
    Charlie 110, 146,
    147, 182
Bowmore 160
Branklyn Garden 130
Brig o' Doon 104, 105
British Golf
    Museum 132
Brodick Castle 109
Buachaille Etive
    Mór 145
Bucinch 123
Burns, Robert 104–7
Burns Country
    104–7
Burns' House
    Museum 106
Burns' Monument
    106
Burrell Collection
    70, 72–4
buses 33, 34

Cairngorms 156–9
Caledonian Canal
    146, 181
Callander 127
Calton Hill 60
Camera Obscura 60
camping and
    caravanning 37
car hire 35
Castle Trail 172
Ceardach 123
ceilidhs 13
Celtic Connections
    Festival 13
Central Scotland
    117–38
    accommodation
    136–7
    Angus Glens 131
    RRS *Discovery*
        121, 132
    Dundee 131–2
    Dunkeld 130
    East Neuk of Fife
        132
    eating out 134–5
    entertainment
        138
    Loch Lomond
        122–5
    map 118–19
    Perth 119, 130
    St Andrews 132,
        133
    Scone Palace
        121, 130–1
    Scottish Fisheries
        Museum 133
    Secret Bunker 133
    shopping 138
    Stirling 126–7,
        128

three-day
    itinerary 120
Trossachs 127–8
children 192
Cia-aig Waterfall
    182
Clan Cameron
    Museum 182, 183
climate and seasons
    188
clothing sizes 190
Cobb Memorial 155
Commando
    Memorial 181
Connery, Sir Sean 7
consulates and high
    commissions 192
Corrievreckan
    Whirlpool 160
Coylumbridge 159
Crail 118, 132
credit cards 189
crofting 14–15
Cuillins 150
Culloden Moor 162
Culzean Castle and
    Country Park 99,
    109
currency 189

dental services 192
Dewar, Donald 30
disabilities,
    travellers with
    192
RRS *Discovery* 121,
    132
Doyle, Sir Arthur
    Conan 8, 10
driving 35, 188
drove roads 184–6
drugs and
    medicines 192
Drumnadrochit 155
Dryburgh Abbey
    110, 177
Dumfries 105–6
Dun Carloway
    Broch 152–3
Dundee 131–2
    Barrack Street
        Museum 131
    Dundee
        Contemporary
        Arts 131–2
    McManus
        Galleries 131
    Mills Observatory
        131
    St Mary's Tower
        131
    Verdant Works
        132
Dunkeld 130
Dunvegan Castle
    152, 153

East Neuk of Fife 132
eating out 38–9
    see also
    individual areas
Edinburgh 43–66
    accommodation
        63–4
    Arthur's Seat 60
    Calton Hill 60
    Camera Obscura
        60
    eating out 61–2
    Edinburgh Castle
        46, 48–51
    entertainment 66
    Georgian House
        56
    Gladstone's Land
        57
    Grassmarket 58
    literary pub tours
        9
    map 44–5
    Mary King's
        Close 58–9
    Museum of
        Scotland 52–4
    Nelson's
        Monument 51
    New Town 55–7
    Old Observatory
        60
    one o'clock gun
        50, 51
    one-day itinerary
        46–7
    Our Dynamic
        Earth 59
    Palace of
        Holyroodhouse
        45, 59–60
    People's Story 59
    Pets' Cemetery
        51
    Rebus Tours 10
    Royal Yacht
        Britannia 60
    St Giles Cathedral
        58
    Salisbury Crags 60
    Scotch Whisky
        Heritage
        Centre 50
    Scottish National
        War Memorial
        49
    Scottish
        Parliament 29,
        30, 58
    Scottish United
        Services
        Museum 51
    Shaping a Nation
        6
    shopping 65
    tourist
        information 33

Witches' Well 51
Writers' Museum 9
Edinburgh Airport 32
Edinburgh Festival 21–2
Edzell 131
electricity 191
emergency telephone numbers 191
England–Scotland relationship 27–30
entertainment 40–2
see also individual areas

Falls of Braan 130
Falls of Clyde 103
famous Scots 6–7
ferry services 34
festivals and events 42
Fingal's Cave 161
fishing 41
food and drink 23–6, 38–9, 40
see also eating out
Fort William 146, 148, 181
West Highland Museum 181, 183
Foyers 182
Fyvie Castle 174–5

Georgian House 56
Gladstone Court 98, 108–9
Gladstone's Land 57
Glasgow 67–94, 178–80
accommodation 91–2
The Barras 85–6
Botanic Gardens 88
Burrell Collection 70, 72–4
Celtic Connections Festival 13
eating out 89–90
entertainment 94
Gallery of Modern Art 87
Glasgow Botanic Gardens 69, 88
Glasgow Cathedral 86, 178
Glasgow City Chambers 70, 75–6, 178
Glasgow Green 85, 179

Glasgow School of Art 19–20, 87–8, 180
SV *Glenlee* 88
Holmwood House 84
House for an Art Lover 84–5
Hutcheson's Hall 76
Italian Centre 76
Kelvingrove Museum and Art Gallery 81–3
Lighthouse 87
literary pub tours 9
maps 68–9, 178–9
Merchant City 75–7
Museum of Transport 88
one-day itinerary 70–1
People's Palace 85
Provand's Lordship 86, 178
St Mungo Museum of Religious Life and Art 86
Scotland Street School 85
shopping 93
Templeton's Carpet Factory 19, 85, 179
Tenement House 71, 78–80
Tolbooth Steeple 179
tourist information 33
Trades House 76
Wellpark Brewery 86
Willow Tea Room 87
Winter Gardens 85
Glasgow International Airport 32
Glasgow Prestwick International Airport 32
Glasgow Style 18–20
Glencoe 142, 144–5
Glenfiddich Distillery 173, 174, 175
Glenfinnan Monument 146
Glenfinnan Railway Museum 146
SV *Glenlee* 88
golf 16–17, 41, 132

Grantown-on-Spey 159
Grassmarket 58
Great Glen 181–3
Greenhill Covenanters Museum 109
Gruinart 160

Haddington 111
Harris 150, 151–2
health 188, 192
Hebrides 149–51
Highland Folk Museum 158
Highlands and Islands 139–70
Aberdeen 162
accommodation 168–9
Cairngorms 156–9
Culloden Moor 162
eating out 166–7
entertainment 170
five-day itinerary 142–3
Glencoe 142, 144–5
Inverness 161–2
Iona 161
Islay 160
Jura 160
Loch Ness 154–5
map 140–1
Mousa Broch 165
Mull 161
Orkney 163–4
Road to the Isles 146–7
Shetland 165
shopping 170
Skye and the Western Isles 149–53
hiking and climbing 41, 122, 159
Hill House 20
Holmwood House 84
Holy Isle 109
Honours of Scotland 48
hotels 36
see also individual areas
House for an Art Lover 84–5
Huntly Castle 172, 175
Hutcheson's Hall 76

Inchcailloch 123
Inchfad 123
Inchgalbraith 123

Inchmahome 128
Inchmurrin 123
insurance 188, 192
Invermoriston 155, 182
Inverness 161–2
Inverness Castle 143, 161
Kiltmaker Centre 162
Iona 161
Islay 160
Italian Chapel 164

Jacobite Steam Train 146, 148
Jarlshof 165
Jedburgh 177
Jedburgh Abbey 110, 177
Jura 160
Corrievreckan Whirlpool 160
Isle of Jura Distillery 160
Paps of Jura 160

Kelso 177
Kelso Abbey 110, 177
Kelvingrove Museum and Art Gallery 81–3
Kilmarnock 104–5
Kilt Rock 149
Kiltmaker Centre 162
Kingussie 158
Kirkoswald 104
Kirriemuir 131
Kylerhea Otter Haven 150

Lairig Ghru 159
Lake of Menteith 128
Lead Mining, Museum of 110
Leadhills Gold Panning 109–10
Lerwick 165
Lewis 151, 152–3
Arnol Blackhouse 153
Dun Carloway Broch 152–3
Lewis Loom Centre 153, 170
Standing Stones of Calanais 150–1, 152, 153
licensing laws 39
Lighthouse 87

literary Scotland 8–11
Loch an Eilein 157
Loch Garten 159
Loch Insh 157
Loch Katrine 120, 129
Loch Leven 145
Loch Lomond 122–5
Loch Morlich Water Sport Centre 156
Loch Nan Uamh 147
Loch Ness 154–5
lost property 192
Lower City Mills 130
Luib Folk Museum 152
Luss 122

Machrie Moor 108, 109
Mackintosh, Charles Rennie 18, 19–20, 84–5, 87
McManus Galleries 131
Maes Howe 164
Mallaig 147
Malt Whisky Trail 172
Marine World 147, 148
Mary King's Close 58–9
Mary, Queen of Scots 60, 128
Mary Queen of Scots' House 177
Mauchline 105, 106
Melrose Abbey 110, 177
Merchant City 75–7
Military Tattoo 22
Mills Mount Battery 51
Mills Observatory 131
Moat Park Heritage Centre 108, 109
money 189
Mons Meg 50
Morar 147, 148
Mousa Broch 165
Mull 161
Tobermory 161
Toronsay Castle 161
Munro-bagging 124
museum opening hours 190
music and dance 12–13, 41, 165
national holidays 190

Nelson's Monument 51
Neptune's Staircase 146, 147, 181
New Lanark 97, 100–3
New Town, Edinburgh 55–7
North and South Uist 151

oats 23
Old Man of Hoy 140
Old Man of Storr 149
Old Observatory 60
Old Town Jail 126
opening hours 190
Orkney 163–4
    Italian Chapel 164
    Maes Howe 164
    Ring of Brodgar 163
    St Magnus Cathedral 164
    Skara Brae 163
    Stones of Stenness 163
ospreys 159
Ossian's Cave 130
Ossian's Hall 130
Our Dynamic Earth 59
Owen, Robert 100, 101

Palace of Holyroodhouse 45, 59–60
passports and visas 188
People's Palace 85
People's Story 59
personal safety 191
Perth 119, 130
    Bell's Cherrybank Garden 130
    Black Watch Museum 130
    Branklyn Garden 130
    Lower City Mills 130
Pets' Cemetery 51
pharmacies 190, 192
Pittenweem 132, 133
police 191
Poosie Nancie's Tavern 105
postal services 190–1
Prince's Cairn 147
Provand's Lordship 86, 178
public transport 32–3, 34–5
pubs and clubs 39, 41

Queen Elizabeth Forest Park 118, 128
Quiraing 149

Raasay 150, 153
Rannoch Moor 145
Ring of Brodgar 163
Road to the Isles 146–7
Rob Roy 118, 127, 129
Rob Roy and the Trossachs Visitor Centre 127, 128
Robert the Bruce 27, 28–9, 97, 110, 132
Robert Burns National Heritage Park 104, 106
Rosslyn Chapel 96, 99, 111
Rothiemurchus Estate 157–8
Rowling, J K 11
Royal and Ancient Golf Club 16, 132
Royal Yacht Britannia 60
Ruthven Barracks 158

St Andrews 132, 133
    British Golf Museum 132
    Royal and Ancient Golf Club 16, 132
    Sea Life Centre 133
St Giles Cathedral 58
St Magnus Cathedral 164
St Monans 132
St Mungo Museum of Religious Life and Art 86
Salisbury Crags 60
Scapa Flow 164
Scone Palace 121, 130–1
Scotch Whisky Heritage Centre 50
Scotland, Museum of 52–4
Scotland Street School Museum 85
Scott, Robert Falcon 132
Scott, Sir Walter 8, 110, 129, 176
Scottish Fisheries Museum 133
Scottish National War Memorial 49

Scottish Parliament 29, 30, 58
Scottish United Services Museum 51
Scottish Wool Centre 128
Scott's View 177
Sea Life Centre 133
Secret Bunker 133
Selkirk 176
senior citizens 192
Shaping a Nation 6
Shetland 165
    Jarlshof 165
    Lerwick 165
    Up Helly Aa Exhibition 165
shopping 40, 190
Signal Rock 145
Sir Walter Scott 129
Skara Brae 163
Skye 149–51
    Cuillins 150
    Dunvegan Castle 152, 153
    Kilt Rock 149
    Kylerhea Otter Haven 150
    Luib Folk Museum 152
    Old Man of Storr 149
    Quiraing 149
    Skye Museum of Island Life 150, 153
    Skye Serpentarium 150–1, 153
    Talisker Whisky Distillery 151
    Trotternish Peninsula 149
Smailholm Tower 176
South of Scotland 95–116
    accommodation 114–15
    Arran 109
    Biggar 108–9
    Border abbeys 110
    Burns Country 104–7
    Culzean Castle and Country Park 99, 109
    eating out 112–13
    entertainment 116
    Falls of Clyde 103
    Haddington 111
    Leadhills Gold Panning 109–10
    map 96–7
    New Lanark 97, 100–3

Rosslyn Chapel
96, 99, 111
shopping 116
Summerlee
Heritage Park
108
three-day
itinerary 98–9
Traquair 110–11
Speyside Cooperage
173, 175
sport and lesiure
41–2
Staffa 161
Standing Stones of
Calanais 150–3
Stevenson, Robert
Louis 8, 57
Stirling 126–7, 128
Bannockburn
126–7
Old Stirling
Bridge 126, 127
Old Town Jail 126
Stirling Castle 126
Wallace Monument
28, 126

Stone of Destiny 27,
48
Stones of Stenness
163
Strathisla Distillery
173–4, 175
students and young
travellers 192
Summerlee Heritage
Park 108
sun safety 192

Talisker Whisky
Distillery 151
Tarbet 122
taxis 35
Teddy Melrose
Museum 111
telephones 191
Templeton's Carpet
Factory 19, 85, 179
Tenement House 71,
78–80
theatre 41
time differences
189, 190

tipping 191
Tobermory 161
toilets 192
Tolbooth Steeple
179
Toronsay Castle
161
tourist information
33, 188–9
Trades House 76
train services 32–3,
34, 189
Transport, Museum
of 88
Traquair 110–11
travellers' cheques
189
Trossachs 127–8
Trotternish
Peninsula 149
Ullapool 184–5
Up Helly Aa
Exhibition 165
Urquhart Castle 155

Verdant Works 132

Wade Bridge 158
Wade Road 158, 183
Wallace Monument
28, 126
Wallace, Sir William
28, 126
Wanlockhead 109
websites 188
Wellpark Brewery
86
West Highland
Museum 181, 183
West Highland Way
122
Western Isles
151–3
whisky 25–6, 39,
173–4
Wigtown 10
Willow Tea Room 87
Winter Gardens 85
Witches' Well 51
wreck diving 164
Writers' Museum 9

youth hostels 37

Picture credits

Abbreviations for terms appearing below: (t) top; (b) bottom; (l) left; (r) right; (c) centre.

Front and back cover: (t) AA Photo Library/E Ellington; (ct) Ian Dawson Landscape; (cb) AA Photo Library/K Paterson; (b) AA Photo Library.

Aberdeen & Grampian Tourist Board 174(l), 174(r); Marius Alexander Photo Library 12(l), 13(t), 13(r), 21(l), 21(r), 22(t); Ian Atkinson 25(cb); Anthony Blake Photo Library 23(t) (Anthony Blake), 23(b) (Joff Lee), 24(t) (Martin Brigg), 24(b) (Philip Wilkins); Bloomsbury Publishing Inc. 11(l); Bridgeman Art Library 7(tl) Alexander Graham Bell in his laboratory by Dean Cornwell (1892-1960), (Private Collection), 8(l) Sir Walter Scott (1771-1832), 1822 by Sir Henry Raeburn (1756-1823), (Scottish National Portrait Gallery, Edinburgh, Scotland), 9(c) Robert Louis Stevenson (1850-94), 1892 by Count Girolamo Pieri Nerli (1853-1926), (Scottish National Portrait Gallery, Edinburgh, Scotland), 28(r) Robert the Bruce and De Bohun (oil on canvas) by Eric Harald Macbeth Robertson (1887-1941), (The Fleming-Wyfold Art Foundation); Bruce Coleman Collection 158(t); Corbis 2(i) (AFP), 5 (AFP), 7(r) (AFP), 14/15 (Wild Country), 14(t) (Hulton Deutsch), 14(c) (Hulton Deutsch), 15(t) (Tony Hamblin, Frank Lane Picture Agency), 15(c) (Patrick Ward), 22(b) (Peter Turnley), 28/9 (AFP), 30(t) (AFP); Mary Evans Picture Library 6, 8(r), 8(b), 9(tr), 9(b), 16/17, 17(c), 100; Glasgow Museums 72(b), 73, 74, 83; Glasgow School of Art Enterprises Ltd 88, 180(r); Greater Glasgow & Clyde Valley Tourist Board 12(r), 13(l) (Gordon Hotchkiss); Robert Harding Picture Library 45, 48/9, 51; Historic Scotland 49; Image Bank 3(iii), 139; Images Colour Library 18, 21(background), 22(c); David Morrison 25(ct), 26(b), 27; National Trust for Scotland 80, 175; Popperfoto 2(i), 5, 7(bl), 29; Rex Features Ltd 10, 11(r), 30(b); Scottish Highland Photo Library 28(l), 142(b), 143(t), 144, 145, 148, 156/7, 165, 186; Scotland in Focus 3(iv), 77, 97(b), 103, 106/7, 108, 110/1, 124, 127(t), 128, 129(t), 140, 142(c), 143(b); 150/1, 152, 159, 162, 163, 164, 171, 176, 184; Phil Sheldon Golf Picture Library 17(t); Trustees of the National Museums of Scotland 52, 53(t), 53(b), 54; S J Whitehorne 20(b), 97(t), 101(t), 101(b), 102, 119(t), 119(b), 122/3, 125, 149, 151, 156. All remaining pictures are held in the Association's own library (AA PHOTO LIBRARY) with contributions from the following photographers:
M Alexander 2(iv), 3(i), 67, 95, 96, 98, 99(b), 104(t), 107; J Carnie 146; S L Day 3(ii), 26(t), 117, 118, 120(c), 120(b), 121(b), 126, 127(b), 129(b), 130, 133, 141, 147(t), 181; E Ellington 25(t), 172; R G Elliott 56(b), 160, 161; S Gibson 20(cr), 78, 82(r), 85; J Henderson 154/5, 158(b); K Paterson 2(ii), 2(iii), 31, 43, 44, 46(t), 46(b), 47(t), 47(c), 48, 50, 55, 56(t), 57, 58, 59(t), 59(b), 60, 104(b), 105, 104/5, 106, 110, 121(c), 147(b), 191(t), 191(c), 191(b); R Richards 182; P Sharpe 99(t); S J Whitehorne 3(v), 18/9(t), 18/9(b), 18/9(cb), 19, 69, 70(t), 70(b), 71(t), 71(c), 72(t), 75, 76, 79(t), 79(b), 81, 82(l), 84, 86, 87, 178, 179, 180(l), 187.

Acknowledgements

The authors would like to thank the following individuals and organisations for their help during the research of this book:
Caroline Keith, Scottish Tourist Board; Mike Blair, Calmac; Alan Mclean, Virgin Trains; John Yellowlees, Scotrail; Andy Naylor, GNER; Sheila Hamilton, Dan McGrory; Logonair.

Atlas

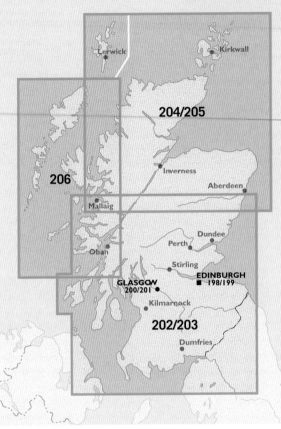

Lerwick

Kirkwall

204/205

206

Inverness

Aberdeen

Mallaig

Dundee

Perth

Oban

Stirling

EDINBURGH
■ 198/199

GLASGOW
200/201 ●

Kilmarnock

202/203

Dumfries

Regional Maps

| 0 | 10 | 20 | 30 | 40 km |

| 0 | 10 | 20 miles |

—·—·— National boundary

═══════ Motorway

────── Main road

────── Other road

·········· Trail

—·—·— Ferry

☐ City

▫ Major town

◦ Large town

◦ Town, village

▒ Built-up area

■ Place of interest

✈ Airport

City Plans

| 0 | 100 | 200 | 300 metres |

| 0 | 100 | 200 | 300 yards |

──────── Pedestrian street

▨ Important building

▨ Featured place of interest

[i] Information

● Subway station

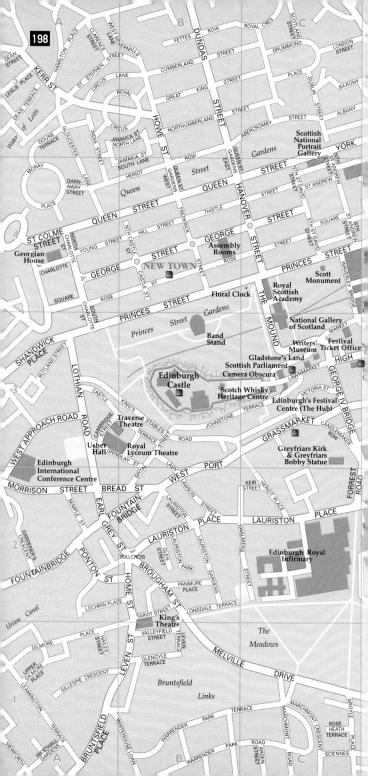

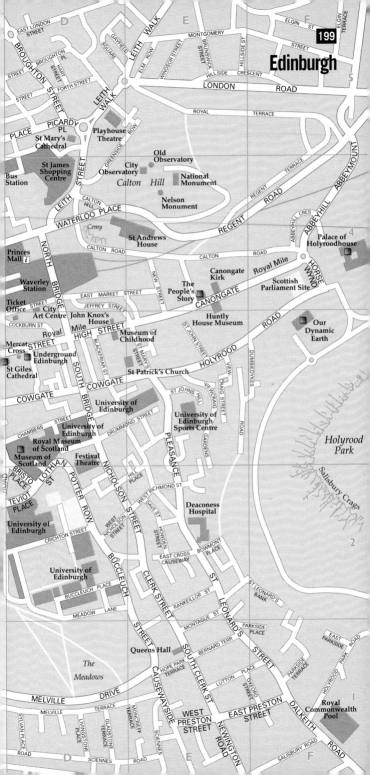

Edinburgh

EAST LONDON STREET

BROUGHTON STREET

LEITH WALK

GAYFIELD SQUARE

ELM ROW

MONTGOMERY STREET

BRUNSWICK STREET

HILLSIDE ST

ELGIN ST

ELGIN TERRACE

BROUGHTON STREET

HART STREET

FORTH STREET

WINDSOR STREET

HILLSIDE CRESCENT

LONDON ROAD

PICARDY PL

Playhouse Theatre

ROYAL TERRACE

St Mary's Cathedral

GREENSIDE ROW

Old Observatory

St James Shopping Centre

City Observatory

Calton Hill

National Monument

TERRACE

Bus Station

LEITH STREET

NORTH BRIDGE

CALTON HILL

Nelson Monument

REGENT ROAD

ABBEYMOUNT

Princes Mall ℹ

WATERLOO PLACE

Cemy

St Andrews House

CALTON ROAD

CALTON ROAD

ABBEYHILL CRES

ABBEYHILL

Palace of Holyroodhouse

4

Waverley Station

EAST MARKET STREET

NEW STREET

The People's Story

Canongate Kirk

CANONGATE

Royal Mile

HORSE WYND

Scottish Parliament Site

Ticket Office

City Art Centre

JEFFREY STREET

John Knox's House

HIGH STREET

Huntly House Museum

Our Dynamic Earth

Royal Mile

COCKBURN ST

Museum of Childhood

BLACKFRIAR ST

ST MARY'S STREET

ST JOHN STREET

HOLYROOD ROAD

DUMBIEDYKES

Mercat Cross

SOUTH BRIDGE

St Patrick's Church

St Giles Cathedral

Underground Edinburgh

COWGATE

JOHNS HILL

VIEWCRAIG STREET

CRAIG STREET

COWGATE

University of Edinburgh

DRUMMOND STREET

University of Edinburgh Sports Centre

Holyrood Park

CHAMBERS STREET

University of Edinburgh

PLEASANCE

GARDENS

Royal Museum of Scotland

Museum of Scotland

Festival Theatre

NICHOLSON STREET

HILL PLACE

Salisbury Crags

BRISTO PLACE

LOTHIAN ST

POTTER ROW

WEST RICHMOND ST

Deaconess Hospital

2

TEVIOT PLACE

CRICHTON STREET

WEST NICHOLSON STREET

DAVIE ST

HOWDEN STREET

University of Edinburgh

BUCCLEUCH PLACE

BUCCLEUCH STREET

EAST CROSS CAUSEWAY

BOWMONT PLACE

ST LEONARD'S

RANKEILLOR ST

ST LEONARD'S STREET

BANK

EAST PARKSIDE

University of Edinburgh

MEADOW LANE

MONTAGUE STREET

PARKSIDE PLACE

HOLYROOD PARK ROAD

The Meadows

CLERK STREET

Queens Hall

SOUTH CLERK ST

BERNARD TERR

PARKSIDE TERRACE

Royal Commonwealth Pool

HOPE PARK TERRACE

LUTTON PLACE

OXFORD STREET

1

MELVILLE DRIVE

CAUSEWAYSIDE

WEST PRESTON STREET

EAST PRESTON STREET

DALKEITH ROAD

MELVILLE TERRACE

MONCRIEFF TERRACE

GLADSTONE TERRACE

SCIENNES

NEWINGTON ROAD

SYLVAN PLACE

LIVINGSTONE PLACE

ROAD

SCIENNES

ROAD

SALISBURY ROAD

D

E

F

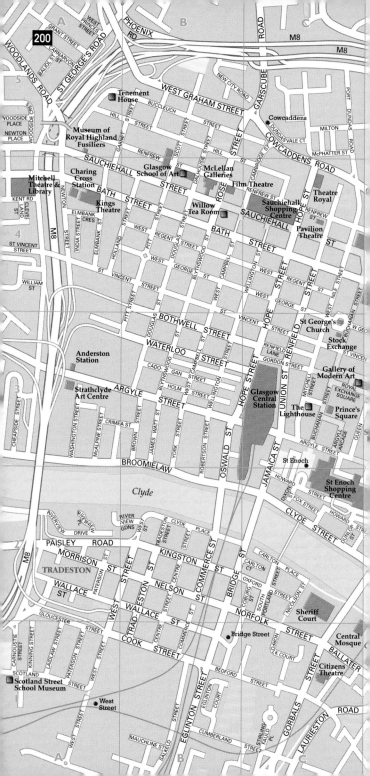

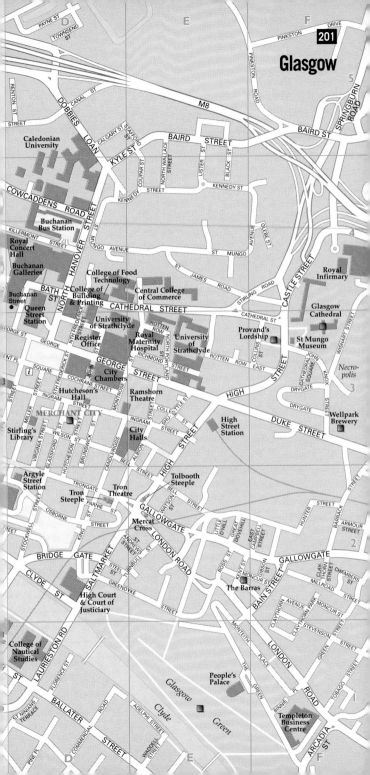

Glasgow

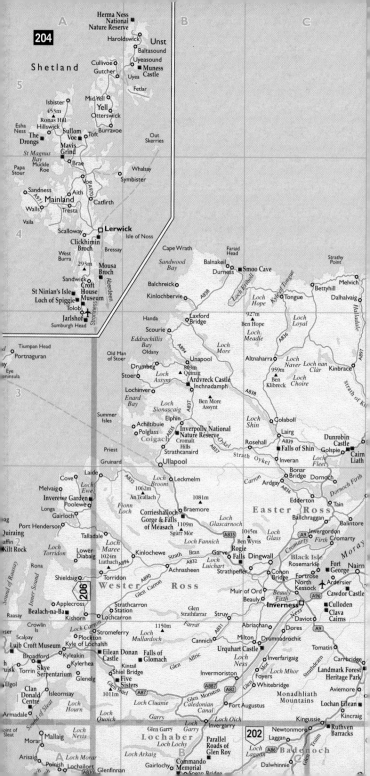

D   E   F

Lerwick

Noltland Castle
Westray
The North Sound
Papa
Westray
North
Ronaldsay

5

Westray
Firth
Rapness
Fara
Sanday
Kettletoft

Rousay
Brinyan
Eday
Egilsay
Wyre
Backaland
Stronsay
Whitehall
Sanday Sound

Stronsay
Firth
Stronsay

Birsay
Dounby
Loch of
Shapinsay
Auskerry

Marwick Head Nature Reserve
Harray
Skara Brae
Maes Howe
Finstown
Balfour

Ring of Brodgar
Stones of Stenness
Stromness
Mainland
Kirkwall
Orkney

Houton
Gritley

477m.
St Mary's
Italian Chapel

Old Man of Hoy
Dwarfie
Stane
Fara
Scapa Flow
Burray

Rackwick
Lyness
St Margaret's Hope

Hoy
Martello Tower
Flotta
South Ronaldsay

Swona
Burwick

P e n t l a n d   F i r t h

4

Dunnet
Head
Stroma
Duncansby Head

Scrabster
Dunnet Bay
Mey
John O'Groats

aunreay
Thurso
Castletown
Stacks of
Duncansby

eay
Halkirk
Keiss
Sinclair Bay

Caithness
Watten
Castle Girnigoe & Sinclair

Mybster
Wick
Wick

Grey Cairns of Camster
Ulbster

Thurso
Achavanich
Whaligoe
Hill O'Many Stones

Laidhay
Croft Museum
Lybster
Latheron
Dunbeath

Berriedale

Timespan Heritage Centre
Helmsdale

Ousdale Broch

Tarbat
Ness
ortmahomack

Lossiemouth
Burghead
Spey Bay
Portknockie
Portsoy
Macduff
Rosehearty
Fraserburgh

Findhorn
Elgin
Spey Bay
Cullen
Banff
Pennan
Inverallochy

odie
astle
Forres
Pluscarden Abbey
Fochabers
Bridge of Alvah
New
Pitsligo
Rattray
Head

Dallas Dhu
Keith
Aberchirder
Turriff
Buchan
St Fergus

Ferness
Rothes
Isla
Deveron
New Deer
Peterhead

Dava
Aberlour
Craigellachie
Huntly
Fyvie Castle
Boddam

ochindorb
Dufftown
Glenfiddich Distillery
Strathbogie
Aden Country Park
Cruden Bay

rantown-
on-Spey
840m.
Ben
Rinnes
Loanhead Stone Circle
Haddo House
Ellon

Nethy
Bridge
Glenlivet
Leith Hall
Insch
Oldmeldrum
Pitmedden Garden
Newburgh

Boat of Garten
Loch Garten
Cabrach
Rhynie
Correen
Hills
Bennachie
Pitcaple
Inverurie
Balmedie

Strathspey Railway
Tomintoul
Ladder Hills
Kildrummy Castle & Gardens
Mossat
Grampian Transport Museum in Alford
Kintore
Dyce

oylumbridge
Cock
Bridge
Strathdon
Craigievar Castle
Lumphanan
Castle Fraser
ABERDEEN

orlich 1245m.
Corgarff Castle
872m.
Dinnet
Torphins
Drum Castle
Peterculter

Ben Macdhui
1309m
203
Crathie
Balmoral Castle
Ballater
Aboyne
Dee
Crathes Castle
Banchory
Storybook Glen
Portlethen

irngorms
Braemar
115m.
Inverey
Lochnagar
Muick
Strachan
Stonehaven

an
115m.
E
D
Lochnagar
E
F
Dunnottar Castle

Questionnaire

Dear Traveller
Your comments, opinions and recommendations
are very important to us. So please help us to improve
our travel guides by taking a few minutes to complete
this simple questionnaire.

You do not need a stamp (unless posted outside the UK). If you do not
want to remove this page from your guide, then photocopy it or write your
answers on a plain sheet of paper.

Send to: The Editor, Spiral Guides, AA World Travel Guides,
FREEPOST SCE 4598, Basingstoke RG21 4GY.

Your recommendations…
We always encourage readers' recommendations for restaurants, night-life or shopping
– if your recommendation is used in the next edition of the guide, we will send you a
FREE AA Spiral Guide of your choice. Please state below the establishment name,
location and your reasons for recommending it.

_____

_____

_____

_____

_____

Please send me AA Spiral _____
(see list of titles inside the back cover)

About this guide…
Which title did you buy?

_____ AA Spiral

Where did you buy it? _____

When? m m / y y

Why did you choose an AA Spiral Guide? _____

_____

_____

_____

Did this guide meet your expectations?

Exceeded ☐   Met all ☐   Met most ☐   Fell below ☐

Please give your reasons _____

_____

_____

_____

_____

continued on next page…

Were there any aspects of this guide that you particularly liked?

_____
_____
_____
_____

Is there anything we could have done better?

_____
_____
_____
_____
_____

About you...

Name (Mr/Mrs/Ms) _____

Address _____

_____ **Postcode** _____

Daytime tel nos _____

Which age group are you in?

Under 25 ☐ 25–34 ☐ 35–44 ☐ 45–54 ☐ 55–64 ☐ 65+ ☐

How many trips do you make a year?

Less than one ☐ One ☐ Two ☐ Three or more ☐

Are you an AA member? Yes ☐ No ☐

About your trip...

When did you book? m m / y y   **When did you travel?** m m / y y

How long did you stay? _____

Was it for business or leisure? _____

Did you buy any other travel guides for your trip? ☐ Yes ☐ No

If yes, which ones? _____

Thank you for taking the time to complete this questionnaire. Please send it to us as soon as possible, and remember, you do not need a stamp (unless posted outside the UK).